Joseph Barber Lightfoot

Sermons Preached in St. Paul's Cathedral

Joseph Barber Lightfoot

Sermons Preached in St. Paul's Cathedral

ISBN/EAN: 9783744744324

Printed in Europe, USA, Canada, Australia, Japan

Cover: Foto ©Lupo / pixelio.de

More available books at **www.hansebooks.com**

SERMONS

PREACHED IN

ST PAUL'S CATHEDRAL

BY THE LATE

JOSEPH BARBER LIGHTFOOT, D.D., D.C.L., LL.D.,
LORD BISHOP OF DURHAM
SOMETIME CANON OF ST PAUL'S

PUBLISHED BY THE TRUSTEES OF THE LIGHTFOOT FUND

London
MACMILLAN AND CO.
AND NEW YORK
1893

All Rights reserved

TO THE MEMORY

OF

RICHARD WILLIAM CHURCH

SOMETIME DEAN OF ST PAUL'S
GREAT ALIKE IN THOUGHT LITERATURE AND COUNSEL

THESE SERMONS ARE DEDICATED
IN TOKEN OF THE
REVERENCE AND AFFECTION
IN WHICH THEIR WRITER HELD
THE HEAD OF THAT ILLUSTRIOUS BODY
WHICH IT WAS HIS JOY TO SERVE
FOR EIGHT YEARS

EXTRACT FROM THE LAST WILL AND TESTAMENT OF THE LATE JOSEPH BARBER LIGHTFOOT, LORD BISHOP OF DURHAM.

"I bequeath all my personal Estate not herein-
"before otherwise disposed of unto [my Executors]
"upon trust to pay and transfer the same unto the
"Trustees appointed by me under and by virtue of a
"certain Indenture of Settlement creating a Trust to
"be known by the name of 'The Lightfoot Fund for
"the Diocese of Durham' and bearing even date
"herewith but executed by me immediately before
"this my Will to be administered and dealt with by
"them upon the trusts for the purposes and in the
"manner prescribed by such Indenture of Settle-
"ment."

EXTRACT FROM THE INDENTURE OF SETTLEMENT OF 'THE LIGHTFOOT FUND FOR THE DIOCESE OF DURHAM.'

"WHEREAS the Bishop is the Author of and is
"absolutely entitled to the Copyright in the several
"Works mentioned in the Schedule hereto, and for the

"purposes of these presents he has assigned or intends "forthwith to assign the Copyright in all the said "Works to the Trustees. Now the Bishop doth "hereby declare and it is hereby agreed as follows :—

"The Trustees (which term shall hereinafter be "taken to include the Trustees for the time being of "these presents) shall stand possessed of the said "Works and of the Copyright therein respectively "upon the trusts following (that is to say) upon trust "to receive all moneys to arise from sales or otherwise "from the said Works, and at their discretion from "time to time to bring out new editions of the same "Works or any of them, or to sell the copyright in "the same or any of them, or otherwise to deal with "the same respectively, it being the intention of "these presents that the Trustees shall have and "may exercise all such rights and powers in respect "of the said Works and the copyright therein re-"spectively, as they could or might have or exercise "in relation thereto if they were the absolute bene-"ficial owners thereof....

"The Trustees shall from time to time, at such "discretion as aforesaid, pay and apply the income "of the Trust funds for or towards the erecting, "rebuilding, repairing, purchasing, endowing, sup-"porting, or providing for any Churches, Chapels, "Schools, Parsonages, and Stipends for Clergy, and

"other Spiritual Agents in connection with the
"Church of England and within the Diocese of
"Durham, and also for or towards such other pur-
"poses in connection with the said Church of
"England, and within the said Diocese, as the
"Trustees may in their absolute discretion think fit,
"provided always that any payment for erecting any
"building, or in relation to any other works in con-
"nection with real estate, shall be exercised with due
"regard to the Law of Mortmain; it being declared
"that nothing herein shall be construed as intended
"to authorise any act contrary to any Statute or
"other Law....

"In case the Bishop shall at any time assign to
"the Trustees any Works hereafter to be written or
"published by him, or any Copyrights, or any other
"property, such transfer shall be held to be made for
"the purposes of this Trust, and all the provisions
"of this Deed shall apply to such property, subject
"nevertheless to any direction concerning the same
"which the Bishop may make in writing at the time
"of such transfer, and in case the Bishop shall at any
"time pay any money, or transfer any security, stock,
"or other like property to the Trustees, the same
"shall in like manner be held for the purposes of this
"Trust, subject to any such contemporaneous direc-
"tion as aforesaid, and any security, stock or pro-

"perty so transferred, being of a nature which can lawfully be held by the Trustees for the purposes of these presents, may be retained by the Trustees, although the same may not be one of the securities hereinafter authorised.

"The Bishop of Durham and the Archdeacons of Durham and Auckland for the time being shall be *ex-officio* Trustees, and accordingly the Bishop and Archdeacons, parties hereto, and the succeeding Bishops and Archdeacons, shall cease to be Trustees on ceasing to hold their respective offices, and the number of the other Trustees may be increased, and the power of appointing Trustees in the place of Trustees other than Official Trustees, and of appointing extra Trustees, shall be exercised by Deed by the Trustees for the time being, provided always that the number shall not at any time be less than five.

"The Trust premises shall be known by the name of 'The Lightfoot Fund for the Diocese of Durham.'"

CONTENTS.

                                                                        PAGE

I. BALAAM AND BALAK.

And Balaam rose up, and went and returned to his place: and Balak also went his way.
                        NUMBERS xxiv. 25. . 1

II. THE FORGIVENESS OF DAVID'S SIN.

And David said unto Nathan, I have sinned against the Lord.
                        2 SAMUEL xii. 13. . 16

III. THE CONSEQUENCES OF DAVID'S SIN.

The king covered his face, and the king cried with a loud voice, O my son Absalom, O Absalom, my son, my son!
                        2 SAMUEL xix. 4. . 31

IV. CÆSAR'S TRIBUTE AND GOD'S TRIBUTE.

Render to Cæsar the things that are Cæsar's, and to God the things that are God's.
                        S. MARK xii. 17. . 46

CONTENTS.

PAGE

V. THE FALL OF JUDAS.

Jesus answered them, Have not I chosen you twelve, and one of you is a devil? He spake of Judas Iscariot the son of Simon: for he it was that should betray Him, being one of the twelve.
S. JOHN vi. 70, 71. . 53

VI. THE COUNSEL OF CAIAPHAS.

And one of them, named Caiaphas, being the high-priest that same year, said unto them: Ye know nothing at all, nor consider that it is expedient for us, that one man should die for the people, and that the whole nation perish not.
S. JOHN xi. 49, 50. . 75

VII. PILATE'S QUESTION.

Pilate saith unto Him, What is truth?
S. JOHN xviii. 38. . 91

VIII. THE ONE TAKEN AND THE OTHER LEFT.

And he went out, and wept bitterly.
S. MATTHEW xxvi. 75.

And he went and hanged himself.
S. MATTHEW xxvii. 5. . 105

IX. THE TRIUMPH OF FAILURE.

Then all the disciples forsook Him, and fled.
S. MATTHEW xxvi. 56. . 122

X. CHRIST'S GIFT OF PEACE.

Peace I leave with you, My peace I give unto you: not as the world giveth, give I unto you.
S. JOHN xiv. 27. . 136

XI. WHY STAND YE GAZING UP INTO HEAVEN?

Why stand ye gazing up into heaven?
ACTS i. 11. . 150

CONTENTS.

XII. CHRISTIAN FORETHOUGHT AND UNCHRISTIAN ANXIETY.

Take therefore no thought for the morrow: for the morrow shall take thought for the things of itself.
S. MATTHEW vi. 34. . 164

XIII. TRUE BLESSEDNESS.

But He said, Yea rather, blessed are they that hear the word of God, and keep it.
S. LUKE xi. 28. . 178

XIV. HASTY JUDGMENT.

Judge nothing before the time, until the Lord come.
1 CORINTHIANS iv. 5. . 193

XV. THE SPIRIT AND THE LETTER.

The letter killeth, but the spirit giveth life.
2 CORINTHIANS iii. 6. . 206

XVI. S. PAUL OUR EXAMPLE.

If I be not an Apostle unto others, yet doubtless I am to you.
1 CORINTHIANS ix. 2. . 218

XVII. THE PHILIPPIAN GAOLER.

Sirs, what must I do to be saved?
ACTS xvi. 30. . 230

XVIII. THE CONSTRAINING LOVE OF CHRIST.

The love of Christ constraineth us.
2 CORINTHIANS v. 14. . 243

XIX. MADNESS AND SANITY.

I am not mad, most noble Festus; but speak forth the words of truth and soberness.
ACTS xxvi. 25. . 255

XX. THE MESSAGE TO LAODICEA.

Unto the angel of the church of the Laodiceans write; These things saith the Amen, the faithful and true witness.
REVELATION iii. 14. . 269

XXI. THE HOLY TRINITY.

Go ye, and teach all nations, baptizing them in the name of the Father, and of the Son, and of the Holy Ghost.
S. MATTHEW xxviii. 19 . 287

XXII. THE GREAT RENEWAL.

And He that sat upon the throne said, Behold, I make all things new.
REVELATION xxi. 5. . 304

I.

BALAAM AND BALAK.

And Balaam rose up, and went and returned to his place: and Balak also went his way.

NUMBERS xxiv. 25.

Third Sunday after Easter, 1873.

EACH went his own way. Each returned to his own place. This strange intercourse between men so different in position and character has come to an end. Despite the eager desire on both sides to arrive at some mutual understanding, to agree on some common policy, they could find no meeting-point. Again and again, at the very moment when they seemed to be realising their common hope, an invisible power rose up, like a spectre, between them, and beckoned them asunder. They shifted their position: they framed and reframed their plans. It was all in vain. Still this unseen presence haunted the ground—a purpose, a will, which, however much they desired it, they could not put aside. The conspiracy against God's chosen people, and God's eternal design, had come to nought. The worldly diplomacy of Balak, and the spiritual diplomacy of Balaam, had alike been futile. Their negociations were ended.

And so they parted. Each went on his own way, to his own place. Their careers hitherto had been separate: their destinies henceforth will be distinct. How then had they been affected by this crisis? They had found themselves—both the one and the other—face to face with a revelation from heaven, a visitation of God, in the prosecution of a common design. How had it left them?

A revelation from heaven! The words suggest to our minds some striking manifestation, which appals the outward senses, dazzling the eye and stunning the ear, as when Jehovah descended amid the thunders and the lightnings of Sinai, and the mountain trembled under the tread of the Almighty Presence. A visitation of God! When we hear this phrase, we think of some sudden and terrible physical catastrophe; as when the vessel strikes on the coral reef, and plunges its whole cargo of living souls into eternity without time even to breathe a hurried prayer: or when a plague suddenly appears, smites down one and another, then scours a whole region, sweeping thousands into an unforeseen and premature grave: or when the falling timber singles out the chance passer by, and widows the wife and orphans the household without a moment's warning. We are awe-stricken with revelations like this; we count such visitations as these fearful and solemn indeed. And so they are. But it is not in the mighty and strong wind which rends the mountains, nor in the shuddering of the earthquake, nor in the devouring flame of fire, nor by any outward demonstrations of majesty and awe, that God most commonly and most fearfully reveals Himself to the individual soul; but in the still small voice, which speaks to the conscience in some passing opportunity, some sudden temptation, some moral crisis, when the whole man is tried, is sifted, is saved or is lost. These moments will pass unnoticed by others. The voice is so low, that it penetrates one ear alone. The man will go about his daily task, will pursue his daily amusements once more, as if nothing had happened. To others he will appear just the same as he ever was. There is no outward sign of the moral catastrophe which has overtaken him. But he himself knows—he cannot help knowing—that God has visited him, that he has stood face to face with the Eternal One, that he is morally a changed man— changed for better, or for worse, by the awe and the glory of that presence.

And just in proportion to his endowments and his

advantages will be the effects of such a visitation on his character. Greater gifts carry with them greater capacities of evil as well as of good. The man of the world cannot sin so deeply, cannot fall so low, as the man of the Spirit. For the latter, everything is cast in a grander scale—his temptations, his lessons, his triumphs, his defeats. The same event is not the same to one man, and to another. The magnitude of the opportunity is measured, not by the magnitude of the actual occurrence, but by the magnitude of the inward capacity.

Of these two types of character—the man of the world, and the man of the Spirit: the man of vulgar capacities and vulgar aims, and the man of high insight and keen moral sensibilities—we have examples in Balak and Balaam.

Balak is essentially a man of the world. He desires to compass common ends by common means. He does not trouble himself about the morality of his actions one way or the other. Here is an enemy to be conquered, and he will use every effort to conquer him. Here is a people to be cursed, and he will leave no stone unturned to get them cursed. He does not at all understand Balaam's scruples. He takes that low, depreciatory view of man's nature, which the worldling always takes. He has no belief in human integrity, or human honour. His maxim is the worldling's maxim, that every man has his price. So he feels confident that, if he will only bid high enough, Balaam's services will be secured. He offers him honour, offers him wealth. He tries the bribe, which is the most insidious and most efficacious, when offered by the prince to the subject—the bribe of personal deference and respect. Then, when he is frustrated, he loses all patience. 'Balak's anger was kindled against Balaam, and he smote his hands together.' It is so unreasonable, so discourteous, so stupid, to refuse a request, preferred with this studied respect and backed by these tempting offers.

And, again, his idea of God's purpose is just on a par with his idea of man's integrity. He has a vague notion that religion cannot be dispensed with. He pays all outward respect to its representatives. But, by some means or other, religion must be made to bend to the political situation. He will have religion on his side, cost what effort it may. Of God, as an Eternal, Invincible Will, as One Who cannot change and cannot lie, he knows nothing. Religion is, in his eyes, as pliable as state-craft. He trusts to the arts of diplomacy in dealing with God, just as he would trust to them in dealing with a rival prince. He will increase the number of his victims; he will change the position of his altars. He will bribe God; or, if bribes fail, he will coax Him into compliance; and then all will be well. Balak is the very type of the man of the world.

Of Balak's future nothing is told. It is not probable that this crisis made any strong impression on his character. He 'went his way.' He had been thwarted in his design. He had failed, and there was an end of it. He returned to his ordinary pursuits—to his wars, to his diplomacy, to his feasting. He was a worldling before, and he remained a worldling still. Of him no terrible fall is recorded in the sequel. God's visitation had passed away, leaving him not indeed any better, but probably not much worse, than it found him.

But with Balaam the case was wholly different. Balaam was a man of high capacities, both moral and spiritual. And, in the face of a great emergency, such a man must gain or must lose appreciably.

Can we doubt his *moral* capacities, or even his moral attainments? Read his repeated refusal to abandon his convictions, or to tamper with the truth, under each repeated temptation. Have we not here, we are disposed to ask, a man of strictly conscientious principles? Does not his whole language bespeak the very soul of honour? 'I cannot go beyond the word of the Lord my God, to do less or more.' 'The word that God putteth in my mouth, that shall I speak.' 'He hath blessed, and I cannot reverse it.'

And, corresponding to his moral elevation, was his *spiritual* intuition also. He it was who 'heard the words of God' and 'saw the vision of the Almighty.' He, a child of an alien stock, beheld spread out as a map before him, like that wide landscape on which he was even then gazing from Peor's height, the glorious history of the race, whom wishing to curse he was constrained to bless; and in that remote age, to that obscure tribe, foretold the advent of a Star, which should rise and glorify a whole world, the domination of a Sceptre, whose kingdom should have no end. Truly it was no empty vaunt, when he described himself as 'the man whose eyes are open.' Here was a seer, if seer there ever was.

And so he parts from Balak, having shown himself, as we might think, a man of unblemished honour, a man of far-sighted prescience. 'He rose up, and went and returned to his place.' Then there is an interruption, a pause, an interval of silence: and Balaam reappears on the scene. We find just one passing reference to his after career, to his sin, to his fate. Can it be the same man—so changed, so fallen, so vile and profligate? The man, who foretold Israel's glory, has conspired for Israel's shame. Balaam and Balak have changed places. Balaam is the tempter and Balak the tempted now. Balaam's name becomes a byword and a proverb for almost fiendish profligacy.

Balak could not have sinned so deeply. The man of the Spirit has fallen lower, incomparably lower, than the man of the world.

A strange and perplexing transmutation; and yet is it after all so very far removed from the common experiences of life, that we are at a loss either to understand, or to appropriate, the lesson? Have we known no instance in which the man of the highest endowments, of the keenest insight, of the loftiest moral perceptions, has sunk below the level of the common worldling, even of the common criminal; and thus all confidence in human integrity, and honour and purity, in all that is best and most precious in heaven or earth, is shaken by that one man's act? The prophet of God casts the stumbling-block in the way of the people of God.

Is it not so, when the poet, whose divine gift of imagination has enabled us to realise with a keener zest, and to acknowledge with a deeper thanksgiving, the manifold glories of nature, whose insight into the workings of the human heart has stirred our sluggish sensibilities, lifting us above ourselves and inspiring us with larger and more generous sympathies, then uses the ascendency, which he has gained, to corrupt the wells of his country's literature with the poison of sensuality? Is it not so, when some representative of the majesty and power of the law, whose legal decisions are admired for their acuteness and their breadth, and on whose professional integrity no breath of suspicion has passed, is suddenly detected in acts of mean and petty dishonesty, to which even men of not very scrupulous honour would never have stooped; as when once the judicial ermine was sullied in the person of its chief representative, and over the memory of the most illustrious Chancellor of England, and the most famous philosopher of modern times, whose writings for originality of thought and aptness of illustration and dignity of sentiment stand unrivalled in the prose literature of our country, the cruel epitaph was inscribed, 'The greatest, wisest, meanest of mankind'? Is it not so, when one who has taken a chief part in every philanthropic movement, and occupied the foremost seat on every religious platform, suffers a felon's punishment for some gigantic fraud, which has spread a panic far and wide, and involved whole families in ruin? Is it not so, when a minister of religion, whose soul-stirring eloquence has stung the conscience and moved the hearts of awe-stricken thousands, is detected in some shameful act, and he that has preached so often and so forcibly to others has himself been found a castaway?

These things have been. Keen insight, refined imagination, generous sympathies, a profound intuition into abstract truth, a lofty sense of moral obligations, even a high appreciation of spiritual mysteries, have not saved a man from ruin; when the discipline of the life has been relaxed. We carelessly set down such painful inconsistencies to hypocrisy. We are sure that the man did not mean what he said, because his base actions have belied his noble words. It is an easy and ready solution; but it is utterly false. O there is a much more profound and subtle lesson underlying such frailties than this! Balaam was *not* a hypocrite. There is a ring of sincerity in his every word. He spoke, we cannot doubt, from the inmost convictions of his heart, when he said : ' I cannot go beyond the commandment of the Lord, to do either good or bad of mine own mind.' It was not in his utterances, but in his actions, that he was untrue to himself.

And how came he to be untrue to himself?

Follow the narrative of his successive negociations with Balak. Analyse the conflict of motives—God's purpose here, his own aggrandisement there. Why it is the very history—perhaps on a grander scale, but still the very history—of your own temptation, your own weakness, your own vacillation, which you seem to be reading. And as you trace each alternation in his mind—the resolute resistance, the feeble concession : the conscientious scruple, the eager desire : the triumph, the defeat—the voice of conscience within you points the moral of the parable, reminding you of some great crisis in your own inner life, and startling you with the direct home-thrust, 'Thou art the man.'

Observe, first, that the conflict between the higher and the lower motives is unmistakeable. There could be no doubt on which side Balaam's worldly interests lay. He would secure wealth and honour; he would indulge his antipathy to an unfriendly people; he would confer a personal service on a friendly prince —if he could only bring himself to act in one way. Here was an accumulation of inducements, beckoning him in one direction. On the other hand, the will of God is clear and explicit, forbidding him to take this path. Has this never happened to any one here?

And, if so, have you dealt with your conflict and your temptation as Balaam dealt with his? His worldly interests could not be made to change. That was clear. So he took these as his starting point, and set himself to manipulate God's eternal purpose. He would not defy, would not confront and oppose it. Conscience was too strong for this. But he would circumvent it by some means or other. 'Peradventure the Lord would come to meet him.' Is this the first or the last time, when reliance has been placed upon a 'peradventure' to tamper with the inviolable and to change the unchangeable? Is this the only instance, where a man, eager to escape from an obvious duty, has thought to silence or to convert God's protest within him by shifting his position or by multiplying his sacrifices? He hastens from height to height, hiding some features in the scene here and revealing others there; and, having thus altered the relative position of the objects, he fondly hopes that a curse may after all be pronounced on some part at least of this duty which is so imperative and yet so hateful to him. He has changed his own point of view, and he vainly imagines that God will change His also. He multiplies his religious services; he increases his charitable gifts; as if these forsooth could purchase immunity, or could make that right which is not right.

Thus Balaam lingers over his temptation; he dallies with it; he familiarises himself with it. These things are an allegory. 'What men are these with thee?' You too have heard at the outset the divine voice asking within you in no uncertain tones; 'This design which thou art lodging in thy heart, this temptation with which thou art courting familiarity— what manner of thing is this?' You were at no loss for an answer. The question was its own answer. And yet you thought that you might entertain the project, that you might at least turn it over in your mind, that you might just see whether 'peradventure' it would assume some brighter aspect as you got to know more of it. And so you involved yourself deeper and deeper. If you had only spurned it at first, your path would have been easy. Your character would have been strengthened; your temptation would have passed away. But this you would not do. You fortified yourself by strong asseverations to yourself that under no circumstances would you do wrong; but you would reconsider the matter, and just see whether, somehow or other, the blessing and the curse could not be made to change places. Do not suppose that Balaam's repeated professions of integrity and obedience were intended to overawe Balak. It needs no deep penetration into man's heart to see a different motive from this. Their object was to quiet and to reassure Balaam's own conscience, when he felt that his footsteps were tottering.

And then comes the apparent contradiction in terms. God bade Balaam go with the messengers, and yet God was angry with Balaam because he went. A strange moral paradox, it will be said. Yes: but, like all moral paradoxes in the Bible, instinct with the deepest meaning. It is a law which regulates our probation here, that each concession to temptation involves us still further, and increases the difficulty of resistance. The law itself is God's ordinance, is God's will; but the frailty on our part, which brings us under the operation of the law, is hateful in His sight.

Thus it was the inevitable consequence of Balaam's fingering the temptation in the first instance, that he should be drawn into closer proximity with it afterwards. And so he went forward, entangling himself more and more in the meshes of the tempter.

But Balaam escaped. Balaam was true to his word. Balaam did not transpose the blessing and the curse. Balaam did declare God's will neither more nor less without reservation and without stint. His integrity was saved. Yes: it was saved this once, but saved only 'as by fire.' Herein lies the solemnity of the lesson. He escaped this once. But the next incident recorded of him is a shameful, irretrievable fall. How this came about, we are not told. Yet was not his yielding to the later temptation the only too obvious consequence of his tampering with the earlier? He had overcome once. God's voice within him was still too strong for his own baser desire. But he had caressed and fondled the temptation; he had suffered himself to be fascinated by it. A man cannot do this without moral deterioration. His sense of right and wrong is blunted by such trifling. His power of resistance is diminished. He may escape once, but he will not escape again.

If to any one here the history of Balaam's temptation, of Balaam's weakness, of Balaam's escape, has seemed like a parable of some past crisis in his own inner life, let him take the warning to heart in time; lest the last scene also be only too faithfully reproduced in him, when the prophetic voice of conscience shall be once more heard—no longer in warning, but now in condemnation—bringing the parallel home to him, and stinging him with the conviction: 'Thou art the man.' Let him that standeth, but even now is tottering, 'take heed lest he fall.'

II.

THE FORGIVENESS OF DAVID'S SIN.

And David said unto Nathan, I have sinned against the Lord.
2 SAMUEL xii. 13.

Third Sunday after Easter, 1878.

THE incident, to which these words refer, occurred at the most brilliant epoch of a singularly brilliant career. The despised shepherd lad, the youngest of a large family, starting in life without wealth, without connexions, with no external advantages of any kind, had raised himself by his abilities and his exertions to a height of power which none of his race had ever reached before, and which none after him succeeded in maintaining—his favourite son and immediate successor alone excepted.

A youth of bold exploit and persevering endeavour, spent amidst trials and dangers and vicissitudes the most varied—the hard and precarious life of an outlaw at one time, the not less perilous service at the court of a jealous and moody king at another—all these had passed away. The severe discipline of youth had been crowned with the triumphant success of manhood. He had sown in tears, and he was now reaping in joy. Called from the sheepfold to a throne, environed with personal enemies and political malcontents, yet by firmness, by courage, by a lofty generosity and a wise discretion, by the ascendency of a personal character which united in itself a rare combination of gifts the most diverse, he had silenced all opposition. At length rebellions had been crushed, and feuds were dying out. He reigned the sole and undisputed sovereign of Israel.

Nor was this all. In internal administration and in foreign conquest alike his vigour and ability had triumphed. He had wrested the last important stronghold from the idolatrous inhabitants of the land; and had built there a fortress and a city, destined now to be the capital of his own dominions, but marked out hereafter as the religious metropolis of the civilised world—Zion and Jerusalem, the most cherished of all cherished names, the holiest of all holy places, the monuments of a past history unique in the annals of mankind, the symbols of all the deepest thought and the fondest hopes of the human heart to the end of time, the earthly types of our final and eternal home. He had organized an army with the regularity and the precision of Macedonia or of Rome. He had developed a striking and magnificent ceremonial of religious worship. He had surrounded himself with something at least of the pomp and splendour of an Oriental court. A succession of victories had crowned his arms abroad. One by one the hereditary enemies of his country had fallen before him. Philistia, Moab, Syria, Edom, all were humbled. At this very moment he was engaged in his final and successful struggle with the Ammonites. Here too he was triumphant. From the Mediterranean to the Euphrates he had no rival.

And, if his eye could have pierced through the veil of the future, and the scroll of the world's history had been opened before him, he might well have felt a proud self-complacency, as he read the enduring effects of his empire and administration. To us at least, who can trace these effects through long centuries of the past, who see in this empire and administration the channel whereby the truths, which have moulded the thoughts and guided the actions of men in successive generations, were diffused far beyond the limits of his own race, till they flooded and fertilised the whole civilised world—to us, I say, even if we could close our eyes for a moment to the eternal issues of the Gospel, this reign of David will appear to have set upon the history of mankind a stamp deeper and more enduring even than the conquests of an Alexander, or a Cæsar, or a Timour, or a Napoleon.

But not only has he been thus triumphant as a monarch. His private designs also have been crowned with success. At this very moment he is enjoying the fruits of a secret and cherished project which was carefully planned and has been prosperously executed. An object very near to his heart has been attained. The risks were great, but they have been surmounted. Obstacles have been removed; publicity has been avoided; no scandal has been created. Uriah has been slain fighting valiantly in the hottest of the battle; and Uriah's wife has become the wife of David.

At this crisis, when success culminates and self-satisfaction is complete, the blow comes. His tower of pride is crumbled into dust by some unseen hand. Henceforth he is a changed man. He is no more light-hearted and joyous and hopeful. He has tangled a coil of difficulties about him, from which he can never again extricate himself. He has loaded himself with a burden of sorrow, under which he must stagger through life, only to bury it finally in the grave. Troubles gather thick upon him, troubles the most acute and numbing—gross crimes and irregularities in his own family, the rebellion of his sons, even of a favourite son, annoyances and perplexities and trials of all kinds. He has placed himself at the mercy of an unscrupulous and arrogant relation—the agent in his stratagem and the master of his secret. Everything goes wrong henceforth. From this time onward 'the sword never departs from his house.'

And yet, at this very moment, when the greatness of the crisis is revealed to him, his thoughts do not turn to any of these things. Not the gathering storm-cloud, not the fatal ascendency of Joab, not the existence of a perilous secret, not the loss of respect and of power, not any of the thousand perplexities and troubles in which this one act may involve him—rise up before him now. One thought dominates his soul. He remembers only One, Whom he has grieved and alienated, One Who is invisible and yet very present, One—this is the terrible thought which overwhelms and crushes him—One Who is 'of purer eyes than to behold evil'. 'And David said unto Nathan, I have sinned against the Lord.'

The feeling, which is here concentrated in one despairing sentence, is amplified in the 51st Psalm. 'Against Thee only have I sinned, and done this evil in Thy sight.' 'Wash me throughly from my wickedness, and cleanse me from my sin.' 'Lo, Thou requirest truth in the inward parts.' 'Turn Thy face from my sins, and put out all my misdeeds. Make me a clean heart, O God; and renew a right spirit within me.' 'O give me the comfort of Thy help again, and stablish me with Thy free Spirit.' 'The sacrifice of God is a troubled spirit; a broken and contrite heart, O God, shalt Thou not despise.'

The oldest tradition regards this 51st Psalm as the outpouring of David's soul at this crisis, when the crowning sin of his life was brought home to him in all its heinousness. The ancient heading in our Bibles so describes it. Nor need we question the truth of this tradition. To the thoughtful mind it will appear to bear the very stamp of that terrible crime and that deep penitential sorrow. It would be difficult to fix on any incident, or any man, in the whole range of history, to whom the language and the feelings would be so appropriate, as to the man after God's own heart in the first revulsion of spirit after his terrible fall. One objection only is offered to this ancient and wide-spread belief. The concluding verses seem to speak of a later period, when the city was rebuilding after the return from Babylon. But is it not reasonable to suppose that these two verses were a later addition to adapt the psalm to liturgical uses? Quite independently of any difficulties which they create in connexion with David's authorship, they are marked off, as it were, from the rest of the psalm by their inherent character. They have no reference to the struggles of the individual heart; they are a national appeal to the God of Israel. They dwell not on the sacrifices of a broken spirit, but on the sacrifices of burnt offering. They utter the language no more of penitent sorrow, but of confidence and hope. The building of the walls of Jerusalem, the offering of bullocks upon God's altar—have we not here the language of the prophets and priests after the restoration, probably of Ezra himself, adapting the penitential utterances of the Psalmist King to congregational worship, now that the Second Temple was rising, and the service of the God of Israel was once more reinstated?

But I need not dwell on this point. It is sufficient that this psalm represents the very spirit of David at this crisis—the absorbing consciousness of the presence of a Being of infinite purity and holiness, the deep sense of alienation from that Being by sin, the loathing of self and the yearning towards God.

The interview between Nathan and David is better known and better remembered than almost any passage in the Old Testament. The lesson which it conveys is a very plain lesson. The preacher can have nothing to say beyond what must have occurred to any one who has bestowed more than a passing thought on it. Questions indeed there are in connexion with the narrative, on which much has been written and spoken. This signal fall of one who is commended as the man after God's own heart, this sudden plunge into an abyss of crime, may well be the starting-point for much serious reflection on the mixed good and evil which divide the empire of the human heart. The direct consequences of David's sin, following by an inevitable moral order and embittering his whole after life —the disorders of his family and the disturbances in his realm—will furnish an instructive example of the laws by which crime works out its own penalty. This latter point may supply matter for consideration on another occasion. Today I would ask your attention rather to the view which David himself takes of his act. At the moment when the veil of self-deception is torn aside, when he sees his conduct in all its hideous deformity, one thought alone possesses his soul—one absorbing, overwhelming, painfully bitter thought—'I have sinned against the Lord.' 'Against Thee only—against Thee only—have I sinned.'

Was David right in this, or was he wrong? Is there indeed a Being of infinite perfection, before Whom our hearts lie open, to Whom we are responsible for our acts, against Whom sin is treason, and from Whom guilt is alienation? Or is this mode of regarding human conduct a play of fancy, a trick of education, the result indeed of habits of thought handed down through many generations, but nevertheless illusory and unreal? If so, the Bible is the falsest of all books; for this is the one leading idea, the one unbroken thread which runs throughout from the first Chapter of Genesis to the last of the Apocalypse. In other things it exhibits growth, development, increasing light, successive revelation. Material conceptions gradually give place to spiritual. National privileges expand till they embrace all mankind. The doctrines of a future life, a judgment, a redemption, a Christ, grow ever clearer, as the dawn spreading on the mountains, till the sun arises and all at once the world is flooded with a blaze of light. But is the foundation, on which this imposing superstructure is built, altogether hollow and rotten? Is the very light darkness? This day of the Lord, is it night after all?

I should not dare to use such words, but that it is only possible to state the momentous nature of the issue by a strong contrast such as this. It is obviously (I need not dwell on what must be self-evident) it is obviously the most important question, which can occupy the thoughts of any person. There cannot be any compromise or any halting between two opinions here. The one view must be false, and the other true; and the view that is false—whichever it may be—must be utterly, hopelessly, incurably false. It is a question which infinitely concerns every person in this congregation, young or old, learned or ignorant, rich or poor; for it affects the conduct of every day and every hour. According as a man answers it himself rightly or wrongly, so will his career be; if wrongly, an entire mistake, a more than life-long failure, a dazzling failure possibly—for he may go down to his grave rich in wealth, in fame, in popularity, in friendships—yet a disastrous failure nevertheless; but if rightly, then full of strength, of power, of vitality, of truth.

And, when I speak of answering this question, I do not mean answering it in a mere mechanical way, but answering it morally, answering it practically. It is not the response of the lips, but the response of the life, which I wish to elicit from you, from myself, from every one here. I cannot think that anyone in this congregation, if the question were pressed home to him, could boldly take the atheist's side. His presence in this church is a sufficient guarantee so far. But there are voices abroad, which obscure, where they do not deny, the idea of God—and with the idea of God the idea of sin stands or falls; and not a few, though they may not turn a direct ear to such voices, do yet suffer their spiritual senses to be confused by the din which they hear around them, till they hardly know what they believe.

If any such there be here, I do earnestly entreat him to reflect on the danger of allowing himself to drift he knows not whither from mere carelessness, because he will not make the necessary effort and face the momentous alternative which rises up before him. There are many points on which we may be content to wait for more light. But this is not one. It cannot be a trifling matter, for it affects every corner of human life. It is a matter, in which beyond all others we are bound to have clear views and to act upon them. It is a matter, in which it is perilous to court doubt and confusion.

But, as I said before, it is not the answer of the intellect, but the answer of the conscience, of the heart, of the life, which I desire to evoke. 'I have sinned against the Lord.' 'Against Thee only have I sinned and done this evil in Thy sight.' 'Against Thee only.' Has this been the one paramount, absorbing, overwhelming thought with you, as it was with David, when you were betrayed into sin? Or were you occupied with other considerations? Were you sensible of the presence of God, or did your thoughts turn solely, or chiefly, on the presence of man?

The wrong deed is done. What then? What is the chief anxiety which occupies your mind? Are you vexed with yourself, that in one moment of recklessness you should have coiled a chain around you which you will drag about to your dying day? Do you curse your folly, that for a transient gratification you should have bartered your good name, should have sacrificed (if so be) the ambitions of a lifetime? Are you distressed and anxious, lest by any means the law should get you into its clutches? Is it your first concern to hide away your wrong-doing that, hiding it away, you may avert its consequences? Or perhaps it is a secret sin. Do you congratulate yourself on its secrecy? Alas, it might have been a thousand times better for you, that your fall had been published to all the world, so that its publicity had taught you its heinousness. And meanwhile of God's image marred, of God's purity outraged, of God's truth defied, of God's love—of your heavenly Father's love—scorned and trampled under foot, how much or how little do you think?

Or perhaps your thoughts rise higher than this, but still are arrested far below the throne of God. You are really grieved that you have done a wrong to another. You are dissatisfied with yourself, because you have forsaken your ideal, and your self-respect has been wounded in consequence. Nay, ask yourself, this ideal, what is it, but God's image and superscription stamped upon your soul, though the legend be worn and the features blurred, so that you fail to trace the identity? This wrong done to another, what is it but a wrong done to God—to God in the person of Christ? 'Inasmuch as ye did it to one of the least'—aye, the poorest, the meanest, the feeblest —'of these my brethren, ye did it to Me'—to Me and none other. And so we return to the same point. 'Against Thee only, O Lord, have I sinned.' 'Against Thee only.' 'Thou alone hast been wronged, and Thou alone canst forgive.'

'Thou alone canst forgive.' No interposition of priests, and no multiplication of sacrifices, can dispense with that direct, immediate, personal confronting with the Eternal Presence, that absolving, purifying, renewing converse with God, wherein the sin is laid bare before the Throne of Grace, and the burden cast down at the foot of the Cross. Surely David, if any man, would have had recourse at this crisis to the sacrifices of the Mosaic hierarchy, if the slaughter of bulls and of goats could have taken away sin. Yet the very thought is abhorrent to him in the moment of self-revelation. Not the blood of hecatombs could wash out one single spot from his soul saturated with crime. The sacrifice which God asked was far other than this. 'The sacrifice of God is a troubled spirit; a broken and a contrite heart, O God, shalt Thou not despise.'

You know well—each man knows well, if he will cast a glance within, what is his special danger. He can lay his finger at once on the dark spot which stains his character. He feels instinctively where the burden presses, which weighs down his soul. Is it eating away your spiritual life by a slow, continuous, almost imperceptible process? Or does it, like the sin of David, after slumbering awhile, break out suddenly in some flagrant deed, startling and stunning you in the midst of your false security? Whatever it may be, take it at once into the presence of God. Single out your special sin; realise its heinousness; loathe its degradation; feel how it shuts out the light of heaven from your heart. If you have shunned God's presence, shun it no more. Seek Him. Dare to be alone with Him. He, and He only, can put away your sin. He only can cleanse your heart, and renew a right spirit within you.

Only do not expect that you are undertaking a light task. An inveterate habit (if such it be) is not soon laid aside. A diseased heart is not easily healed. It will be a sharp, painful, probably a prolonged, struggle. Persevere and conquer. If you play the courageous part, if you are firm and unflinching, if in spite of weariness, in spite of loneliness, in spite of darkness overhead, you wrestle with the angel from nightfall till dawn of day, be assured you will not depart without the blessing. If without reserve you cry from the depths of your heart, 'I have sinned against the Lord,' then too without reserve the prophetic voice will answer, 'The Lord also hath put away thy sin.'

The sin itself; but perhaps not its temporal consequences. It was not so with David. In a thousand ways the temporal consequences may remain. But the clean heart and the right spirit will be yours. You will live henceforth a true life. You will be free, as you never have been free before. Is this an ideal picture? Strive to realise it. He who does so has learnt the true lesson of the season; for he has indeed died with Christ; he has indeed risen with Christ; he is indeed living in Christ.

III.

THE CONSEQUENCES OF DAVID'S SIN.

The king covered his face, and the king cried with a loud voice, O my son Absalom, O Absalom, my son, my son!

2 SAMUEL xix. 4.

Fourth Sunday after Easter, 1878.

ON Sunday afternoon last, I took for my subject the interview between Nathan and David. I asked you to consider the circumstances of David's life at the moment when the incident occurs. Attention was called to the successes of his administration at home and the triumph of his arms abroad. This crisis was the culmination of his good fortune. No Israelite before or after achieved such great things as he achieved. In strong contrast to this unexampled career stands his sin and his humiliation. It is no comfort, no compensation to him that he has succeeded in everything to which he has put his hand. The one painfully bitter thought absorbs him, 'I have sinned against the Lord.' Without seeking excuses, without calculating consequences, without any afterthought of any kind, he concentrates his whole soul on the sin of the deed. Thus his *contrition* is complete.

And not less complete is his *pardon*. This immediate confronting with God, this absolute abasement of self, this piercing cry for forgiveness, is not unheeded. The answer is prompt, and it is unreserved. The same prophetic voice, which had denounced the offence, absolves the offender, 'The Lord hath put away thy sin.' A clean heart is made, and a right spirit renewed within him.

But the lesson of David's fall would not be complete without the sequel. Though the sin was put away, the consequences of the sin remained. Though the guilt was pardoned, the penalty was not foregone. Let this be the subject of our meditations this afternoon. We will consider the culminating sorrow of David's after-life—the revolt and death of Absalom —as the retribution which by an inevitable moral law his crime had brought upon him.

The narrative is in every way very striking. There is a deep pathos in it which is scarcely surpassed elsewhere even in the Bible, the most pathetic of all books. It appeals to our hearts with a freshness, which no repetition can blunt. The record moreover is singularly minute in this portion. The flight of David is told with a circumstantiality of detail which has no parallel elsewhere. There is no single day in Jewish history—it has been truly said—of which so full an account is preserved. We have vividly before our eyes the long train of exiles following the king, as he turned his back on the Holy City, the scene of his greatest exploits, and crossed the brook Kidron and ascended the slopes of Olivet. 'All the country wept with a loud voice, and all the people passed over.' 'David wept as he went up, and had his head covered, and he went barefoot: and all the people that was with him covered every man his head, and they went up, weeping as they went up.' And so we follow him on his mournful way, till the pathos of the story and the awe of the lesson reach their climax in the fierce execrations and brutal insults of Shimei, who seizes this opportunity of trampling on the conscience-stricken broken-hearted king, 'Come out, come out, thou man of blood and thou man of Belial.' 'Behold, thou art taken in thy mischief, because thou art a man of blood.' Then it is that the depth of the king's contrition reveals itself. Alas! it was only too true—it was truer even than Shimei knew—that he was a man of blood. With a noble forbearance he restrains his followers from punishing this savage miscreant. Let him curse, and throw stones, and cast dust to his heart's content. How can he add to a grief, which already surpasses all griefs? How can he deepen a humiliation, than which no humiliation could be lower? 'Behold, my son seeketh my life: how much more now may this Benjamite do it?' These curses—are they not after all God's judgment denounced against the sin? These outrages —are they not after all God's discipline sent to chasten the penitent? 'Let him alone' therefore: 'let him alone, and let him curse; for the Lord hath bidden him. It may be that the Lord will requite me good for his cursing this day.'

The tide of events turns. The rebellion is crushed; the rebel is slain; the exiles retrace their steps homeward. Now at length, we might have supposed, all would be joy and thanksgiving for the great deliverance wrought. Nay, the return is sadder than the departure; the triumph is more depressing than the humiliation. 'The victory that day was turned into mourning unto all the people; for the people heard say that day how the king was grieved for his son. And the people gat them by stealth that day into the city, as people being ashamed steal away when they flee in battle.'

Of the intense horrors of a civil war or of intestine revolution we Englishmen have been spared the cruel lesson. While the powerful nation, which is separated from ourselves only by a narrow strip of sea, has passed through a succession of such bloody conflicts within our recollection; while the great transatlantic people, who are bone of our bone and flesh of our flesh, was torn asunder by a mighty civil war within very recent memory, England's experience is buried in a remote and forgotten past. But if it be true, as our own great general said, that next to a defeat a victory is the saddest sight which a man can witness, what must not be the case, when to the ordinary calamities of war new and unwonted horrors are added, when the only way to triumph leads over the slaughtered bodies of fellow-countrymen, perhaps even of relations and friends, and when each successful blow recoils on him who aims it! In such a conflict it must ever be the case that 'the victory that day is turned into mourning.'

Not less sad—far sadder—than this was the short, sharp struggle, of which the narrative is brought to a close in the words of the text. It was civil war in its most terrible form. It was a combat, not only between fellow-countrymen, but between fellow-citizens. And the hostile chiefs were father and son.

The crime of Absalom is not isolated. It has had

not a few parallels in the history of great dynasties, where the natural heir to the throne, impatient of delay, has anticipated the slow course of events, and snatched at the power which in due time would have been his own by inherited right. It has had its sad counterpart too in not a few private homes. Many a father and many a mother can tell of a child, whose winning ways have wound themselves round their affections, whose personal charms have shed a radiance of joy on their homes, and who yet has wrung their hearts by dark ingratitude or cruel selfishness. The sacred writer dwells with fondness on the endowments of Absalom, his faultless beauty, his attractive graces. It is clear that he himself is not proof against those fascinations which others found irresistible. There is a terrible irony in Absalom's career which consciously or unconsciously each fresh stroke of the narrative brings out more strongly—the contrast between the outward charms and the worthless character of the man, the contrast between the bright hopes of the outset and the deep gloom of the close, the contrast between his rich endowments and his hapless fate. He unto whom 'the soul of king David longed to go forth' in the midst of his sorest displeasure, he of whom it is said that 'in all Israel there was none so much praised for his beauty,' in whom 'there was no blemish from the sole of his foot even to the crown of his head,' who by his winning courtesy 'stole the hearts of the men of Israel,' would, we feel sure, have stolen our hearts also.

Outside the walls of Jerusalem over the brook Kidron stands an ancient monument traditionally reputed to be the tomb of Absalom. Its sides, we are told, are 'buried deep with the stones which' the Jews 'throw against it in execration.' It is a religious duty with the modern Israelites to curse the memory of this prince who stole the hearts of their forefathers. Let the contrast speak for itself.

The lesson is one of common and very painful experience—dark treachery underlying an easy gaiety of manner, intense selfishness veiled by a graceful courtesy of demeanour, a worthless heart set in a beautiful frame. Are there any, whom God has endowed with gifts resembling these, who are conscious of possessing a certain power which secures them an easy victory over the hearts and minds of others— whether personal graces or conversational fluency or ready tact? Let them be ever on their guard against themselves. These are precious endowments, if used rightly. They force a way, where a way is barred to others; they smooth the path of life through its roughest obstructions; they light up the journey of life through its darkest and dreariest wastes. But they have their special dangers also. The very ease, with which such persons pass through life, removes the most valuable trials of life. When ascendency over others is gained without an effort by the attraction of personal graces, the heart will stagnate, because it receives no discipline and learns no lessons of self-denial. And hence, unless he keeps constant watch over himself, the possessor must become unfeeling and selfish. So too with the possession of natural tact— an equally valuable and equally dangerous gift. It tempts men to trust to the management, rather than to the goodness, of their cause, to match versatility against truth; and thus, though they began perhaps by being not less single or upright than their neighbours, they fall imperceptibly into disingenuousness and fraud. We forebode ill of the spoilt child of a household; but these are the spoilt children of a neighbourhood, of a people, of society at large.

Such, we may imagine, were Absalom's temptations; such certainly was Absalom's fall. But in choosing the subject I did not intend to dwell so much on the faults of the son, as on the sorrows of the father. I wished to consider the sequel of David's life as the consequence of David's sin.

God has not so willed that the laws of His spiritual interference shall supersede the laws of natural sequence. The 'water spilt on the ground' 'cannot be gathered up again.' The sinful deed is an accomplished fact; it is done and it cannot be undone; the pardon is granted, but the consequences are not evaded. Thus expositors have pointed out (and the lesson is eminently instructive) how each one of the calamities, which overwhelmed the repentant king, flowed from some source of guilt. They have bidden us observe that the shameful deed of Amnon, which aroused Absalom's bloodthirsty revenge, and thus led to his banishment, his estrangement from his father, his rebellion and his death, grew out of the irregularities which must prevail in a household where polygamy is the rule. They have noticed that Ahithophel, the cunning and treacherous counsellor of Absalom, appears incidentally to have been the grandfather of Bathsheba, and that therefore his desertion and hostility may have been provoked by David's crime. They have observed also that the increased power and ascendency of Joab (to which the king's sorrows and perplexities henceforth were mainly due) must be traced to his possession of the fatal secret, to his virtual complicity in the murder of Uriah. They have suggested, moreover, that some rumours of David's guilt, having spread, would relax his hold on the affections of his people, and thus prepare the way for the revolt. They might have added (if they have not added), that the sins of the father must have lowered the moral tone of the houschold, and encouraged (if they did not suggest) the sins of the sons; for it is the very nature of such crimes to spread by contagion. At all events, he who himself had done a deed of shame could not reprobate Amnon for a deed of shame; he who himself had committed a virtual murder from guilty passion could not punish Absalom for a murder committed in revenge and under exasperation, with the crushing moral force, the lofty freedom, of conscious innocence.

But indeed this is no arbitrary inference from the facts of the history, no subtle but unwarranted theory of modern expositors. The very prophet, who declared the pardon, foretold at the same time the consequences of the sin. 'Now therefore the sword shall never depart from thy house.' 'Thus saith the Lord, Behold I will raise up evil against thee out of thine own house.' 'Thou didst it secretly; but I will do this thing before all Israel, and before the sun.' God's law of cause and consequence cannot be suspended. 'Be not deceived.' 'Whatsoever a man soweth, that shall he also reap.' Such as the seed is, such will also be the harvest.

'There are some,' said the great Augustine, 'for whom it is good to fall.' He who thus spoke had himself sinned deeply in youth, had himself fallen, and had risen from his fall. In him, as in the repentant king, God had created a clean heart and renewed a right spirit. Thus cleansed and regenerated, he was permitted to pass behind the veil and to declare the hidden things of God with a spiritual insight rarely equalled since Apostolic times. And yet our moral instinct, not less than David's example, forbids us to accept this unguarded saying. It cannot be good for any one to fall.

Not good to fall. For what in common language we understand by the fall, is not the fall itself. The fall itself has been accomplished long before. The one startling act, the one concentrated sin, whether of thought or of word or of deed, is only the indication of an evil state of mind, fostered, encouraged, developed by a slow growth, only the consummation of a gradual decline. The entertaining and the cherishing of the propensity to evil (whatever form this propensity may take) the ever advancing deterioration of the soul—this is the true fall. The other is only the outward symbol, the concrete embodiment, of the fall. It is good for a man to find out that he has fallen; but it never can be good for him to fall.

Not good to fall. For though God may create a clean heart and renew a right spirit in a man, his sin has left behind a bitter heritage of trial, a heavy burden of suffering, which he can only lay down with his life. So at least it was with David. Is there any one, who, dissatisfied with his insensibility to sin and wearied with the deadness of his heart, is tempted to escape from this moral torpor by some overt act of evil, who in despair would embrace penitence as a spiritual luxury, would in the Apostle's language 'sin that grace may abound'? Is not David's history enough to banish such a perilous thought? If he is too weak to shake off the burden of spiritual sloth, is he strong enough to bear the intolerable load which his sin will lay on him in its consequences? We can well imagine that David's heaviest sorrows, as he mourned over the troubles of his household, over the desertion of his friends, over the rebellion and death of his favourite son, was the thought that all these trials were the legitimate consequences of his own fall; and that with a bitter pang of self-reproach he would see, as many a father has seen, in the sins of his children the reflection and the legacy of his own sins. His guilt had indeed been cleansed by the copious streams of God's mercy; but the consequences of his guilt he must bathe in his own tears, without hoping to wash them away in this life.

With such tears—the tears of mingled sorrow and self-reproach—he bade farewell to his own new capital, his beautiful Zion, when the rebellion broke out. 'And David went up by the ascent of mount Olivet, and wept as he went up, and had his head covered.'

We are reminded by these words of a later scene

where another, resting on the slope of this same hill, shed tears over this same Jerusalem. 'And when He was come near,' says the Evangelist, 'He beheld the city and wept over it, saying, If thou hadst known, even thou, at least in this thy day, the things which belong unto thy peace. But now they are hid from thine eyes.'

The place and the incident are the same; and yet what a contrast is there in the situation and the feelings of the two mourners! A great moral gulf separates the one from the other; and this gulf is the consciousness of past sin. David's Son, like David himself, shed tears over a rebellious city, bewailed the abuse of rich opportunities, the eclipse of bright hopes. But in His grief there mingled no bitter aftertaste of remorse, no shame, and self-reproach for the past. It was the pure, calm sorrow, which can be felt only by one looking down from the lofty heights of innocence on a people infatuated in its sin and hastening to its ruin. He shed tears, but He did not cover His head.

With still more bitter tears and with still keener self-reproach, now that the rebellion is crushed, the broken-hearted king abandons himself to his grief. He would give anything now—his wealth, his kingdom, his life—to have his son back. And yet he himself (he cannot shut out the thought) he himself must bear the blame—at least in part—for the crimes, the rebellion, the death, of his handsome, winning, wayward boy. Ah! was he not indeed taken in his mischief? Was he not indeed 'a man of blood'?

Soon or late each man will have his sorrows in life. It is not good for any one that he should escape them. By suffering even the Son of Man was made perfect; by suffering we must be taught, as He was taught. Well then will it be for us, if, when the hour of trial comes, we meet the struggle, not like David with accumulated agony and shame as those reaping the harvest of seeds they themselves have sown, but in the likeness, however faint, of David's greater descendant with a saintly heroic sorrow as those mourning over sins from which they are free, and bearing calamities which they did not cause.

But if, when the trial comes, it should find us otherwise; if the type of our sorrow must be sought in the son of Jesse, not in the Son of Man; if we have sinned by some violation of God's laws, whether of honesty or of truth or of purity or of mercy or of love, so that our sufferings may be directly traced to our sin; if, like another rude Shimei, our conscience from its vantage-ground above hurl stones and cast dust and heap curses on us, as we pass mournfully through the valley of our humiliation, reproaching us with being taken in our own mischief; yet nevertheless even so it is good for us; even so let us take heart. God's blessing is wrapped up in Shimei's curses, as the fertilising rain is held in the black thunder-cloud. 'Let him alone, and let him curse: it may be that the Lord will look on mine affliction. It is no sign to us this, that God's arm is shortened, that God's pardon is qualified. It is the very token of His presence; it is the very message of His love. It is His discipline, assuring us that He has not overlooked our needs. It confirms to ourselves individually the joyful tidings which the Church proclaims to all at this season, and which nature herself with her fresh awakening glories enforces by type; for it speaks of resurrection, of renewal, of life.

IV.

CÆSAR'S TRIBUTE AND GOD'S TRIBUTE.

*Render to Cæsar the things that are Cæsar's,
and to God the things that are God's.*

S. MARK xii. 17.

I SUPPOSE that the selection of these words will seem to many to allow the preacher no alternative as to the subject which he proposes to consider. The text, and the application of the text, are too familiar to leave his hearers in any uncertainty. The preacher must desire to say something on the relations of Church and State. He must intend to discuss the advantages and disadvantages of an Establishment. He must wish to adjust and apportion the obligations which we owe to the civil and the spiritual powers respectively.

Let me say plainly at the outset, that I have no such intention. I do not underrate the importance of such questions, but I do not purpose speaking of them to-day, simply because (if I understand the text aright) it has nothing at all to do with such topics, or at least it has only a very remote and indirect bearing upon them. This language perhaps will seem startling to some. They have been accustomed to regard this text as the chief authority on the subject. They have seen it quoted so frequently in the newspapers; they have heard it so applied again and again in sermons. Churchmen and Nonconformists—friends of Establishment and foes of Establishment—have alike accepted it in this sense.

But can this possibly be its bearing? If this were so, it must be intended to draw a broad line of demarcation between two sets of duties. 'Here is one set of obligations which we owe to Cæsar and not to God, and there is another set which we owe to God and not to Cæsar. Keep the two quite distinct. Do not think at all of God's pleasure or displeasure, when you are doing Cæsar's work; and do not regard Cæsar's approval or disapproval, when you are doing God's work.'

If the purport of the precept, I say, is distinction, then the distinction must be as sharp and definite as this. The text must proclaim a duality of authority. Yet we are startled, when the issue is thus set before us. Can anything be imagined more unscriptural— I might well say, more irreligious, more blasphemous

—than this? Is not the Bible from the first chapter of Genesis to the last chapter of Revelation one unbroken protest against this sharp distinction of the secular and the spiritual? Does it not teach us that our religion must be everywhere, because God is everywhere? And more especially, when it enforces our duties towards our temporal rulers, what language does it hold? Are we not plainly told that we owe obedience to kings and governors, because they are God's instruments, God's representatives, God's vicegerents? See how S. Paul emphasizes this view; 'There is no power but of God.' 'The powers that be are ordained of God.' 'He is a minister of God to thee for good.' 'He is a minister of God to execute wrath.' 'For this cause pay ye tribute also, for they are ministers of God.' Not less than six times in as many verses does the Apostle reiterate this statement, that allegiance to our temporal rulers is allegiance to God. And in the last passage, as you will observe, the precept has reference to this very matter of paying tribute.

It is plain, therefore, that the words cannot mean this. But, if we desire to know what is their real purport, we must investigate the circumstances which called them forth. Who were the questioners? What was their motive?

The questioners, we are told, were the Pharisees

and the Herodians. With the Pharisees we are well acquainted. Of the Herodians we know nothing, except what this incident reveals. Whether they were a religious sect or a political party, we are not informed. Their name merely shows that they were favourable to the ascendency of Herod and Herod's family.

The Pharisees and the Herodians alike must have had a genuine interest in the question which they asked, 'Is it lawful to give tribute to Cæsar or not?' It was not a mere speculative question. It was a direct, pressing, personal, practical matter; 'Shall we give, or shall we not give?' Here is the tax-gatherer at my door, and it is a case of conscience with me, whether I may give, whether I can give, or whether I ought not rather to submit to all the untold consequences of refusal. To the Herodian probably the question presented itself as the alternative between his allegiance to a native or quasi-native dynasty, and the demands of a foreign ruler. But to the Pharisee it would assume a far higher aspect. To him it was essentially a matter of conscience, of religion. This Cæsar was the arch-heathen, the arch-enemy of Israel; he had his throne on the Babylon of the seven hills; he had set his heel on the neck of the covenant people of God; everything about him was profane. The sound of the Roman language in the law courts offended the ears of the Pharisee; the sight of the Roman eagles hovering over the temple area itself shocked his eyes. Could he—a son of Abraham and Isaac and Jacob—by an overt act acknowledge the sovereignty of this profane tyrant? Was it not a question between king Cæsar, who was there, and king Messias, who was to come? And, if so, ought he to hesitate for a moment? Had he not here in another form the same alternative which was offered to Israel of old on Carmel; 'If Jehovah be God, then follow Him; but if Baal be God, then follow Him?'

Thus it was a question, which a perfectly sincere but somewhat bigoted Pharisee might well have asked. But these men were not sincere. The Evangelists speak of their craftiness, their hypocrisy; our Lord addresses them as hypocrites. S. Luke describes them as 'spies who feigned themselves upright men.' Their object was not to solve their own difficulties, but to entangle Him in difficulties. In scriptural language they were tempting Him, luring Him on, that they might weave their meshes about Him. Hence the unnatural alliance. The Pharisees and the Herodians had nothing in common. But they would band themselves together to destroy Jesus— just as the Pharisees and Sadducees made common cause, just as Jews and Romans were leagued together, just as Herod and Pontius Pilate shook hands over their victim—because, though they hated one another, they hated Him far more. Had they not both alike cause to hate Him? Could the Pharisees love Him, when He denounced their zeal as cunning, and their piety as pretence, when He held them up as a scorn and byword to the people, whose professed leaders they were? Could the Herodians wish Him well, when He denounced the leaven of Herod, and when He stigmatized their chief as a fox? Therefore they conspire. They appeal to His courage. 'Thou art true, and carest for no man.' They will flatter His pride, and lure Him on to His ruin. The question placed Him in a dilemma; 'Shall we give tribute to Cæsar, or not?' If He answered 'Yes,' He would lose caste. He would forfeit His character for boldness; He would offend the scruples of the religious patriots; He would sink into a mere truckler and time-server. If He had any design of becoming a popular leader—possibly a Messiah—this would be its death-blow. Antagonism to foreign rule was the only standing-ground for such a leader. But this was not what they hoped. They desired that He should answer 'No.' By praising His courage and independence of spirit, they strove to elicit this answer. And, if He should so answer, their work was done. It was overt treason; it was rank rebellion. The iron grip of the

Roman authorities would close upon Him at once; and there would be an end of Him. Their conduct was of a piece with the shameful hypocrisy which afterwards raised the cry, 'We have no king but Cæsar'—Cæsar whom they detested, Cæsar against whom their heart of hearts rebelled, Cæsar whose yoke they would throw off to-morrow, if they could.

Our Lord does not answer them directly 'Yes' or 'No.' He asks for a denarius—the common silver coin of the day. What do they see there? The broad brow laurel-crowned, the stern, cruel, mysterious visage of Tiberius the reigning Emperor; or perhaps the singularly handsome, regular, finely-cut features of his predecessor, the now deified Augustus. And this portraiture, this name thus stamped on the coin, is in some sense a mark of ownership. It comes from Cæsar's mint, and must be restored to Cæsar's exchequer. It symbolizes the obligations which are due to the civil power. It tells of a fixed and orderly government, which secures their lives and properties to them, which provides for the impartial administration of justice, which watches over and regulates commercial transactions, which has assigned its weight and its value to this very coin, which in short makes life possible and worth living for them. Cæsar's head, Cæsar's superscription, is engraved upon this coin, just as it is engraved upon the institutions under which they live. The question was not rightly put; 'Is it *lawful* to give tribute to Cæsar?' The answer is; 'You are not only permitted, you are *bound* to give tribute.' The payment is a repayment for the inestimable benefits which you have received from the State. This then is the purport of our Lord's answer. He declares not indeed the Divine right of an Augustus or a Tiberius, not the Divine right of kings or of emperors, nor yet the Divine right of democracies, but the Divine right of established government, the Divine right of law and order. 'Render to Cæsar the things that are Cæsar's.' The argument would have been just as valid, if instead of an Augustus or a Tiberius the emblem of the Roman Republic had been stamped upon that coin.

'Render to Cæsar the things that are Cæsar's.' Here is a complete answer to their question. But this is not enough. The opportunity is seized. A rebuke is administered, and a lesson is enforced. These Pharisees were very scrupulous about the lower duties of religion, but very forgetful of the higher. They paid their tithe on mint and anise and cummin to the extreme farthing, and yet they omitted the weightier matters of the law, judgment and mercy and truth. They washed the outside of the cup and the platter, but within they were full of extortion and excess.

So here. They are infinitely scrupulous, or at least they feign to be so, about the political aspects of religion; but are they equally anxious about the moral and spiritual?

This is the frame of mind, which our Lord would correct. 'Yes,' He seems to say, 'Ask what is your duty with regard to Cæsar. But do not stop here. Do not rest content with dwelling on the politics of religion. Rise above your relations towards Cæsar, and face your relations towards God. This silver-piece is a type, is a parable, for you. Is there no other tribute, think you, which you owe to a higher than Cæsar? Is there no other coinage, which bears the image and the superscription of One greater than Cæsar? Aye, for is it not written that God created man in His own image; in the image of God created He him? His effigy is stamped upon thee; His name and attributes are written around thee. From His mint thou wast issued, and to His treasury must thou be repaid. If to Cæsar thou owest the tribute of these perishable coins, to God thou owest the tribute of thy soul, thy mind, thy life, the tribute of thyself.'

I suppose that for every one man who is really eager about the spiritual and personal aspects of religion, who hungers and thirsts after righteousness, whose soul pants after the living God, scores of persons take an active and sincere interest in its polemics—the controversy between Romanism and Protestantism, the disputes between Churchman and Nonconformist, the relations of Church and State, the conflict between faith and unbelief. This is not a disease of any one time or any one place. It was characteristic alike of the orthodox Pharisee and the heretic Samaritan. When the Samaritan woman suddenly finds herself face to face with a prophet, how does she use her opportunity? 'Sir, teach me how to lay aside this burden of wickedness; Sir, help me to cleanse my sin-stained life; Sir, bring me nearer to God?' Not this, but 'Sir, tell me whether at Jerusalem or on this mountain men ought to worship;' a question not unimportant in itself, a question to which there was a right and a wrong answer, but a question infinitely little, infinitely valueless to her then and there—to her with her sin-stained heart, to her with her sullied life.

Whose is this image and superscription—this, which is stamped on thyself, O man? It was not an uncommon metaphor to speak of men as coins; the dishonest and bad, as spurious and counterfeit; the upright, as genuine currency with the true ring. So an Apostolic father writes in the next age: 'There are two coinages,—the one of God, the other of the world; and each is stamped with its own device. The unbelievers bear the impress of this world; the believers, of God the Father through Jesus Christ in love.' When then, having first asked, 'Whose is this image,' our Lord closes with the injunction, 'Render to God the things that are God's,' is it too much to infer that the connecting link between the symbol and the application was that familiar text, 'In the image of God created He him?'

Whose is this image? Look into yourself and see what lineaments are traced there. What is this conscience, approving, stimulating, terrifying, punishing, but the impress of the Righteousness of God? What is this capacity of progress, which distinguishes you from the beasts that perish, which urges you ever forward eager and restless, but the signet of the Perfection of God? What is this power of memory and imagination, which annihilates time and space, penetrating into the pre-historic past and projecting itself into the boundless future, traversing the heavens with more than the speed of lightning, but the stamp of the Omnipresence of God? What is this anxiety about the hereafter, this desire of posthumous fame, this interest in descendants yet unborn, this witness of your immortality within you, but the seal set upon you by the Eternity of God? Yes, everywhere are God's features stamped upon your soul, however blurred by ill-usage and however corroded by rust.

But again. Whose is this image and superscription—this which is stamped on thee, O Christian? When your brow was sealed in baptism, with whose signet was it sealed? Remember how the Apostle speaks of admission into the Church of Christ, and to the privileges of the Gospel, as a re-creating, a renewing after the image of God. In this second creation the same image was restamped upon you. The blurred lines were sharpened, as you passed once again through the mint of God. The obverse is still the face of God, while the reverse is the Cross of Christ. The old ownership is doubly affirmed. You are bought—bought with the costliest price which even God Himself could pay. Henceforth you are not your own. You are God's—God's by redemption now, as you were His by creation before. 'Render to God the things that are God's.'

V.

THE FALL OF JUDAS.

Jesus answered them, Have not I chosen you twelve, and one of you is a devil? He spake of Judas Iscariot the son of Simon: for he it was that should betray Him, being one of the twelve.

S. JOHN vi. 70, 71.

Thirteenth Sunday after Trinity, 1871.

THE one crime, which society judges hardly, for which it holds no penalty too severe, is treachery. Of other sins the world is a lenient critic. It deals very gently with the profligate; it is full of excuses for the self-willed and violent. It has a sympathy with passion—the passion of the sensualist, or the passion of the headstrong—which softens its judgment. But the traitor receives no mercy at the bar of public opinion. The instinct of self-preservation does not leave society a choice. It could not hold together, if perfidy were overlooked. The betrayal of a friend, the betrayal of a cause, the betrayal of one's country —these are unforgiven and unforgotten crimes. Even treachery to a treacherous cause is barely tolerated. The law employs it, and disguises it with a specious title. We call it 'turning Queen's evidence,' but still it is repulsive. We avail ourselves of the treachery, but we loathe the traitor. It is an ugly name and an ugly thing, to which no social or political necessity can altogether reconcile us.

And here in the text we are confronted with the arch-traitor himself—the one man, before whose one act the darkest treacheries recorded in the annals of crime seem pale and colourless, whose name is handed down to all generations branded with the reproach of a never-dying infamy. For he betrayed the Friend, Who was the very impersonation of Love; he betrayed the cause, in which the eternal interests of mankind are bound up; he betrayed the country, of which we all are citizens, the kingdom of heaven, where we all aspire to dwell.

Is not the case of Judas, we are led to ask, so exceptional, that his temptation is not our temptation, that his crime cannot be our crime, and that therefore his fall has no lesson of warning for us? Nay, his sin seems so unnatural and monstrous, that we have some difficulty in even realising it. The contrast is too violent between the Apostle and the traitor—the intimate communion with the Holy One here, the vile perfidy to the Friend and Saviour there: the unique advantages here, the unparalleled baseness there. The perfect example of the Master, the elevating society of the fellow-disciples, the words of truth, the works of power, the grace, the purity, the holiness, the love—all these forgotten, spurned, trampled under foot, to gratify one miserable, greedy passion, if not the worst, at least the meanest, which can possess the heart of man. On this moral contrast our Lord lays special emphasis in the language of the text. 'Have I not chosen you, the twelve, chosen you out of the many thousands in Israel, in preference to the high-born and the powerful, in preference to the rabbi and the scribe and the priest, chosen you a mere handful of men to be My intimate friends, My special messengers now, to sit on twelve thrones judging the twelve tribes of Israel hereafter; and yet one among you is not faithless only, not unworthy, not sinful only, but a very impersonation of the Accuser, the Arch-fiend himself.'

Our experiences may recall some faint type of such a contrast, where the circumstances of the criminal and the baseness of the crime seem to stand in no relation to each other. We may have seen some one member of a family, brought up under conditions the most favourable to his moral and religious development, watched over by parents whose devoted care was never at fault, growing up among brothers and sisters whose example suggested only innocence and truthfulness, breathing in short the very atmosphere of holiness and purity and love; and yet he has fallen—fallen we know not how, but fallen so low that even the world rejects him as an outcast. He is a traitor to the family name, he has dragged the family honour in the mire. And yet, until lately, he was, to all outward appearances, as one of the rest— sharing the same companionships, joining in the same amusements, learning the same lessons, nay, even wearing the same family features, speaking with his father's voice, or smiling with his mother's smile.

But, though such experiences may serve in some measure to account for the fall of Judas, yet we feel that much still remains unexplained. The exceptional circumstances have not yet been taken into our reckoning. There is a theological difficulty, and there is a moral difficulty. The theological difficulty relates to the part taken by our Lord Himself; the moral difficulty relates to the part taken by Judas.

1. There is the theological difficulty. If our Lord did indeed read men's hearts, if with Divine insight He could forecast the future, how did He admit into His little band one, in whom even then He saw the germs of a base passion, and whose fall

hereafter He must have foreknown by His omnipresent intuition? There is something strangely contradictory, we are apt to think, between the selection to the Apostleship and the prescience of the betrayal.

But is it really so? If, when Judas was chosen to his high office, his heart had been already cankered with avarice, and his character debased, then indeed the difficulty would be great; then indeed his selection would have been (we cannot think the thought without irreverence) a solemn unreality, a mere dramatic display. But we have no reason to suppose this. When he was chosen, he was worthy of the choice; he was not a bad man; he had, we must suppose, no common capacities for good; there was in him perhaps the making of a S. Peter or a S. John. His whole history points to this view of his character. Can we suppose that he alone had made no sacrifices, suffered no privations, met with no reproaches, during those three years, in which through good and evil report he followed that Master, Who was despised and rejected of men, Who had not where to lay His head? Can we imagine that he alone had given no pledges of his earnestness, that he alone escaped the bitter consequences of discipleship, that from him alone Christ's unpopularity glanced off without leaving a bruise or a scar behind? And does not his terrible end read the same lesson? The sudden revulsion of feeling, the bitter remorse, the crushing despair, so fatal in its result, serves but to show what he might have been, if one vile passion had not been cherished in him till it had eaten out all his better nature. And so it was, that throughout the Lord's ministry, even to the last fatal moment, he seems to have been unsuspected by his brother Apostles, moving about with them, trusted by them, appearing outwardly as one of them. On that night when the Master announces the approaching treachery, each asks sorrowfully, 'Is it I?'—not enduring to entertain the thought of himself, and yet not daring to suspect the evil in another. All this while Judas was on his trial, as we are on our trial. He was selected for the Apostleship, as we are called into Church-membership. But, like us, he was allowed the exercise of his human free-will; he was not compelled by an irresistible fate to act worthily of his calling; he was free to make his election between good and evil; he rejected the good, and he chose the evil.

And therefore the theological difficulty no longer remains. We cannot say how God's foreknowledge and our free-will should coexist. The prescience of Christ is as the prescience of God. It is subject to the same conditions, is attended with the same difficulties. His little company was not intended to be perfect. Otherwise it would have conveyed no lessons to us. It had its coward in Peter; its sceptic in Thomas; and it had also its traitor in Judas.

2. But the second difficulty, the moral difficulty, still remains. Granted that there is nothing inconsistent with God's known dealings elsewhere in our Lord's selection of Judas to the Apostleship, yet how are we to explain the conduct of Judas himself? With these advantages, amidst these associations, before this Presence, how could he so fall? Have we not here a moral impossibility?

Had he not, day after day, and month after month, and year after year, listened to the voice of Him, Who spake as never man spake, Whose single utterances have had power to turn from evil to good and to change at once the whole tenour of a life, Whose words ringing through all the ages now after the lapse of eighteen centuries speak to the hearts of every man and every nation with a force and a distinctness and a penetration peculiarly their own? Had he not heard Him, as He denounced the cares of this world and the deceitfulness of riches; as He declared the impossibility of a divided worship between God and Mammon? Amidst all distractions, through every discouragement, Judas had remained, had persevered, had listened; listened to all that He had uttered from that first conscience-stirring sermon on the Galilean Mount to these last solemn discourses on Olivet and in Jerusalem; and yet he was a traitor.

And had he not also witnessed those mighty works—works which no man could do, except God were with him, which were the very credentials of His Messianic claims? Had he not been present when those five thousand were fed on the few loaves in Galilee, and those four thousand in Decapolis? Had he not seen the lame walk, and the dumb speak, and the lepers cleansed, by that voice and under that touch? Had he not witnessed the very devils unwillingly confessing His name? Nay, had he not, only a short time ago, not far from this very spot, seen the crowning miracle of all, when the friend, who had been dead already four days, was restored to life again, and seated at table with his Master; and yet he was a traitor.

I know that some have sought an escape from this difficulty by supposing that the motives of Judas were not so very bad after all. He was very wrong, no doubt, they would say; but his fault was quite as much an error of judgment as an obliquity of moral principle. He did not intend his Master to be put to death. He believed in His Messianic claims. He knew that He was the predicted King of Israel. But he was impatient that Jesus did not declare Himself. He was dissatisfied that so many golden opportunities had been lost, that year after year had passed and nothing was done. And so he would put an end to this long suspense; he would compel his Master to assert His sovereignty; he would concentrate upon Him the antagonism of the rulers in such a way that He must declare Himself, must confound His enemies by the exercise of His supernatural powers, and stand forth confessed the Anointed, the Chosen One, the King of Israel.

To this there is one decisive answer. The Gospel narrative gives no intimation that this, or anything like this, was his motive. On the contrary, they suggest a very different view of Judas's character. 'This he said, not that he cared for the poor; but because he was a thief, and had the bag, and bare (or purloined) what was put therein.' He had misappropriated the general funds, as we should say, in delicate modern phrase; the Evangelist knows nothing of delicate modern phrases, and calls it thieving. He had allowed one vile passion to grow unchecked in his heart. His office, as treasurer of the little company, had given him opportunities of indulging this passion. He had yielded, and so fell.

But after all does this painful history really contradict our experience? Experience may not carry us to the extreme point where Judas's transgression lies; but, so far as it goes, it only confirms this strange contradiction. For it teaches that the moral character by no means keeps pace with the moral opportunities;

nay, it shows that, when a man, placed in a position eminently favourable to the development of his higher self, does nevertheless give the rein to some vicious tendency within, his vice seems to gain strength by this very fact. It can only be indulged by resistance to the good influences about him, and resistance always gives compactness and force, always braces the capacity, whether for good or for evil. Moreover, such a man gets to isolate his vicious passion from the surrounding circumstances, even from the better impulses within himself. If he did not, his relations with those about him would be intolerable; the conflict in his own heart would be too agonizing. But when, gradually and half-unconsciously, he has got to treat his special temptation as something apart, to concede to it a special privilege, to regard it as a law to itself; then the moral checks are removed; then it thrives, uninterrupted and almost unnoticed; until at length it casts away its disguises, it throws off all control, and reveals itself in all its vile deformity.

This then is the first stage in the traitor's fall. It is the often-told tale of a single sin springing up and luxuriating in secret, till in its rank growth it has twined itself around all the fibres of the heart, and choked and killed with its poisonous embrace whatever there was of pure and noble and good in that soul. The process had been a gradual process. It is an old and a true saying, that no man ever became utterly base at once. Utter baseness requires a long education ; but it is carried on in secret, and so we do not notice it. The heinous, shocking crime first startles us, but it is only the end of a long series. It was so no doubt with Judas. He had had, as every man, whether good or bad, has in some form or other, an evil tendency in his heart. Here was his trial ; here might have been his moral education. But he made it his master, and it plunged him in headlong ruin. There was, first of all, the pleasure of fingering the coin ; then there was the desire of accumulating ; then there was the reluctant hand and the grudging heart in distributing alms ; then there was the silent appropriation of some trifling sum, as indemnification for a real or imagined personal loss ; then there was the first unmistakeable act of petty fraud—and so it went on and on, until the disciple became the thief, the trusted became the traitor, the Apostle of Christ the Son of Perdition. For there was no external check upon him. The moral checks—the influences, the companionships, the Divine Presence, ought to have been more than a compensation for the absence of material checks. This was his spiritual probation. The incomings and the outgoings of the common purse were alike precarious. There was no balancing of ledgers, no auditing of accounts in the little company. No one knew what was received and what was spent. Each trusted, and each was trusted by, the other.

Up to the time of his fall Judas had been avaricious, miserly, fraudulent. Let us use the plain language of the Evangelist, he had been a thief. But a traitor, an arch-traitor—this was far from his thoughts. To betray, to ruin, to kill the Master Whom he respected and feared, Whom perhaps after his poor fashion he loved, Whose fortunes he had followed so long, Who (he must have felt it in his heart of hearts) was the destined deliverer, the anointed King of Israel—this was too terrible, too shocking, even for the imagination to entertain.

Let us follow this history now through its second stage—the temptation and the struggle. The opportunity came. The match was put to the train, which long inveterate habit had laid. And could the result be otherwise?

The opportunity came. I do not doubt that he reasoned about it. There was much to be said for his yielding; there always is much to be said for yielding, when a temptation courts acquiescence. He might argue thus. Either Jesus is the Christ, or He is not. If He is the Christ, my act will do no harm— nay, it will be a positive good. It will be the means of eliciting the truth. He will be confronted with His opponents; He will wrest Himself from their grasp; He will crush them by His divine power; He will ride triumphant over His foes, and seat Himself on the throne of Israel. If He is the Messiah, no act of mine can touch Him.

But what if he is not the Messiah? What if those works of power, which I have witnessed, were wrought, as the priests and Pharisees have said, not by the finger of God, but by Beelzebub, the prince of the devils? What if He is a mere pretender, a rank impostor? Then there can be no doubt about the wisdom, the propriety of this course. By exposing this gigantic imposture, by terminating these blasphemous assumptions, I shall confer a substantial benefit on my generation and my country.

Thus he might argue. Whatever of belief there was in him, and whatever of scepticism there was in him, pointed in the same way. With the evil-hearted all things turn to evil. The argument was without a flaw. It had only one fault: it was wholly beside the question. It did not touch the motive of the act, and therefore did not touch the character of the act. Believe me, if there is one maxim more sound, more saving, more universal in its application than another, it is this—never to reason, never to argue, in the face of temptation; but to spurn it from your presence, if you are strong enough; if not, to flee from its presence.

Of all cases this is the one where to argue, and so to hesitate (for if you argue you must hesitate), is to be lost. Logic and argument have their high and noble functions; but this is not their place. Here we want not reasoning; we want love and conscience—conscience which directs, and love which inspires. Love is better than reason. If you would realise the contrast between the two, recall the scene in Simon's house at Bethany six days before. There too Judas reasons, while Mary loves. 'Why was not this ointment sold for three hundred pence, and given to the poor?' Here also the reasoning is faultless; it has been repeated again and again in diverse forms, when an excuse is sought for niggardliness. But it was said without love, and it is repeated without love. Better, a thousand times better, the unreasoning devotion, the uncalculating abandonment of love in Mary, than the prudential logic, the strong practical common-sense of Judas. Of her it is said, 'Wheresoever this Gospel shall be preached in the whole world, there shall also this be told for a memorial of her.' Of him, 'Woe unto that man by whom the Son of Man is betrayed; it had been good for that man if he had not been born.'

And so Judas fell. Love might have saved him: reason killed him. He fell; and the heinousness of his crime, the greatness of his fall, lay in this, that he sinned against light. He, whose feet this very night the Master had washed as an example to His disciples, he, who this very night had partaken of the sacramental bread and wine, went out and forthwith betrayed his Lord. This violent contrast is ever present in the narratives of the Evangelists. 'Judas, which betrayed Him, being one of the twelve,' says S. John. 'He was numbered with us, and obtained part of this ministry,' says S. Peter. And all the incidents connected with his fatal act are symbolical of the contrast—the favours, the privileges, the light, vouchsafed on the one side: the meanness, the ingratitude, the blackness of the treachery on the other. 'He it is, to whom I shall give the sop, when I have dipped it.' And the transition is as sudden as the contrast is violent. 'And after the sop Satan entered into him. He then having received the sop immediately went out: and it was night.'

'It was night.' In the full presence of the glorious Sunlight it was night to that traitorous, fallen man. With darkness overhead, and deeper darkness still within, he did the deed of eternal, irretrievable infamy.

The deed is done; the Master is condemned; the reward is secured. And then the revulsion comes. What is now the value of those few paltry coins? What is now the use of that persuasive, flawless logic? Is there any one here in this congregation, who has passed through any similar experience; who has sacrificed his probity and honour, the pillar of his inward self-respect, to the temptation of some sordid gain; who has bartered his purity—the royal robe of his Christian birthright—for the gratification of some hasty passion, and found out, then when it is too late, in the bitterness of remorse, that the bright, tempting, full-ripe fruit was turned to rottenness in his grasp— loathsome to the eye and poisonous to the taste? If so, he may realise, faintly realise, the despair of Judas, when he awoke from his moral trance. It was night, when the deed was done; now there is light—only too much light—striking in upon his soul, and piercing its darkest and most dreaded recesses with a painful glare.

The end we know. He flung back the accursed coin, the seal of his guilt, to those who had tempted to the fatal act. He could not bear the light, could not bear life, could not bear himself.

An ancient writer, impressed by the bitterness of his grief and the sincerity of his confession, 'I have sinned in that I have betrayed the innocent blood,' would interpret his suicide favourably. In the agony of his condition he could not bear to wait; his Master was doomed, and he would anticipate Him; would rush at once into the world of the unseen, seek His presence there, and confess the heinousness of his

guilt, and throw himself on His infinite compassion—
'with his bare soul.' It is a striking thought. 'With
his bare soul'—stripped of those hands which sealed
the fatal compact by their grasp, of those eyes which
gloated over the accursed gain, of those lips which
gave the final, fatal, treacherous kiss. And yet this,
we feel, is not the Judas of the Evangelists, the Son
of Perdition. 'With his bare soul.' It had been bare
enough throughout in the sight of God, with all its
dark windings, all its treacherous subterfuges—bare
with that blackened guilt, which a long life of penitence were too little to wipe out, and which a suicidal
death could only fix there the more indelibly.

'He went to his own place'—this is S. Peter's
simple phrase. The veil is drawn over his fate. We
dare not, cannot lift it. There let us leave him;
there to the mercy of the Righteous Judge, and the
justice of a merciful God; there 'with his bare soul,'
in the presence of the Christ, Whom he betrayed and
crucified. It is not ours to judge. Only his history
remains; not as a discouragement, for that it cannot
be, but as a warning to us, how the greatest spiritual
privileges may be neutralised by the indulgence of
one illicit passion, and the life, which is lived in the
face of the unclouded sun, may set at last in the night
of despair.

VI.

THE COUNSEL OF CAIAPHAS.

And one of them, named Caiaphas, being the high-priest that same year, said unto them: Ye know nothing at all, nor consider that it is expedient for us, that one man should die for the people, and that the whole nation perish not.

S. JOHN xi. 49, 50.

Fourteenth Sunday after Trinity, 1871.

LAST Sunday I took as the subject of my sermon one of the principal agents in the passion of our Lord; to-day I purpose taking another. Last Sunday it was Judas; to-day it shall be Caiaphas. By the collusion of these two the result was attained, the death was compassed—fatal at once to Judas, fatal soon after to the Jewish priesthood, but bringing light and life and hope to untold generations of men and women yet unborn. Caiaphas spoke truly. It *was* expedient, though not as he understood it—not expedient for himself, the speaker, or for his order; not expedient for the Jewish priesthood or for the Jewish polity; but expedient for the saving of the nations, that this one man should die.

And what a contrast between the two chief conspirators in this crime! Last Sunday we followed the history of an isolated individual cherishing a fatal passion in secret. We traced the temptations, the misgivings, the self-excuses, the dark windings of that single, silent, traitorous heart. Now we are thrown into the midst of an ecclesiastical assembly, with its many voices, its diverse counsels, its tumultuous passions, till at length the master-spirit by force of character, and prestige of office, and definiteness of purpose, sways it to his own view, and all unite in the resolution, 'It is expedient for us, that one man—this one man—should die.' There we had the tempted; here we have the tempters. There we had the intimate friend, the chosen disciple, allured into the basest perfidy: here we have at least consistent enemies, who felt instinctively that the doctrine of this new Teacher must be fatal to their ascendency, and were only abiding their time to compass His destruction. And when the conspiracy is successful, and the deed is done, what a contrast still! Look at the agony of despair there; the heartless satisfaction here. 'I have sinned in that I have betrayed the innocent blood.' 'What is that to us? See thou to that.' It were almost better, we are tempted to think, to be like Judas crushed under the burden of that one unremitted sin, than like Caiaphas, and the colleagues of Caiaphas, rejoicing in the success of their criminal stratagem, and answering with a cold, cutting sneer the agonized remorse of their miserable dupe.

And I think too that in applying the lesson to ourselves, we feel something of this contrast. We cannot realise the crime of Judas; we repudiate it; we do not recognise any likeness to ourselves; we try to persuade ourselves that his history has no warning for us. His sin is so unique and monstrous. But, when we turn to the Jewish priesthood and the Jewish populace, the case is different. A secret misgiving arises in us that, if we had been there, we might have been found in the majority, nay, more probably than not, we should have been found in the majority. And a cold shudder creeps over us at the bare thought that, seated in that priestly gathering, we should have agreed with Caiaphas in the expediency of this one man's death; that, standing among that popular throng, we should have cried out to save Barabbas the robber, and to crucify Jesus the Christ.

Not that we have any sympathy with the counsel

of Caiaphas. How could we have any? Even if no world-wide issues had depended on the result, even if He, Whose life was trembling in the balance, had been an ordinary man, still this counsel would have been base, utterly base. It was unjust; it did not even profess to take account of right or wrong; whether the accused deserved to die or not, was wholly beside the question; there was a political necessity, and to this He must be sacrificed; it was expedient for them that He should die. Again, it was untruthful; the reasons, which Caiaphas and those with him put forward, were not the reasons which influenced them in their secret heart. They pleaded the danger of a popular demonstration and the anger of the Romans in consequence. 'They will come and take away our place and nation.' But mark them at a later stage, and judge whether the avowed pretext was the real motive. Then it was Pilate, the Roman governor, who could have saved Jesus; while by clamour and threat and insult these chief-priests drove him against his inclinations and against his judgment to shed the innocent blood. Again it was based on a conspiracy. This assembly was a motley group, composed of various members differing on essential questions of doctrine, and agreed only on this one point, that this Galilean must at all hazards be put out of the way. The greater part were Pharisees; Caiaphas himself, and the heads of the priesthood, were Sadducees. The Pharisees believed in the immortality of the soul; the Sadducees denied it. Could any more vital difference be conceived? But now they made common cause. Jesus was hateful to both alike. He was hateful to the Pharisees; for He had denounced their pride, their formalism, their hypocrisy, their spiritual tyranny, in no measured language. He was hateful to the Sadducees; for the raising of Lazarus, wrought in the very suburbs of Jerusalem and attracting crowds from the city itself, was a flat refutation of their leading doctrine, the denial of a resurrection. So they conspired against Him. And lastly it was selfish, intensely and cruelly selfish; for why should He, the blameless Galilean teacher, He Who had ever inculcated obedience to the powers that be, Who had enjoined His hearers always to render to Cæsar the things that are Cæsar's—why should He be sacrificed—in pretence, that the whole nation might not perish: in reality, that they, the priests, they, the Pharisees—their order, their prestige, their interests, they themselves—might not suffer?

And now, when we look back on the act in the light of revelation, with the experience of time—now, when we realise the full significance of putting this one man, this Galilean carpenter, to death, the injustice, the hypocrisy, the collusion, the selfishness, the baseness of the deed excite a repulsion and an abhorrence which no words can describe.

And yet, notwithstanding our abhorrence of the crime, we are half-forced to acknowledge that we, with the Jewish priests, with the Jewish mob, might have been partners in the guilt, that we with them might even have claimed as a privilege the responsibility of the act; 'His blood be on us, and on our children'—words lightly spoken then, words terribly significant afterwards.

Nay, we feel a half inclination to palliate their conduct. Their religious feelings were excited; their leaders worked upon their fears and their fanaticism; what was first the deliberate counsel of a few bold spirits was accepted as the thoughtless resolution of all. They did that collectively, which they would have shrunk from doing individually.

There is something inexpressibly shocking in the thought that the injustice and the wickedness of a large assembly—even of a deliberative assembly—is greater than the injustice and the wickedness of an individual. Yet so it is. The passionate are excited; the timid are silenced; the immoral feel themselves shielded from any evil consequences by numbers; the more moral calm their consciences by pleading divided responsibility.

Yes, here is the crowning delusion. A divided

responsibility! How can you divide your responsibility? Is there any other man, or any other body of men, master of your conscience, or you of theirs? You may have the majority with you, or you may have it against you; but for your voice, your sentiment, your vote, you will give as strict an account before the All-righteous and All-seeing Judge, as though it had stood alone, as though it singly were the sole arbiter of the event. He, who raises his voice for the murder of a man, is equally a murderer, though it be drowned in ten thousand others, clamouring for the same man's death. Does not the law itself teach this? When a conspiracy to commit a crime is proved, it treats the conspirators as all guilty; it does not divide the legal penalty into so many fractions and apportion one to each; but it visits all alike with the full punishment due to that crime. Apply this righteous principle then to responsibilities of members composing an assembly. If as a member of a board you vote for an unrighteous or oppressive measure, because your party puts some pressure upon you; if as a member of a synod you condemn or denounce the innocent, because it is expedient for your Church or your order that he should be condemned; if as a member of a body of electors you vote for an unfit or a less fit candidate, because your interests or your fears prevail with you; if as a member of a trades union you consent to or connive at an act of violence and tyranny against a fellow-workman or an employer, because you do not like to go against the rest of your class; then be assured, that for that unrighteous measure, for that unjust verdict, for that unfit election, for that act of coercion, you are equally guilty as though it were your own doing, for you have made it your own. In that forest of uplifted hands your hand may have passed unnoticed; in that hubbub of clamorous voices your voice may have been unheard; but be assured it has gone up to heaven—clear and distinct, with all its individuality, with all its peculiar emphasis—as though it had startled the silence and awakened the echoes in the solitude of a desert.

'But,' you will say, 'let all this be granted; suppose that I feel the full responsibility of my individual vote, yet what safeguard can I have that I should not have gone wrong, conscientiously wrong, in such a case as this? Here was prestige, authority, office on one side. The priests, the rulers, the rabbis, recommended this course. Could I refuse to obey those who sat in Moses' seat?'

To this the obvious answer is; that the cause which pleads, 'It is expedient,' and cannot plead, 'It is right, it is just, it is true,' must be bad, by whatever authority it may be recommended. Though an angel from heaven should preach this doctrine to you, yet hold it accursed. No expediency can make the condemnation of the innocent right.

'But the religious question—the doctrine of Jesus and the doctrine of the Pharisees—how judge between these? What faculty is given to me, what faculty had these Jews, by which they could discriminate between the two? Was it not excusable, was it not natural, nay, was it wrong, to follow constituted authority and time-honoured prescription here?'

Yes, give its proper weight to authority, to prescription; and yet show we you a more excellent way. There are times, when God wills to break down the barriers of the past, to lead men into unexplored fields of truth, in short to give them a new revelation. The crisis, of which we are speaking, was one of these—the most momentous of them all. At such times the hearts of the thoughtful and conscientious and devout will be filled with anxiety. At such times authority fails, and reason fails, and liberalism fails. The only safe guides, counsellors, confessors, are love and the Spirit.

To the Pharisees both these were wanting. Love was the fulfilling of the law: and yet they saw in the law only a rigid system, which gave into their sole keeping the keys of heaven, which enabled them to bind on men's shoulders a burden too heavy for them to bear. Love is the mind of God; and those who have no love cannot enter into His mind, cannot read His purposes. Love is that electric sympathy, which finds its like, which is drawn by a natural attraction to whatever is lovely and beautiful and good. The mission, the words, the life, the love, of Christ spoke to the loving heart. They spoke to Peter and to John and to Nathanael, to Israelites without guile, in tones clear enough. But to Caiaphas and to the Pharisees they were inarticulate, unmeaning—to Caiaphas, the cold and heartless, who for his own selfish ends ruthlessly put the innocent One to death; to the Pharisees, the proud and self-complacent, who devoured widows' houses, while for a pretence they made long prayers.

And the close ally of love is the Spirit. I use the term as opposed to the letter, the form. I mean that faculty, which pierces the outside shell, and discovers the hidden soul of things. I mean that habit of mind, for which mere formalities without any accompanying idea are valueless, which seeks to endow all its acts with a meaning, a reality, a life. Time was when the strict observances of the Pharisees were not mere formalities. At a great national crisis the Pharisees had banded themselves together to resist aggression from foreign tyrants; they had set themselves to preserve the commandments of the Law and the teachings of the Old Testament intact against the degrading polytheism and the low morality of the surrounding nations. To effect this, it was necessary to be strict, over-strict, in ceremonial observances. Thus they had deserved well of their country: they had wrought and suffered in the cause of true religion. This we must not forget. But lapse of time, and change of circumstance, and increase of worldliness had done their work; and while the forms remained, the spirit had gone; just as one will go on repeating the hymn learnt long ago at the mother's knee year after year in a heartless, listless, unmeaning way, because through indifference and apathy he has allowed the cold shadow of the world to deepen upon him, and has neglected to renew his spiritual faculties from day to day at the source of all true freshness of life, at the fountain of the Holy Spirit.

Only by the spiritual faculty are things spiritual discerned. To the Pharisees their rabbinical learning, their strict observances, their religious zeal, were useless here. Their spiritual vision had been blinded by long disuse, and they could not see.

So will it be with us. Without love, without the Spirit, we cannot judge aright. When the alternative is offered, we shall blindly follow the counsel of Caiaphas; we shall prefer Barabbas the robber to Jesus the Christ; and in a moment of recklessness, perhaps in an excess of religious zeal, we shall crucify the Son of God afresh.

Man proposes, but man cannot dispose. Man devises means, but man cannot control the event. God takes our rough-hewn counsels and shapes them to His finer ends. He uses the worldly ambition of one prince for the overthrow of idolatry, the selfish profligacy of another for the establishment of a reformation. The injustice and the cruelty and the arrogance, the scheming and the success of Caiaphas are supple as clay in His hands.

'It is expedient, that one man should die.' We all acknowledge the truth of this prophecy, as the Evangelist acknowledged it. But what would Caiaphas himself have said if he had foreseen the result? I turn over the pages of history, and I find that a few years after these words were uttered, Caiaphas was deposed from the high-priesthood by these very Romans whom he was so very eager to conciliate. I look further, and I read that some thirty years later still, while many present at this council of priests and Pharisees were yet living, the Romans did come and take away both their place and nation; and this, because in place of believing on the true Christ Whose kingdom was not of this world, Who commanded to give tribute to Cæsar, they chose as their leaders false Messiahs, political adventurers, whose schemes of earthly dominion were dangerous to the power and the majesty of Rome.

So it is that God takes our selfish, arrogant, empty utterances, and fills them with a meaning of His own. A powerful European people only the other day, having declared war against a neighbouring nation and thirsty with the greed of conquest, sped forth its departing armies on their errand of expected victory with cries, 'To the enemy's capital.' To the enemy's capital they indeed go; but they go as prisoners, not as conquerors. By a Divine irony the letter of their wishes is granted; the substance is withheld. They entered upon the war with a light heart; they came out of the war in much sorrow and heaviness, their finances broken, their armies destroyed, their empire curtailed, their prestige and their supremacy gone.

Thus an overruling providence guided and interpreted the words of Caiaphas. Moreover there was eminent fitness in the witness chosen for this prophetic announcement. 'This he spake,' says the Evangelist, 'not of himself, but being high-priest that year.' To him as high-priest the duty pertained of offering the yearly sacrifice of atonement, and entering within the veil to make intercession for the people. That year —the year in which he spoke, the year of all years, the acceptable year of God—the one great Atoning

Victim was offered, in Whom these continually recurring sacrifices were abolished at once and for ever, Who was Himself 'a full, perfect, and sufficient Sacrifice, oblation and satisfaction for the sins of the whole world.' By the iniquitous counsel of Caiaphas the Victim was slain; by the unconscious testimony of Caiaphas the Atonement was foretold. In this exercise of his high-priestly functions the irony of Divine providence was complete. The wisdom of God triumphed over the passions and the follies of men.

But let us turn for a moment, before we part, to another scene. Let us leave the conspirators, and let us seek the Victim. At the very time, when these priests and Pharisees were holding their latest assemblies and perfecting the designs of Caiaphas, He with His chosen few has retired from that last supper to the solitary garden, and there, in the stillness of the night, bowed down with agony is pouring out His soul to God.

Look at the contrast. Against the overbearing insolence of Caiaphas, 'Ye know nothing at all,' set the perfect resignation of Christ, 'Not My will, but Thine be done.' Against the selfish and cruel policy of Caiaphas, 'It is expedient for us—for you and for me—that one man should die,' set the absolute renunciation of Christ, 'I lay down My life for My sheep.' 'It is expedient for you, that I go away.'

THE COUNSEL OF CAIAPHAS.

The law of life with Caiaphas is to sacrifice others to himself; the law of life with Christ is to sacrifice Himself for others. Could any contrast more complete be imagined? Was it possible that Caiaphas could be other than the determined antagonist, the relentless persecutor, of Christ?

And to you and to me—to every member of this congregation—the alternative is offered, and the choice must be made. Do you adopt as your guide in life the rule of Caiaphas, or the rule of Christ? If the former, then you will endeavour to get through life easily, to avoid everything that is inconvenient and unpleasant, to throw your burdens on other men's shoulders, to give as little and to take as much as you can; and, if you are clever, you may get the reward you seek; you may be successful, as the world counts success; you may secure ease or pleasure or position. But I know that no one here would consciously and deliberately reject the better and choose the worse. I know that, however specious may be the suggestions of a so-called utilitarian doctrine, however strong and however over-mastering may be your individual temptations to selfishness in practice, still the spirit and the conscience of everyone here would revolt against the baser alternative. You do acknowledge—you cannot help acknowledging—in your heart of hearts that it is better to live for others than to live for yourselves, it is higher and nobler to suffer for others than to let others suffer for you. If you acknowledge it, then practise it. Spurn the counsel of Caiaphas henceforward in your conduct, as you have spurned it already in your conscience. Leave Caiaphas to his selfish intrigues and his transient successes. And follow the Son of Man, Who went about not receiving but doing good, notwithstanding His troubles and His failures. Choose the better part at once. As you go home this afternoon, determine by God's grace that you will devote yourself more unselfishly to those, with whom your existence is bound up. Search out at once some dark spot in the life of parent, or child, or brother, or friend, or neighbour, which may be made purer, brighter and happier by your care. Begin with this, and from this beginning go on; that so, advancing daily step by step on the path of self-denial, you may at length confess with perfect conviction and with heartfelt gratitude, that it is indeed 'more blessed to give than to receive.'

VII.

PILATE'S QUESTION.

Pilate saith unto Him, What is truth?
S. JOHN xviii. 38.

First Sunday after Trinity, 1875[1].

S. JOHN is especially distinguished among the four evangelists for his subtle delineation of character. We do not commonly remember, it costs us an effort to remember, how very largely we are indebted to the fourth Gospel for our conceptions of the chief personages who bear a part in the evangelical history, when these conceptions are most distinct. If we analyse the sources of our information, we find again and again, that while something is told us about a particular person in the other Gospels, yet it is S. John who gives those touches to the picture, which

[1] Preached before the Lord Mayor and the Judges.

make it stand out with its own individuality as a real, living, speaking man. The other Evangelists will record a name, or perhaps an incident. S. John will add one or two sayings, and the whole person is instinct with life. The character flashes out in half-a-dozen words. From the abundance of the heart the mouth speaketh. So it is with Thomas, with Philip, with Martha and Mary, with several others who might be named.

This vividness of portraiture is our strongest assurance (if assurance were needed) that the narrative was indeed written by him whose name it bears, by the beloved disciple and eyewitness. For there is no effort at delineation of character; there is no delineation of character at all, properly so-called. The Evangelist does not describe the persons whom he introduces. They describe themselves. The incidental act, the incidental movement or gesture, the incidental saying, tells the tale. That which he had heard, that which he had seen with his eyes, that which he had looked upon, that which his hands had handled, of the Word of Life, that and that only he declared.

Pilate furnishes a remarkable illustration of this feature in the fourth Gospel. Pilate is the chief agent in the crowning scene of the Evangelical history. He is necessarily a prominent figure in all the four narratives of this crisis. In the three first Gospels we learn much about him; we find him there, as we find him in S. John, at cross purposes with the Jews; he is represented there, not less than by S. John, as giving an unwilling consent to the judicial murder of Jesus. His Roman sense of justice is too strong to allow him to yield without an effort; his personal courage is too weak to persevere in the struggle when the consequences threaten to become inconvenient. He is timid, politic, time-serving, as represented by all alike; he has just enough conscience to wish to shake off the responsibility, but far too little conscience to shrink from committing a sin.

But in S. John's narrative we pierce far below the surface. Here he is revealed to us as the sarcastic, cynical worldling, who doubts everything, distrusts everything, despises everything. He has an intense scorn for the Jews, and yet he has a craven dread of them. He has a certain professional regard for justice, and yet he has no real belief in truth or honour. Throughout he manifests a malicious irony in his conduct at this crisis. There is a lofty scorn in his answer, when he repudiates any sympathy with the accusers, 'Am I a Jew?' There is a sarcastic pity in the question, which he addresses to the Prisoner before him. 'Art *Thou* the King of the Jews?'

'Art *Thou* then a King, Thou poor, weak, helpless fanatic, Whom with a single word I could doom to death?' He is half-bewildered, half-diverted, with the incongruity of this claim. And yet there is a certain propriety that a wild enthusiast should assert his sovereignty over a nation of bigots. So he sarcastically adopts the title: 'Will ye that I release unto you the King of the Jews?' Even when at length he is obliged to yield to the popular clamour, he will at least have his revenge by a studied contempt. 'Behold your King.' 'Shall I crucify your King?' And to the very last moment he indulges his cynical scorn. The title on the cross was indeed unconsciously a proclamation of a Divine truth, but in its immediate purpose and intent it was the mere gratification of Pilate's sarcastic humour. 'Jesus of Nazareth (could any good thing come out of Nazareth?), Jesus of Nazareth, the King of the Jews.' He has sacrificed his honour to them; but he will not sacrifice his contempt: 'What I have written, I have written.'

But it is more especially in the sentence which I have chosen for my text that the whole character of the man is revealed. The Prisoner before him had accepted the title of a king. He based His claim to this title on the fact that He had come to bear witness of the truth. He declared that those, who were themselves of the truth, would acknowledge His claim; they were His rightful subjects; they were the enfranchised citizens of His kingdom. Strange language this in the ears of a cynical, worldly sceptic, to whose eyes the most attractive type of humanity was a judicious admixture of force and fraud. 'Pilate saith unto Him, What *is* truth? And when he had said this, he went out.' The altercation could be carried no further. Was not human life itself one great query, without an answer? What was truth, what else, except that which each man thought?

Truth! This helpless prisoner claimed to be a king, and He appealed forsooth to His truthfulness as the credential of His sovereign rights. Was ever any claim more contradictory of all human experience, more palpably absurd than this? Truth! When had truth anything to do with founding a kingdom? The mighty engine of imperial power, the iron sceptre which ruled the world, whence came it? Certainly it owed nothing to truth. Had not Augustus established his sovereignty by an unscrupulous employment of force, and maintained it by an astute use of artifice? And his successor, the present occupant of the imperial throne, was he not an arch-dissembler, the darkest of all dark enigmas? The name of Tiberius was a byword for impenetrable disguise.

Truth might do well enough for fools and enthusiasts, for simple men; but for rulers, for diplomatists, for men of the world, it was the wildest of all wild dreams. Truth! What was truth? He had lived too long in the world to trust any such hollow pretensions. He had listened to the ceaseless din of philosophical disputations till he was weary of them. The Stoics, the Epicureans, the Platonists, all had their several specifics which they vended as truth. All were equally sure, and yet no two agreed. He had witnessed—certainly not without contempt, and yet not altogether without dismay—the rising flood of foreign superstitions, Greek, Syrian, Egyptian, Chaldean, which threatened to deluge the city and empire, and destroy all the ancient landmarks. Could he believe all, or any, of these? In this never-ending conflict of philosophical dogmas and religious creeds, what could he do, but resign himself to scepticism, to indifference, to a cold and cynical scorn of all enthusiastic convictions and all definite beliefs?

'What is truth?' And yet as he turned away, neither expecting nor desiring an answer to a question which he had asked merely to end an inconvenient controversy, some uneasy misgiving, we may well suppose, flashed across the mind of this proud, sarcastic worldling, that he was now brought face to face with Truth, as he had never been brought before. There was a reality about every word and action of this Jewish prisoner, which arrested and overawed him. The calmness with which He urged His claims, the fearlessness with which He defied death, the impressive words, the still more impressive silence, the manifest innocence and rectitude of the man (if he saw nothing more), could not be without their effect even on a Pilate—steeped as he was in the moral recklessness and religious despair of his age. At all events he would save the man, if he conveniently could.

But there had also been a nobler element in Pilate's education than moral scepticism and religious unbelief. He was a Roman governor; and, as a Roman governor, he was an administrator of Roman law. It was their appreciation of law, their respect for law, their study of law, far more than anything else, which gave its greatness to the character of the Roman people. Even in the most degraded ages of their history, and with the worst individual types of men, this is the one bright spot which relieves the gloom. It is the noble prerogative of law to set a standard of morality, clear, definite, precise. I have no concern here with other obligations to the law, which as Christians and as men we are bound to acknowledge—though speaking before the chief representatives of English law and justice I cannot fail to be reminded of them this afternoon.

But this exhibition of a moral standard is a gain, which it is hardly possible to overestimate. The standard will not always be the highest. From the nature of the case it cannot be so. Law deals with some departments of morality very imperfectly; with others it does not attempt to deal at all. But still, wheresoever it is felt and in so far as it penetrates, it creates an ideal, and it begets a habit, which will not be powerless even with the most indifferent and reckless. So it was with Pilate. Theological scepticism had eaten out his religious principles to the very core. Unscrupulous worldliness and self-seeking had shattered his moral constitution. But, though his principles were gone and his character was ruined, still he was haunted by some lingering sense of professional honour. Still the magnificent ideal of Roman justice, of Roman law, rose up before him, and would not lightly be thrust aside. He pleads repeatedly for justice against the relentless accusers. Three times he declares the prisoner's innocence in the same explicit words, 'I find no fault in Him.' Once and again he strives to shift the responsibility from his own shoulders; 'Take ye Him, and judge Him according to your law': 'Take ye Him and crucify Him.' But his efforts are all in vain. They will have none of this. The deed shall be done, and he shall do it.

It was not the first, and it would not be the last time, that Pilate found himself in conflict with the Jews. For ten years he was governor of this turbulent, unmanageable people. This was an unusually long period of office under an emperor like Tiberius, who was constantly changing his provincial governors from mere suspicion and distrust. It must have cost him no little trouble to steer his course so long and so successfully, without foundering either on the suspicions of his jealous master here or on the bigotry of his stubborn subjects there. And yet he was constantly wounding the religious susceptibilities of the Jews. At one time he shocked them by bringing the military ensigns with the effigies of Cæsar within the walls of Jerusalem; at another he persisted by setting up some gilt shields inscribed with a profane heathen dedication in the palace of Herod within the same holy precincts. In both cases, he drove the Jews to the extreme verge of exasperation; in both cases he exhibits the same sarcastic and defiant scorn which is so apparent here; in both cases their obstinate zeal or bigotry triumphs as it triumphs here, and they forced him in the end to retrace his steps and undo his deed.

So then this was only one brief, inobtrusive episode in a protracted struggle between Pilate and the Jewish people. Doubtless, it seemed at the time quite insignificant compared with those other and fiercer conflicts which I have just mentioned. It is passed over in silence by contemporary Jewish writers. It concerned the life of a single person only; it was settled in a single night. And yet it involved nothing less than the eternal destiny of all mankind. Yes, there is a terrible irony in God's retributive justice, which so blinds men to the true proportions of things. A single moment may do a wrong which centuries cannot repair. It is a dangerous thing to defy Truth; the majesty of Truth is inviolable; and he, who insults it in a moment of recklessness, can never forecast the consequences. Time and space and notoriety are no measure of importance here. Our memories are still fresh from the longest trial on record in our English law-courts. For months upon months men read little else and talked of little else. As a monument of the care and patience of English law, it has the highest value; but for the destinies of our race it is, so far as we can see, quite devoid of real significance. The most important criminal trial on record in the history of mankind was hurried through in two or three short hours under cover of night and in the grey of early dawn.

This is the great lesson of Pilate's crime. He was surprised by the Truth. He found himself unexpectedly confronted by the Truth, and he could not recognise it. His whole life long he had tampered with truth, he had despised truth, he had despaired of truth. Truth was the last thing which he had set before him as the aim of his life. He had thought much of policy, of artifice, of fraud, of force; but for truth in any of its manifold forms he had cared just nothing at all. And his sin had worked out its own retribution. Not truth only, but the Very Truth itself, Truth Incarnate, stood before him in human form, and he was blind to it. He scorned it, he played with it, he thrust it aside, he condemned and he gibbeted it. 'Suffered under Pontius Pilate' is the legend of eternal infamy, with which history has branded his name.

So it is now with us. The Lord appears suddenly in His temple—in the shrine of the human heart and conscience—suddenly at a time and in a form which we least expect. The truth visits us very frequently under the disguise of some common event or some insignificant person. It surprises us perhaps in the accidental saying of some little child, or in the insidiousness of some mean temptation, or in the emergency of some trivial choice. It stands before us at once our suppliant and our king. We fail to see its majesty veiled in this humble garb. We treat it as our prisoner, when in fact it is our judge and may become our gaoler. We flatter ourselves that we have power to condemn or to release it. We have no fault to find with it; but still we reject it. We crucify it; and before three days are gone it rises from its grave to bear eternal testimony against us. We could not see the truth, because we were not ourselves of the truth.

Here—in this judicial blindness—is the warning of Pilate's example. Like is drawn to like. Like only understands like. The truth is only for the children of truth.

But we must not unduly narrow the sense of truth and truthfulness. When our Lord called Himself the Truth, when He declared that the Truth should make us free, He meant very much more than is commonly understood by the word. Veracity is indeed truth, but it is only a small part of truth. A man may be scrupulously veracious, strictly a man of his word; he may always say that which he believes, he may always perform that which he promises; and yet he may not be in the highest sense true. He may be the slave of a thousand unrealities. A genuine child of the truth is very much more than a speaker of the truth; he is a doer of the truth, and a thinker of the truth also. He is frank, open, real in all things. Reality is the very soul of his being. He cares for nothing which is hollow, shadowy, superficial. Popularity, wealth, success, worldly ambition and display, are essentially unreal, because they are external, because they are transient. Therefore he estimates them at their true value.

The devotion of scientific men in pursuit of scientific truths wins our highest admiration. It is not without a thrill of national pride that we have just bidden 'God speed' to the gallant company which has started for the Arctic seas. To face untold hardships and possible death in such a cause is a worthy and noble ambition. For these are realities. But obviously there are truths of far higher moment to the temporal and eternal well-being of man, than the laws of magnetism, the causes of the Aurora, or the fauna of the polar seas. Whence came I? Whither go I? What is sin? What is conscience? Is there a God in heaven? Is there a providence, a moral government, a judgment? Is there a redemption, a sanctification, a life eternal? These are the momentous, the pressing questions, which a man can only shelve at his peril.

Christ is the answer to all these questions. Therefore He is the Verity of Verities. Therefore He claims for Himself the title of the Truth, as His absolute and indefeasible right.

An incapacity to see the Truth, when thus presented to us in its highest form, may arise from different causes. It may spring from bigoted partisanship, and religious pride and obstinate formalism, as in the case of the Jews; or it may spring from cold cynicism and worldliness and dishonesty, as in the case of Pilate. These two conspired to crucify the Truth.

As we sow, so also shall we reap. Pilate's life had been spent in untruthfulness. His government had been an alternation of violence and fraud. His aim had not been to rule uprightly, but to rule at all costs. He must calm the suspicions of his jealous master, and he must quell the turbulence of an unruly people. Whatever means would conduce to these ends, were legitimate means. Uprightness, honour, frankness, generosity, truth—what were these to him? He had no belief in them, and why should he practise them? He projected his own motives into his estimate of mankind at large. He read the characters of others in the distorted mirror of his own consciousness. Human life, as he viewed it, was false from beginning to end. It was after all the reflection of his own falsehood which he saw. He was ever looking out for the unrealities of existence; he had no eye for its realities. Men's convictions were their foibles. Men's beliefs were his playthings. Untruthfulness, cynicism, distrust, scorn, had withered his soul. They only will find the truth, who believe that the truth may be found. Pilate had no such belief.

He had gone through life, asking half in bitterness, half in jest, What is truth? He asked it now again, and the question was fatal.

Pilate's temper of mind is a very real danger in an age like ours. Let us beware of thus jesting with truth, lest some time like him we crucify the Truth unawares.

VIII.

THE ONE TAKEN AND THE OTHER LEFT.

And he went out, and wept bitterly.
S. MATTHEW xxvi. 75.

And he went and hanged himself.
S. MATTHEW xxvii. 5.

So God's law was vindicated, and Christ's saying fulfilled: 'I tell you, in that night...two men shall be in the field; the one shall be taken, and the other left. And they answered and said unto Him, Where, Lord?'

'Where, Lord?' The disciples' question is our question also. Where and when and how shall these things be? Does this prediction refer to our own times, our own circumstances? Are we ourselves directly concerned in its fulfilment? Or may we dismiss it at once from our reckoning, as a distant scene which shall be enacted on a foreign stage? 'The one taken, and the other left'—this identity of condition with this separation of destiny, this arbitrary distinction, this unequal distribution, this partiality in the Divine judgments, what does it mean? Where is it realised?

'The one taken, and the other left.' Our thoughts will first revert to some striking physical catastrophe, of which we have read, or which perchance we ourselves have witnessed. We recall with a shudder the terrible railway accident, when our fellow-traveller, seated in the same carriage, with whom just before we conversed familiarly, was silenced at once, and the ghastly vision of his crushed and mangled remains rises before us with all the freshness of that first awful moment of our providential deliverance. Or we think of the terrible lightning-flash, which smote down one of the two friends, wandering together in the forest, and sent the other home, unhurt in body, but awe-stricken in spirit, to live henceforth a changed man. Or we remember the account of the awful avalanche, sweeping down the mountain side and snapping the rope which in all human calculation had bound together the fellow-travellers in a community of destiny, whether for life or for death, hurling this one over the fatal precipice, and sending that other home, stupefied with grief, to tell the tale of his companion's fate.

But no! these are not the true counterparts to our Lord's prediction. A moment's reflection will show that His words must have a far deeper meaning than this. The physical catastrophe is only a type of the spiritual. There is a sense in which the one is taken and the other left, far more awful than the arbitrary action of the railway accident, or the lightning flash, or the mountain avalanche, or the colliery explosion. A separation of moral destiny starting from an identity of moral opportunity—this, *this* is the infallible sign of the presence of the Son of Man, come whensoever and howsoever He will. For this we must be ever on the watch. This will start the question to our lips, 'Where, Lord?'

And so we turn to a wholly different class of facts, as illustrating our Lord's saying. Two school-fellows are brought up together. They have the same natural abilities; they learn the same lessons; they enjoy the same opportunities; they are subject to the same moral influences. The restraints of boyhood end. They become their own masters. They start life with the same hopes. Then the divergence begins. The one rises into merited respect; the other sinks into the abandoned profligate. Christ came to them in the freedom of manhood. The one was taken, and the other left.

Or again; two brothers grow up as playmates. They have the same family interests; they excite the same family sympathies. It would seem that they ought to entertain the same affections and to make the same sacrifices for those affections. But the trial comes. A great catastrophe overtakes some member of the household—a blow to his honour or a blow to his fortunes. The one stands aloof, wrapping himself in his own selfishness, daring nothing, risking nothing. The other is full of generous sympathy. He will share his purse; he will even hazard his good name, confident in his lofty purpose, and resolute at all costs to befriend a friend. In that emergency, that trial of constancy, Christ came—came to those two brothers. The one was taken, and the other left.

Or again; two sisters live in one household. They share each other's confidences; they have the same maidenly pursuits; they are watched over by the same mother's care. We see absolutely no reason why there should be any divergence in after life. And yet, what are they now? The one is a matron, respected and beloved, full of tender sympathy and wise counsels, whose very presence diffuses a radiance of purity and peace and joy around. The other?

Ask about her, and there is silence. Her name is not mentioned now. Her existence is a blank. Her memory is an aching pain in all hearts. Christ came to those two sisters in the unrestrained gaieties of society. The one, aye, the one was taken, and the other left.

I have spoken of such critical moments as comings of Christ. I have applied to the familiar trials and temptations of domestic and social life the description of that awful night, when the great surprise shall come, when the Son of Man shall appear, and the separation of destiny from destiny shall be complete. Is it a legitimate use of our Lord's words? Or is it a mere play of fancy, an edifying application possibly, but still a forced application, neither warranted nor suggested by the Gospel narrative itself?

I cannot think this. The more we read our Lord's predictions of the great and terrible day, the more do they appear instinct with this personal, present, immediate application to ourselves. These trials, these temptations, these siftings, these separations, are more than mere signs and emblems; they are anticipations—to ourselves infinitely important anticipations—of the Advent of Christ. Our Lord Himself has, as if purposely, so combined a temporal judgment with the great and final judgment in one signal instance. The destruction of Jerusalem was such an immediate catastrophe, a great trial of constancy, a great sifting of men. It was in some sense an anticipation of the great day of doom. Hence it is impossible to separate in our Lord's language what refers to the one and what refers to the other. He seems to speak, as it were, through the one to the other. So in like manner our own personal trials are comings of Christ; they are partial, fragmentary realisations of the Great Coming, when all characters shall be sifted, and all hearts laid bare. Hence it is that we are forbidden to say 'lo, here,' and 'lo, there'; hence it is that no revelation of the day or of the hour has been given, but we are commanded to watch; hence it is that in reply to the disciples' question 'Where, Lord?' an enigma takes the place of an answer, 'Wheresoever the carcase is, there will the eagles be gathered together.'

So there are many advents of Christ. Wherever this sign shall be, wherever this condition is fulfilled, there Christ *has* come. And the sign itself? Not the dazzling glory of omnipotence, not the myriads of attendant angels, not the thunders and the lightnings, not the piercing glare of the archangel's trumpet, not these *now*; not any emblems of majesty and power, but an image which speaks of an extinct life and a devouring vengeance. We may not think that this prophecy was exhausted, when the eagles of the

Roman army gathered about the once holy city, to prey upon the corpse of a God-abandoned people. Of *ourselves* the words are spoken. This day, this very day, the scripture is, or may be, fulfilled in our ears. Here are the carcases of blessings spurned, the carcases of opportunities perverted, the carcases of warnings neglected and trials misused, the carcases of ruined souls. As in the desert the vultures scent from afar the dying beast of burden, flocking together from all parts of the heaven and hovering over their prey, till the last convulsive throb ceases and the last feeble moan is hushed and the glaze settles on the eye, and then their foul, greedy work begins; just so, when the crisis has come, and the temptation has come, and the soul has yielded and has died, it lies a prey to a thousand evil influences which wreak their vengeance on its helpless carcase. In such a crisis, such an emergency, such a trial, such an opportunity for good or for evil, Christ comes. Then it is that He is found to be set for the falling of one, and the rising of another. Then it is that the visitation which to one is the savour of life unto life, is to another a savour of death unto death. Then it is, that the one is taken, and the other left.

Such an eventful crisis was the passion and death of our Lord. It was the great probation and sifting of the disciples, of the Jews, of all the agents and all the bystanders in this tragical drama. Whatever of good and whatever of evil lay buried in the hearts of any, was brought out, was tested, was exposed by it. The timidity and the scepticism, the violence and the insolence and the avarice and the fraud, the firm faith, the courage, the endurance, the tenderness, the love, all found expression in this emergency.

Hence it is especially a crisis of moral contrasts. There is the central contrast of all. Two men, prisoners together, both accused of sedition, both tried and condemned as disturbers of the public peace; nay both (according to an ancient tradition) bearing the same hallowed name—Jesus Barabbas, and Jesus the Christ. The chief priests and elders persuade the multitude to ask Barabbas and destroy Jesus. Barabbas is the chosen of the Jews and the rejected of God; Christ is slain by the Jews but lives for ever in God. The one is taken, and the other is left.

And around this central contrast are grouped other pairs, all illustrating the same lesson—oneness of opportunity, separation of destiny. Two members of the Jewish Sanhedrim, both held in honour, both (it would seem) present at that fatal council, both bearing the same name—Joseph surnamed Caiaphas, and Joseph of Arimathea. The one incurs the chief guilt of the crucifixion; the other is the honourable agent of the entombment. The one conspires against the King; the other loyally awaits the kingdom. The one is taken, and the other left.

Two thieves crucified together, both guilty of the same crime, both suffering the merited penalty of their guilt, both in their last hour brought into the same proximity with the Holy One. The one blasphemes; the other prays. The one sinks down into darkness; the other is raised up into Paradise. The one is taken, and the other left.

Two chosen disciples, both belonging to the inner circle of the Twelve, both constant in their attendance on their Master throughout His ministry, both following Him up to the last fatal night, both found wanting in the great emergency, both overwhelmed with an agony of sorrow for their sin; and yet here again, the one is taken, and the other is left.

Of all these severances the last is the most striking. Simon of Bethsaida and Judas of Kerioth had possessed all things in common; common opportunities, common associations, common trials and dangers. They had witnessed the same works, and listened to the same words. They had lived in the same Presence. They had received the same revelation of the same Father from the same hallowed lips. Altogether it might have been thought that their character must have been cast in the same mould. Whence then came this difference?

Whence, but in the use or the misuse of that mysterious, that fatal, that magnificent gift of God to man, his free-will? In whatever other respects their moral capacities or their moral education may have differed, it is here, and here alone, that we have the explanation of the result. This is the secret, silent force, which, working from beneath, produced first the rent, and then the chasm, and then the severance, in their characters and their destinies.

And yet to the last moment the difference has not revealed itself. Both put the same question of misgiving, 'Is it I?' Both were tempted. Both yielded to the temptation. The same night was fatal to the one and to the other. Just at this moment it might have seemed as if there were little to choose between Peter and Judas. The sin of Judas was coarser, was more base, was more heinous; but both had failed at the great crisis of all; and both had forfeited their position. How is it then that Peter rises again, while Judas sinks down, sinks suddenly, sinks irretrievably, sinks for ever?

Certainly, it was not the nature of the sin itself, which made his restoration impossible. It was not what Judas had *done*, but what Judas had *become*, which prevented his rising. His guilt was great, but

8—2

God's mercy is greater. His guilt was great, but God's pardon does not nicely calculate less or more. It is the special characteristic of the Gospel, that, while the condemnation of sin is unbounded, the hope of forgiveness is unbounded also. Other religions fail in the one respect, or they fail in the other. They take a light estimate of sin, or they restrict the operation of pardon. They encourage the sinner, or they scare the penitent. The Gospel alone reconciles both claims. This it does, as the revelation of the Father's infinite love: for in the light of this revelation the sin becomes the more hateful, while the pardon becomes the more assured. Therefore again I say, it was not the *crime*, which excluded forgiveness. If there be any one in this congregation, whose conscience is burdened with the memory of some past sin, who is tempted to doubt whether for him forgiveness is still possible, who seems to himself to be dragged ever downward by a weight which cannot be removed: let him shake off this doubt and spurn it from him, as a vile suggestion of ruin, a shameful libel of the tempter on the goodness of his Heavenly Father, Who desires only his filial submission, and is even now stretching a loving hand through the darkness to save him.

But, if so, if the crime itself was not a bar to forgiveness, where did the repentance of the criminal fail? What difference is there between the remorse of a Judas and the remorse of a Peter, that the one should have been taken, and the other left.

Up to a certain point at least the conduct of Judas appears to contain all the elements of repentance.

For, *first of all*, there is abhorrence of the crime. Judas is racked with agony, when his sin is brought home to him. The revulsion of feeling is complete. His exceeding bitter cry, 'I have sinned, in that I have betrayed the innocent blood', rings piercing through all the centuries, and strikes home to the heart of mankind. Of the intensity of his remorse no doubt can be entertained. Observe too that the whole force of his grief is concentrated on the sin itself, not on the temporal consequences of the sin. He is tortured with agony, not because he has failed, but because he has succeeded. He had shed the innocent blood. Here was the sting of his remorse. Not thirty pieces, nor thirty thousand pieces, of silver could buy this off.

And *secondly*: not only is there inward sorrow for the sin; there is also the outward acknowledgement of the crime. At once he confesses his guilt; confesses it, not in the ear of a confidential friend, but confesses it openly—before that council of priests and elders, before those unsympathetic conspirators, who had bought his services and were partners in his guilt. He faces shame, faces rebuke, faces contempt, faces their lurking hatred, and their undisguised scorn.

And, *thirdly*, he makes reparation for his guilt. The main consequence indeed was irreparable. The thing was done and could not be undone. The innocent was condemned. The blood once shed might not be gathered up again. But at least he would do what he could; he would deny himself all advantage of the transaction. He flung back the accursed gain to his tempters. So far as the past was retrievable, he would retrieve it.

The abhorrence of the sin, the confession of the guilt, the reparation of the crime, these three were complete. So far S. Peter could have done nothing which Judas had not done. But just at this point the severance begins. Remorse and repentance part company. The one is taken, and the other is left.

Faith and hope are the two requisites without which restoration is impossible. With these is life-giving repentance; without these is crushing remorse. Faith in God, and hope for the future.

1. Faith in God. So long as we look only to ourselves, pardon seems wholly beyond our reach. There is nothing in our own hearts, nothing in our past lives, which suggests it. The more we recall our experiences, and the more we examine our motives,

the more distant does it appear. A mere morbid anatomy of self will drive only to remorse. It cannot lead to repentance. It is well that we should grieve over our sins; it is not well that we should give ourselves up to overmuch self-dissection. Our failings must be our steppingstones; they must not be our stumblingblocks. We cannot suffer them to cripple our energies, or to bar our path. But this will always be the case, so long as our gaze is directed solely within. For here we find only feebleness, only vacillation, only ignorance, only failure and sin. Our strength, our consolation, our renewal, are elsewhere. It is only then, when we transcend the limits of self; when our heart goes forth in faith to God, the All-wise and Almighty, God the Merciful, God our Father; then, when the finite is forgotten in the Infinite; that the pardon comes, that the clean heart is made and the right spirit renewed within us. This faith Judas did not realise. He knew God only as an avenging Judge. He did not know Him as a loving Father. What could he hope from a Judge? What might he not have hoped from a Father?'

2. The concentration on self is a denial of faith. The concentration on the past is an exclusion of hope. Judas could not face the future. The past had been an utter failure. He had attempted to make reparation; but he could not retrieve the irretrievable, could

not undo what was done. Yet the future was all before him; the future was uncompromised. The two great preachers of the Gospel were destined to be Peter the denier of Christ, and Paul the persecutor of Christ. Why should not Judas the betrayer of Christ have made up the triad? Why not, except that having lost faith he had lost hope also. His horizon was bounded by the past. Now, now that the past was lost, nothing remained but suicide. This was the remorseless logic of his position.

Do not believe it, when they tell you that hope is a glamour, an illusion, a phantom-light tempting you into a morass, and luring you to your destruction. Hope is the reflection of God's mercy; hope is the echo of God's love. Hope is energy, hope is strength, hope is life. Without hope sorrow for sin will lead only to ruin. It may not end with you, as it ended with him. His was an extreme case. But it must lead to moral paralysis, and moral suicide. We have no time to brood over the errors of the past, while the hours are hurrying relentlessly by; no time to tell our wounds and reckon up our slain, while the fight is still raging and the enemy is upon us. There is enough to occupy all our energies in this warfare of life, without wasting them on lost opportunities and profitless regrets. Have you been tempted? Have you yielded? Have you sinned? Then go out from the scene of your temptation, as Peter went out, and weep bitter tears of repentance before God. But having done this, return, return at once, and strengthen your brethren. In active charity for others, in devoted service to God, is the truest safeguard against the suicidal promptings of remorse. Be the foremost to enter the sepulchre of the risen Lord; the foremost to pledge your devotion to Him, undaunted by recent failure; the foremost to receive the pastoral charge; the foremost to bear witness of Him to an unbelieving world; the foremost in zeal, the foremost in danger, the foremost to do and to suffer. The past is beyond recall. Put it behind you. The future is full of magnificent opportunities. Endeavour to realise them. Be energetic, be courageous, be hopeful. In the agony of your contrition, from the depths of your despair, listen to the Divine Voice which summons you: 'Let the dead bury their dead; dead opportunities, dead regrets, dead failures; yes even, dead sins; and follow thou Me.'

IX.

THE TRIUMPH OF FAILURE.

Then all the disciples forsook Him, and fled.
S. MATTHEW xxvi. 56.

First Sunday after Trinity, 1872.

JUDGED by any human standard, the life of Christ had proved a misadventure and a mistake. With all its beauty and all its heroism and all its sublimity, it was a failure, a gigantic failure. On this point there could not be two opinions. The ministry of Christ had commenced amidst the festivities of a marriage. It had ended in the horrors of a gibbet. In dramatic fiction those tragedies are the most thrilling, which turn upon some sudden and unforeseen reversal of fortune, where the hero's fate overtakes him without a moment's warning. Christ's life was the most tragic of all tragedies. From the bright sunshine of hope it passed at once into the impenetrable gloom of despair. Look at those joyous earlier days of His Galilean ministry. Mark how He is followed about by admiring crowds, thronging on the shores of that inland sea. Everywhere—in Decapolis towards the East, as far as Tyre and Sidon in the West—it is the same. They track His footsteps, and they hang upon His lips. They watch with reverence His every act and His every gesture. Even to the latest moment there is no sign of His impending doom. He enters Jerusalem on His final fatal visit, and He receives the homage of an enthusiastic crowd. The priests and the rulers indeed looked upon Him with no friendly eye. There were scowling visages and murmured reproaches and dark plottings—the first mutterings of the pent-up volcano, which was soon to burst out in devastation and ruin. But the heart of the people seemed sound. He, and He only, knew how hollow, how fickle, how unmeaning, was all this show of respect. Amid the Hosannas of an admiring throng, He entered the Holy City, the elect of the people, the long-expected Son of David, the acknowledged King of Israel. Then came the recoil, the end. The populace turned against Him. His own disciples forsook Him. It would have been some solace at least, amid the angry threats of those priestly conspirators and the cruel taunts of that rude soldiery, to have been cheered by the sympathy of some friendly eye—of Peter whose zeal only a few hours ago had been so fervent, of John whom He loved with more than a brother's love. Even this solace was denied Him. He was left alone—alone amidst the insults of the judgment hall, alone in the agonies of the Cross. In a few hours the work of a life-time had been undone. The web, which He had woven with so much cost, was unravelled and cast aside—a mere mass of tangled threads. Could any failure be more complete than this failure?

If you had asked any of the witnesses to this tragedy, their answer must have been the same. Put the question to Caiaphas and the priests. They would tell you that a dangerous pretender had been crushed, that the temple and the hierarchy were safe. Put it to Pilate and the Romans. They would say that the last had been heard of one more religious enthusiast, who this time at least was innocent, if indeed enthusiasm ever could be innocent. Put it to the bewildered disciples. They would have acknowledged their perplexity and dismay. Their hopes were torn and mangled on that Cross; their joy was buried in that grave. They were stupefied by the unexpected end. Put it to some impartial and calm-judging bystander (if any such there were); and he would have deplored that so much goodness and self-devotion and heroism should have perished, and left no fruit behind. Of all the lessons, which this life of lives has bequeathed to us, the one which addresses itself most directly to the perplexed and troubled spirit, the one which is most fruitful in revived hopes and reinvigorated energies, is this lesson of failure.

To those who have any serious aims in life at all, to those who hear within them a voice summoning them to some nobler task than merely to get through their allotted term of days with comfort and ease and respectability, to those in whom the consciousness of the sin within and the contemplation of the misery and vice without stirs the depth of the soul, the experience of failure is the severest of all trials. It is so very hard to struggle against evil within the heart, and to seem to make no head against it, to return again and again to the conflict, and again and again to retire baffled or defeated. It is so very disheartening to stand forward as the champion of some neglected and despised class, or the opponent of some flagrant but chartered wrong, and to meet only with misunderstanding and want of sympathy, perhaps to succeed for the moment in fanning some flame of enthusiasm in others, then to see it flicker and die out; to be left alone with all those misgivings which isolation brings in its train. At such a crisis, the failure of Christ is the most inspiring of all lessons.

There are three points to which our attention should be more especially directed—first, the necessity of failure; next, the discipline of failure; and lastly, the triumph of failure.

1. First then, failure is inevitable. Success is not the rule of human life. It is the very rare exception. Of all the magnificent possibilities, and all the glorious hopes, of youth only one here and there is ever in any degree realised in after-life. We find here just the same profusion of waste which appears throughout the processes of nature. Nature is lavish of hopes, but she is very frugal in results. One plant produces its hundreds and thousands of seeds. They are sown broadcast by the winds. There is a possibility here, which in a few years might fertilise a desert and feed a city. It is never realised. One seed and another shoots up and grows and blossoms and bears fruit. The rest disappear, and are heard of no more. Failure is written across the face of nature. It is only too true, as our Christian poet has said, that as we are

> Borne down the ebbing stream of life,

we encounter at each turn

> Some mouldering hope or joy.

It is only too true, that the man seems ever 'following

the funeral of the boy', the funeral of bright expectations never realised, the funeral of precious gifts and opportunities neglected or misused. The path of life is strewn with the corpses of magnificent projects and brilliant hopes, crushed and trampled under foot.

We say that this man or that has been eminently successful in life. We mean perhaps that he has amassed great wealth, or won great popularity; that he has been a victorious general, or a famous legislator; that his name will be handed down to after generations, connected with some important enterprise or some brilliant invention. Our estimate of success stops short at these outward tokens. Ask the man himself, and his heart of hearts would often tell you a very different tale. He cannot forget that cruel bereavement, which has left his life a desolate ruin. He cannot put away that domestic wrong, which lies heavy on his heart, and throws a blight over all his successes. He cannot overlook that degrading, unsatisfied passion, which gnaws at his soul within and leaves him no rest. It is a mockery to him to call his life a success.

And, though he should have no such trials as these, though his life should have been one long day of unbroken sunshine, can it ever be called a success, when nothing will avert the doom? You have with much toil secured yourself an easy competency. You have surrounded yourself with the comforts and luxuries of life. You have gathered your friends about you. You have built your soul a lordly pleasure-house, furnished with all the appliances and all the adornments of a refined culture; you have amassed rich stores of knowledge and experience—the work of a life-time. No sooner are your preparations complete, than decay comes and death comes; and all, all is spoilt. When the fruit is full ripe, it suddenly rots. You have sown the seed, but you may not reap the harvest. Death turns the most magnificent success into the most signal failure. The features of the corpse look only the more ghastly for the sparkling jewels and the gay apparel which deck it out. Human life is an inevitable failure.

2. But if so, if failure be inevitable, how can we turn it to account? What are its special uses? This brings us to the second point.

Failure is a discipline. Other trials have their value—sorrow, pain, opposition, obloquy, shame; but the severest, the most searching, most efficient instrument of discipline is failure. As a test of strength, and as a test of faith alike, it is without a rival.

As a test of strength. It is a comparatively easy matter for a man to carry out a great work, so long as public opinion is with him. He will labour night and day, and his toil will be sweetened, for he will be paid to the full in popular applause. Nay, he may not have the world, or even the majority, on his side; and yet he will go on bravely and cheerfully. If only he has secured the approval of his friends, or his party —of those among whom his lot is cast, of those on whose good opinion he is dependent—then he may defy the larger circle without. Their interposition deadens the blows of the external world. He has established a sort of body-guard about him, who repel the thrusts aimed at his comfort or his reputation. He gets just the sympathy and just the praise, which his heart craves most. It is only then, when good men misinterpret his motives and thwart his endeavours, then when the chasm between his principles and his party begins to yawn before him, then when friends look grave and at length fall away, then when he finds that he stands alone, then, in short, when he realises his failure, that the strain on his courage begins. Then indeed he needs all the sympathy and support, which a transcendent example can give.

And this sympathy, this support, he will find in the pattern, the spirit, the life, of Christ. In the absent loneliness of a great purpose, in the utter failure of a self-devoted life, history affords no example which can compare with this. Here he will seek his solace, his inspiration, his strength, his hope.

An old Greek philosopher—the wisest of his race—nearly four centuries before Christ, drew from his imagination a picture of the ideal righteous man. It was an essential feature in the portrait, that he should be tested by the extreme of adversity, that he should be misrepresented and misunderstood; that, though righteous, he should be considered unrighteous; that he should meet with obloquy and persecution and shame; last of all—a strange, instinctive prophecy—he was to die on the gibbet. This old philosopher rightly divined. It was essential that the ideal man should fail, utterly fail, in life. Christ's perfection could only be manifested by entire failure. This failure is the most brilliant jewel in His heavenly crown; the richest portion of the inheritance which He has bequeathed to us.

But failure is not only a test of strength; it is still more a test of faith. So long as a man is successful in his aims, he has no misgivings. He believes in his work, because it progresses under his hands. He believes in himself, because others believe in him. But a time comes when he finds himself on one side, and all the world arrayed against him on the other. He sees before him only discouragement, disappointment, defeat. Then he asks himself whether he alone can be right, and so many thousands wrong. He begins by questioning whether the voice is indeed

God's voice, and he ends by stifling the witness of the Spirit within him.

By stifling the witness of the Spirit. Brothers and sisters in Christ, do not think that this lesson has no reference to you and to you. Do not persuade yourselves, that it is meant only for those who are gifted with exceptionally great capacities, and whom God has therefore designed for some magnificent work. Is there anyone here who has not at one time or another felt some noble enthusiasm burning in his heart—perhaps some aspiration after a higher, purer, more spiritual life, perhaps some desire to devote self to the well-being of relations or friends, perhaps some design for alleviating the miseries or instructing the ignorance or reforming the vices of the outcast poor? This (can you doubt it?) was God's voice speaking within you, was God's Spirit testifying to you; and yet you stifled it. You were discouraged; you tried feebly and failed; and your faith forsook you. You felt that you were left alone; you did not feel that, though alone, you were not alone, for the Father was with you. You appropriated the one half of Christ's experience, the sense of failure; you did not appropriate the other and the essential half, the persistence of faith. There was in you then, there is in you now, if you will only believe it, a power which can defy failure, a power which must be victorious, because it is a power of God, and not of your own. Do you plead that you are young, that you are feeble, that you are unlearned, that you are without position and without influence? What matter? Is not God's strength 'made perfect in weakness?' I spoke before of the waste of the glorious possibilities of youth. What is the cause that they are thus squandered and lost? What, but that we will not trust God's voice speaking through our aspirations and enthusiasms? The first chill of ill-success damps our ardour. We have not faith to forecast the ultimate triumph of God's will.

3. And this brings me to the third and last point, the triumph of failure. History teems with examples illustrating this principle in a higher or lower degree; failure, utter failure at the outset; success, brilliant success in the result. The great Florentine reformer Savonarola commenced his mission. His first attempt was a total failure. He kindled no enthusiasm. His audiences dwindled away. He could not obtain a hearing. So a year passed away, and another and another. It was failure still. But an unquenchable fire was burning within him, and he knew that it was not an earthly flame. Then at length 'on a sudden,' we are told, 'he burst out; appalling, entrancing, shaking the souls of men, piercing to their heart of hearts, and drawing them in awe-struck

crowds before the foot of his pulpit.' No preacher since the Apostolic days produced such striking effects as he produced.

Or take another example from a wholly different walk in life. The great English engineer George Stephenson furnishes a signal illustration of this lesson. He commenced life with the most serious disadvantages of education. He found all scientific men against him. He was confronted with the giant mass of popular *inertia* and distrust. But he was conscious of a great idea; he clung to it; and he persevered dauntlessly. 'I have fought for the locomotive single-handed,' he said, 'for nearly twenty years, having no engineer to help me. I put up with every rebuff, determined not to be put down.' At length the locomotive did triumph. And look at the consequences. Railways have revolutionised the conditions of society, not in England only, but throughout the world.

Throngs of witnesses might be produced to illustrate this same truth—great statesmen, great orators, great generals, great philanthropists, great mechanicians. But all such examples pale into nothing before the lesson of the life of Christ. Here was the most signal failure, followed by the most signal triumph which the world has ever seen. Ask indifferent men; ask unbelievers. They will confess as much as this.

It is the homage which unbelief itself pays to the transcendent glory of Christ's Person and Work, that it allows His influence on the world to have been the greatest and most beneficent which the world has ever known. And yet He died a malefactor's death; and yet all His disciples forsook Him and fled; and yet at that moment His work was stamped out—nothing less. His life's labours and His life's sufferings were simply annihilated.

This is the example of all examples. God's purpose cannot fail. Whatsoever is honest, whatsoever is lovely, whatsoever is pure, whatsoever is truthful, has a strength and a vitality in it, which no time can obliterate and no antagonism can subdue. Believe this, and no failure will be a failure to you. It will only be a triumph deferred. The pains which you have spent in reclaiming that poor outcast are not thrown away, though you see no immediate fruits. The seeds of morality and goodness which you have sown in that wayward child are not lost, though the soil seems hard and barren now. The coldness and the obloquy and the scorn which you incurred in denouncing that social wrong, or that fashionable sin, have not been incurred in vain, though as yet you get no man to hear you. The bread cast on the waters will be found after many days. The echo of your voice will come rolling back, long after it has ceased to articulate, because it has been caught up and reverberated through the everlasting hills. Yes, it was the voice of God after all, and not your own voice. You may not live to see it. Your life may be pronounced a failure. Your sun may set in clouds and darkness. Dare to face this possibility. But your work cannot die. Think of Christ your Master. Think of His unparalleled failure, and His magnificent success. Listen to the witness of the Spirit. Trust God, Who is One: and not the world, because it is many. Then your triumph is assured. 'This, this is the victory that overcometh the world, even our faith.'

X.

CHRIST'S GIFT OF PEACE.

Peace I leave with you, My peace I give unto you: not as the world giveth, give I unto you.

S. JOHN xiv. 27.

Fifth Sunday after Easter, 1871.

ON the first of May, twenty years ago, was inaugurated the earliest of those great international exhibitions which have since taken their place among the recognised institutions of the civilised world. On the first of this present month, the latest of these was opened. These twenty years have been crowded with momentous incidents, which will be ever memorable in the pages of history. May it not be profitable, then, to connect the earliest of these industrial efforts with the latest, to review briefly the intervening period, and to enquire how far they have succeeded, and how far they have failed, in the highest expectations which they excited? Christ's promise in the text, 'Peace I leave with you,' shall strike the keynote of the enquiry.

To those who remember the first exhibition, who witnessed the pomp and the brilliancy of the opening day, who can recall the happy auguries of a new and blissful era, which had broken upon the world with the dawn of that first May morning, the contrast presented in this its latest successor is striking indeed. Crowds doubtless will flock to it; thousands will derive interest and instruction from it. But the sentiment, the enthusiasm, the thrill of delight, the inspiration of hope, is wanting. The magic is gone. It is a mere show-room, a mere display of mechanical contrivances, of industrial products, of artistic design. It is only an international exhibition, not an enchanted world-palace, whence the choicest blessings are to be showered on the nations far and wide.

How shall we account for this change of feeling? Is it that imagination has waned? Is it that the charm of novelty has worn off, and constant repetition deadened the sentiment? This may be a partial explanation, but it is not all. Deeper still lies the consciousness of a grave disappointment; and men resent it by refusing to this later individual effort the tribute of imagination and hope.

For the first, whatever other objects it had in view, was intended before all things to be a Temple of Peace. There under its all-embracing roof the products of the nations were displayed side by side; thither to its wide nave and transepts the representatives of the nations flocked together. It was a novel sight. And in that vast concourse of all kindreds and peoples and tongues men saw the dawning of the happy day, which was to usher in the reign of Peace upon earth. The poet's dream at length had been realised; the roar of the cannon was hushed, and the battle-flag furled. The nations would henceforth live together in harmony, bound to each other by common interests. War had been rendered impossible. International disputes would be settled by international arbitration. And, when after a few months of brilliant success this palace of hope vanished out of sight, it seemed to utter to the world, as its parting benediction, the very echo of our Lord's own words, 'Peace I leave with you.'

Then a few months more and the old warrior, our great champion in the fiercest struggle which the history of Modern Europe had seen, passed away in the fulness of years to an honoured grave; and, as his remains were lowered into the vault of this Cathedral, it seemed as if with him, their representative man, we had also buried with all due respect the last lingering traditions and feelings of the warlike past. The new reign had indeed begun.

And what has been the result? At the first rude touch of human passion the golden chain, which Commerce had thus forged with so much pains to bind the nations in universal amity, snapped and shivered like glass. The voice of this messenger of Peace was still lingering on our ears, when the bugle-note again sounded shrill and loud. And from that time to this wars and rumours of wars have never ceased among us. In all history it would be difficult to find within the same short space a succession of conflicts so continuous, so various in kind, so vast in scale, so momentous in their issues, as those which we in our generation have witnessed within the last twenty years. To us Englishmen only a small share of their aggregate misery has fallen. A Russian war, an Indian mutiny, an Abyssinian campaign—these are enough, and more than enough, to make us realise the horrors of war, and sigh for the blessings of peace. But, compared with those more disastrous struggles which have wasted other nations, our lot may be considered happy indeed. For, in whatever direction we have turned, the same sight has met our eyes. On the continent of America a devastating civil war, spread over a wider area of ground, and waged with larger armaments than any other civil war on record in modern history; among the people of Europe not once nor twice but many times nation grappling with nation in a fierce conflict for supremacy, for vengeance, for life; dynasties overthrown, empires founded, great military powers created or annihilated, peoples made and unmade; a series of wars culminating in this latest and fiercest struggle, which for the fatal magnificence of its operations, the size of its armaments, the capacity of its destructive engines, the rapidity and precision of its movements, the gigantic scale of its battles, its sieges, its capitulations, is quite without a parallel; and which has only ceased, to leave as its legacy to the vanquished a painful civil rebellion, whose horrors are unredeemed by the assertion of any lofty principle, or the championship of any patriotic cause. This is the fulfilment of our auguries, the realisation of our hopes. Our bright vision has vanished like an idle dream. International industry, international commerce, whatever else they have done, have failed to give us peace.

Well then may we turn, in the bitterness of our disappointment, to that older promise, which still invites our acceptance, but which in our self-sufficiency we have neglected for other more specious offers. 'Peace I leave with you, My peace I give unto you: not as the world giveth, give I unto you.'

At this season especially, when in the Gospels for

each successive Sunday the promise of the Comforter is kept before our eyes, and when we are invited to linger over Christ's parting benediction, before He ascends into Heaven, it will be profitable for us to enquire what is the nature of the peace which He offers, and what has been the fulfilment of His promise?

The fulfilment of His promise! I fancy the objector will tell us to look to Christendom for an answer—to look to its past history, and to look to its present condition. We shall be reminded of the incessant conflicts, persecutions, schisms, which have disgraced and devastated the Church from the beginning. The finger of scorn will be pointed to those darker blots which have stained the pages of her annals. We shall be asked not to forget the Albigensian Crusades, and the Massacre of St Bartholomew. We shall be bidden to recall the untold horrors of the Inquisition. Nay, we shall be invited to look nearer home; to reflect on the scenes, of which, at a great crisis in the religious history of England, this very city, these sacred precincts, were witnesses—on the fires of Smithfield and on the fanaticisms of Paul's Cross. We shall be directed to the divisions, the strifes, the hatreds, which at this very moment divide, not only universal Christendom, but individual Churches in Christendom. And then this promise of our Master will be flung in our teeth, and we shall be asked, where is the peace which the Gospel has brought to men?

And yet the answer is simple. The same Christ, Who said, 'Peace, I give unto you,' said also, 'I came not to send peace, but a sword.' The same Christ, Who promised His disciples that in Him they should have peace, in the very next breath warned them that in the world they should have tribulation. Thus the result was foreseen, and foretold.

'Not peace, but a sword.' This is a hard saying. And yet all experience bears witness to its truth. So long as human nature remains unchanged, the result will be the same. Throw down among men any great truth, on the acceptance and interpretation of which momentous issues depend, and it is sure to become an apple of discord. Nay, in exact proportion to its importance will be the zeal—yes, and the bitterness—with which men will wrangle over it. Is this the fault of the truth itself? Is it not rather the fault of human impatience, human obstinacy, human passion?

There have been some—perhaps there are now some—who would put aside Christianity, would get rid of religion altogether, in order that they may get rid of religious zeal and religious fanaticism. What? Would you proscribe the use, that you may prevent the abuse? Would you throw away the most precious thing which God has given to mankind, because its very pricelessness has made it an object of fierce contention? Would you reduce human life to a dull, dead level of moral indifference, that you may leave nothing to inflame the passions, or to stimulate the animosities of men? Does not history tell you that fierce and deadly and hateful as religious wars and religious persecutions have been, yet the misery due to all these causes together is very small, very small indeed, compared with the aggregate of cruelty that outbursts of human passion have inflicted on mankind? Does not all experience teach you, that though you should succeed (which you never will) in thrusting religion wholly out of sight, yet men would still continue to wrangle and to fight over forms of government, over municipal rights, over thwarted ambition, or wounded vanity, or wealth, or power?

For indeed you cannot say that Christianity itself lends any countenance to the quarrelsome or the persecuting spirit. Nay, do we not hear the very opposite charge brought against the Gospel of Christ, that it lays excessive stress on the milder qualities, such as gentleness, humility, patience, submission; that it inculcates too exclusively the feminine virtues, as the phrase is, and too much overlooks the manly? Is not this, in short, the reproach—a just and a glorious reproach—that it follows too assiduously those things which make for peace?

But, if you would learn how Christ fulfils His promise to His true disciples, if you would test the value of this peace which He has left as His parting gift, do not seek it in the heat of controversy, in the wrangling of theological disputants, or in the strifes of religious parties: but go rather to the true disciples of Christ, to the lowly and the poor in spirit, to the suffering and oppressed, to the sorrowful and bereaved, to the sick and dying. Watch the wife cruelly outraged in her deepest feelings by the desertion, or worse than desertion, of a husband, for whose love she has given up all; or the mother wounded at heart by the base ingratitude of a child, for whose advancement she has sacrificed all the comforts, and was ready to sacrifice even the necessities of life. See how, notwithstanding the bitterness of her trial, a deep calm broods over the sufferer, lulling her sharpest pangs, and enabling her to forget her own sorrow, while she ministers to the less poignant sufferings of others. Go to the wretched hovel of the pauper, worn out with age, helpless, unfriended and alone, destitute of everything which could make the burden of life tolerable, and yet cheerful and contented, drawing from an unseen source never-failing draughts of comfort and hope.

Go and stand by the bed of the dying man; watch his last agonies, as the soul struggles to set itself free; see how amid his paroxysms the gleam of joy lights up his features, flushing them with the consciousness of an invisible Presence, and the faint smile and the pressure of the hand bear witness to this inward peace, triumphant over pain, triumphant over death. Go and visit these scenes, and then say, whether Christ is slack to fulfil His promise, whether the peace of the Gospel is a delusion or not.

What then is this peace, which Christ has left us? What is its nature? How can we realise it? Whence comes it?

First of all then; peace is not apathy, not stagnation. Whatever else it may be, it is certainly not freedom from labour, nor suspension of energy; not, in this sense, repose. I fancy that not a few are repelled by the Christian ideal of the present life, as they imagine it to be—a life apart from the interests and the activities of their neighbours, alien alike from public business and private enterprise, a life of dreary listlessness, a tame, unmeaning, savourless life. I believe that more still turn away with a feeling akin to loathing from the Christian ideal of the future life, as it is represented by some, an ideal which separates it from all that interests us now, and reduces it to a level waste of barren nothingness, a dull monotony of existence, a very life in death. What we shall be hereafter, we know not, we can only imagine, now; but of this we may be assured, that our state will afford the amplest scope for the exercise of all our highest faculties, purified, exalted, intensified. What we are expected to be here, we do know with sufficient certainty to guide us. The same Apostle, who describes the peace of God as passing all understanding, is he who laboured more abundantly than all. Let S. Paul be our type. Peace—the peace which Christ has left us—is not only consistent with the manifold occupations, energies, interests, cares of life; but through and in these we must seek it.

But, secondly; peace is not a stifling of the conscience, a deadness of the moral feelings. It cannot be denied that those, who have drugged their moral sensibility, may secure immunity from many misgivings and anxieties—nay, even from some agonies—which a lively conscience will inflict. In one sense they may be said to have attained repose—if a dull, oppressive, unrefreshing torpor, which promises relief and ends in paralysis, can be called repose. In one sense they have found peace, but their peace is a desolation. This narcotic of the soul may afford momentary ease, but it is fatal to life. It may numb the sense of sin in themselves, the sense of responsibility for the sins of others, but it hands over the whole being, motionless and helpless, to awake at length to the agony of a spiritual death.

And, lastly; if the peace of Christ is neither repose from active exertion nor immunity from a sensitive conscience, so also it is not freedom from external trial and suffering. In the same breath Christ offers to His disciples tribulation and peace—not as a choice, an alternative; but the one as accompanying the other, the one as the condition of the other. And their whole after lives were the comment on this strange, paradoxical promise. 'Not as the world giveth, give I unto you.' He holds out no expectation of escape from vexation, from misunderstanding, from calumny, from persecution, from any of the thousand forms of evil which friend or foe may inflict. Such might be the world's idea of peace. But He has promised to endow us with a spirit, which shall rise triumphant over all these things, and bear us up into a region of calm, unbroken, perennial peace.

Two worlds are ours;

this lower world with its privations, its miseries, its distractions, its fretting cares, which we realise only too vividly without an effort; that higher world, into which we are even now translated by faith, where even now the tear is wiped from every eye, and there is no more death, nor sorrow, nor pain.

This promise flows directly from the revelation

of God in the Gospel, the knowledge of the Unity of God, the recognition of Him as our Father, the sense of reconciliation with Him in Christ.

From the knowledge of the Unity of God. The consciousness of one all-powerful, all-comprehensive, presiding will is the first stage. Without unity, there can be no harmony, and therefore no peace. The polytheist's religion was necessarily distraction. With one god of the hills and another of the plains, with one god of strength, and another of beauty, and another of wisdom, and another of vengeance, and another of so-called love, with the necessity of appeasing this and not offending that, peace was impossible. His religion was but the reflex of his worldly life, his conflicting passions, his changing moods, his distracting cares.

And the recognition of this one God as our Father is the second stage. We have earthly parents, to whom we are bound by the closest ties. We obey, reverence, love them. When they are taken away, we realise (some of us for the first time), how much they have been to us. We feel a vacuity, a sense of loss, an overpowering loneliness, which no time can repair. And yet even the relation between father and son, or between mother and daughter, does not satisfy all our yearnings after parental love and parental guidance. The feelings and interests of one generation are not the feelings and interests of the next. There is always some interposing barrier, some reserve, some drawback to unrestrained mutual confidence, to entire communion of heart and spirit. Only when we have learnt to throw ourselves unconditionally on the all-embracing love of our Father in Heaven, shall we find that complete satisfaction, that perfect peace which passeth all understanding.

And this lesson we learn through the Incarnation of the Son. Christ is not so much the realisation, as the manifestation, of the Father's love, for that love was perfect even from the beginning. God taught us His love in the life and teaching of Christ; God sealed for us His love in the Cross and Passion and Resurrection of Christ. Henceforth it is written in large letters, written right across the scroll of this world's history, so that men cannot choose but read. Christ has drawn us to the Father; has reconciled us to Him; has folded us in the arms of His infinite love. Here alone our deepest yearnings are satisfied; here alone we find repose for our weary spirits; repose from distraction and anxiety and temptation; repose 'in all time of our tribulation, in all time of our wealth, in the hour of death, and in the day of judgment.'

XI.

WHY STAND YE GAZING UP INTO HEAVEN?

Why stand ye gazing up into heaven?
ACTS i. 11.

Sunday after Ascension Day, 1877.

ONCE again the disciples had been doomed to a cruel disappointment. Once again, as the cup of happiness touched their lips, it had been snatched from them, and dashed to the ground. Only a few weeks before their faith had undergone a terrible trial. They had borne their part in that triumphal procession—the proudest moment of their lives— when the loud Hosannas of the assembled people had hailed their Master as the rightful Heir of David's line, the long-expected King of Israel, the mighty Conqueror, Who should subdue the nations of the earth. Their hopes then had suddenly set in darkness. They were stunned and paralysed. It was with them, 'as when a hungry man dreameth, and, behold, he eateth; but he awaketh, and his soul is empty.' They had dreamt of a throne; and, behold, a gibbet. They had imagined a palace; and, behold, a tomb. Out of that tomb their hopes had arisen again with their risen Lord. They saw before them, not indeed a throned and sceptred king, not a mighty victor laden with the spoils of his foes, not all that their expectations had forecast; but they saw at least restored to them the same Master, Teacher, Friend. Then came this second shock. The Master discoursed freely with them about the promised kingdom. He led them on point by point, till the last anxious question trembled on their lips, 'Lord, wilt Thou at this time restore again the kingdom to Israel?' What was the meaning of His revival, His resurrection, His presence among them once more, if the long-expected hour had not at length arrived? It seemed doubtless to them, as if every moment the heavens must part asunder, and the celestial hosts descend in glorious panoply to do battle for their King. And yet day followed day in the same monotonous succession. Still there was delay; still there was uncertainty; still there was the wearisome, daily routine of common duties and common cares. They would put an end to this intolerable suspense; they would ask the question point-blank; and thus they would extort an answer by very plainness of speech. 'Lord, wilt Thou at this time?' The answer withheld from them the one thing which they desired to know. It charged them with a difficult and dangerous task, to which henceforth they must devote their lives; it promised them a power, which would enable them adequately to fulfil this task. But to the question 'When,' it vouchsafed no reply at all. 'Here,' it seemed to say, 'here is the work to be done, and there is the means of doing it. Ask for nothing more. It is mere idle curiosity to go beyond this, to penetrate into the impenetrable.' Then, as if to enforce by the strongest practical comment the lesson which His word had conveyed, 'while they beheld, He was taken up, and a cloud received Him out of their sight.' Again it was the phantom of a dissolving dream. They stretched out their hands to clutch at the kingdom, and behold the King Himself had vanished away.

Amazed and uncertain, what else could they do but to gaze up into heaven? Had He really left them, left them for ever? Or had He but retired for a moment, that He might array Himself in His glorious majesty; and would He even now emerge from His celestial chamber, resplendent in glory and attended by countless myriads of His Father's legions? So they stood transfixed, every face upturned and every eye straining, that they might catch the first ray of the descending glory, as it darted through the riven cloud.

From this dream they were startled by the rebuke of the angels. There was something hard and chilling in the very form of address, 'Ye men of Galilee;' not, 'Ye satraps of the King of Kings,' nor 'Ye captains in the mighty Victor's host.' So then the glory had departed. They were humble fishermen and peasants still, simple inhabitants of a despised province, doomed to a life of vulgar toil and commonplace cares. A fit introduction this to the rebuke which follows, 'Why stand ye gazing up into heaven?' 'Face the stern realities of life at once. You have a work to do, which will tax all your energies. There is this tremendous load of sin, under which mankind is sinking, and you are called to remove it; there is this dense cloud of ignorance, which shrouds the heavens from them, and you are charged to scatter it. There is a whole world to be conquered for Christ, and you must conquer it. What matter it to you when He will come—this very moment, tomorrow, next year, centuries hence? Cease to gaze up into heaven. Earth is the scene of your labours now; earth must be the centre of your interests.'

The angels' address is a rebuke to idle speculation in regions beyond the reach of human knowledge. It is a warning against substituting that which is visionary, for that which is real, in religion. It is more especially a denunciation of this over-curious spirit, in those provinces into which it is most eager to intrude itself, in matters relating to the Ascension, the Reign in Heaven, the Second Advent of Christ. At each recurring season of the Ascensiontide therefore it suggests a wholesome check to our thoughts. There is a highly practical way of regarding the Ascension: and there is also an eminently unpractical way. It directs us to the one; it warns us off from the other.

In one sense we cannot help gazing up into heaven. Are we not told elsewhere that 'our conversation,' our citizenship, 'is in heaven?' Are we not charged to 'seek those things which are above, where Christ sitteth on the right hand of God?' Are we not commanded to 'lay up treasures for ourselves in heaven,' for this very reason that 'where our treasure is, there our heart will be also?' And in this spirit have we not prayed during this season that 'as we do believe our Lord Jesus Christ to have ascended into the heavens, so we may also in heart and mind thither ascend, and with Him continually dwell?' In what sense then can we be required to avert our gaze from heaven, and to fix our eyes on the earth?

The circumstances of the Apostles will supply us with a first answer. What was a fault in them, will be a fault in us also. They were eager to know the exact time—the year and the day and the hour—when their King would come and claim His kingdom. They could not submit to wait patiently. The Master Himself had been quite explicit on this point. He had told them again and again, that this knowledge was hidden from them. He had figured this truth in parables; He had enunciated it in plain language. He had bidden them to watch and be ready always, because they knew not what hour their Lord would come. He had warned them that this ignorance was complete, was absolute, was universal. 'Of that day and that hour knoweth no man.' It was hidden even from the angels of heaven—the angels, who serve in the presence of God; it was hidden in some sense from the Son Himself in His mediatorial capacity—the Son, to Whom all things were made known. It was buried deep, dark, inscrutable, in the eternal counsels of the Father. And still, notwithstanding these frequent declarations, the Apostles attempt again and again to probe this secret; still the last words which they address to their risen Lord ignore the oft-repeated warning;

still the last answer which they receive from His lips is a rebuke for desiring to fathom the unfathomable. 'It is not for you to know the times or the seasons.'

The attitude of the Apostles is the type, a forecasting, of the attitude of the Church in aftertimes. The subject has exercised a strong fascination over Christians in all ages. No rebuff and no disappointment seems to have produced any effect. Again and again men have been found to predict the time of the Second Advent. Again and again their predictions have been falsified by the event. In language not less clear than the voices heard by the Apostles of old, the stern logic of facts has rebuked their presumption. 'It is not for you to know the times or the seasons.' 'Why stand ye gazing up into heaven?'

And the wrong done by this lawless speculation is not trifling. It tends to impair that attitude of patient waiting which is enjoined on the Church. It substitutes a spasmodic, intermittent, feverish watchfulness (with intervals of sloth and indifference) for the calm and continuous expectation, which alone becomes the sons of God. It is chargeable with still more fatal consequences than these. It has bred disappointment, and from disappointment has sprung scepticism, and from scepticism, mockery and unbelief. It has given occasion to the enemies of Christ to blaspheme. From the Apostolic age to the present day there have been scoffers, walking after their own lusts and saying, 'Where is the promise of His coming?' From then until now men have been prone to forget 'that one day is with the Lord as a thousand years.' And the guilt lies in no small degree with the lawless speculation of believers. Strange that it should have been so; strange that men should not perceive how each such prediction falsified, each such hope disappointed, is after all only a fresh confirmation of the Master's saying, 'Of that day and that hour knoweth no man.' 'It is not for you to know the times or the seasons.'

This then is one sense, in which we are forbidden to gaze up into heaven—this presumptuous forecasting the day of the Lord's Advent. And the second is akin to it. It has reference to the place and the circumstances of Christ's reign, as the other had reference to the time. 'Christ has ascended into the heaven of heavens; Christ is seated at the right hand of the Father; Christ will descend thence to judge the quick and dead. Where then is Christ now, at this moment? In some far-off star, which sparkles overhead in the midnight sky? In some bright, ethereal region in the mid-air, which we can vaguely imagine?' Nay, we do but perplex ourselves with such idle speculations; we only create difficulties, where there are none, by attempting to realise that which with our present faculties is unrealisable. Only reflect for a moment on the meaning of the terms which you are using. We see now only 'through a glass darkly,' not 'face to face.' We behold, not the eternal things themselves, but only their shadows. God speaks to us not yet plainly, but in parables. Here are metaphors, and we would argue upon them as if they were scientific statements. 'Set your affection on things above.' What do we mean by 'above?' Surely, not overhead. What is above us now will be on a level, will sink below us a few hours hence as the earth revolves on its axis. What is above us at this very moment is beneath the feet of our Australian fellow-disciples of Christ. 'God dwelleth in the heavens!' What again do we mean by 'the heavens?' Not surely the skies. God can no more dwell in the skies, than He can dwell on this solid earth, than He can dwell in the restless ocean. Strain your eyes and rack your thoughts, as you will, to find the place of His abode; and your brain will only grow giddy in vain. Attempt to reckon the myriads upon myriads of miles which separate you from that faint star barely discerned through the most powerful telescope, that star from which the very ray of light now striking the reflector was darted centuries before the human race existed on this earth. Have you arrived one whit nearer to the abode, the court, the throne of God, by all this tension of your senses, by all this play of your imagination? Nay, this heaven, this sky overhead, in its purity, its calm, its glory, its spaciousness, is only an image—a sublime image indeed, but an image still—of an infinitude, which we cannot describe, cannot realise. But the abode of God—God the Infinite, God the Omnipresent—why 'the heaven and the heaven of heavens cannot contain' Him. When the Apostle describes 'the King of kings and Lord of lords, Who only hath immortality,' as 'dwelling in the light unapproachable,' we picture to ourselves such a radiancy as Dante has described, or Angelico has painted. We are obliged to sustain our imagination by such aids. But here too light is only a figure. God Himself dwells no more in the light than He dwells in the darkness. But light is warmth, is geniality, is revelation, is life to us; and therefore it serves as an image of the eternal perfection.

Would we really describe the dwelling-place of God? Then let us adopt the prophet's description, 'The high and holy One that inhabiteth eternity.' Language cannot go beyond this. 'Inhabiteth eternity,' a cross metaphor, it will be said; time and space are confused. Yes, but herein consists the sublimity and power of the image. God has no palace but eternity. And so again, when we say that Christ dwells 'at the right hand of God,' it is still more obvious that we are dealing with a metaphor: God has neither hands nor feet: with God is neither right nor left. It would be blasphemy to think otherwise of Him. Nay, S. Paul says that we ourselves—you and I, Christian men and women—by virtue of our baptism, by virtue of our Christian profession, have been 'seated together with Christ in the heavenly places,' have been enthroned already, where Christ Himself is enthroned. This is an obvious metaphor. And why then should we press the words in the other case, as if they described some visible scene, with Christ sitting on the right hand of God? We recall the court of some earthly sovereign, where the heir-apparent holds the place of honour nearest the throne; and we picture to ourselves some far-off celestial palace, with its rainbow hues, its starry glories, where such a scene is enacted, only with a brilliancy intensified a thousandfold. We have in our mind's eye perhaps the representation of some famous painter, who has described on canvas the session of the Son in glory. And yet—with a strange inconsistency—when the painter attempts to portray the Eternal Father, our mind recoils with horror. We shudder at the profanity, we avert our gaze. Our repulsion, our horror, is a silent witness to us, that the scene cannot be localised, cannot be portrayed.

But 'what then?' it will be said, 'the very purpose, you confess, of the Ascensiontide is to testify to the glorification of humanity in the Session of Christ, as Man still, on God's right hand. Does not this suppose some locality? How can you understand it otherwise?'

Why should you expect to understand it? Is your understanding all-powerful? Nay, do you even understand yourself—yourself, whom you are questioning every moment? Do you understand how it is that, while your body is fixed on this one spot, your mind is traversing all space and all time, soaring into heaven beyond Arcturus and the Pleiades, piercing into the remote past when this earth was peopled with strange monsters, plesiosauri and pterodactyls and labyrinthodons? This is a fact. And, if this is possible, can you not conceive it possible also, that the humanity of Christ—with all the limitations which it implies—may be brought into close proximity, may, in some mysterious way, be placed in a position of unique honour, in relation to the Illimitable, Infinite, Eternal Father, such as is represented to us in a figure, in a parable, by sitting at the right hand of God? Do not presume that you know everything, when in fact you know nothing at all.

Stand no more gazing up into heaven. Spend no more time on barren speculations; they only absorb energy and paralyze action. Nor yet on mystic reveries; they only satisfy the feelings, without stimulating the conscience. Be stirring, be working, be witnesses to Christ.

Stand no more gazing up into heaven; but rather ascend thither as at this season, and there 'in heart and mind continually dwell.' Ascend thither in the contemplation of humanity exalted, enthroned, glorified in Christ, in the presence of the Eternal Father. This thought must purify, must stimulate, must sanctify you, as you remember that you too are seated with Christ—seated with Him even now—in the heavenly places. Ascend thither in the realisation of Christ as still a living Being, still a living Man, Who, though 'touched with the feeling of our infirmities,' has nevertheless entered into the heavenly sanctuary, the true Holy of Holies, and there makes atonement for our sins. Ascend thither in the assurance of His reappearing again, at the great restitution, when there shall be new heavens and a new earth, and when God shall be all in all. Ascend thither in the spirituality of your worship, this knowing, that if Christ had not gone away, the Comforter, the Guide to all truth, could never have come; and that therefore His departure was ordained to wean you from outward, formal conceptions of religion. So rise from earth to heaven; or rather, so call down heaven upon earth. The kingdom of God is within you, is around you; heaven is in your homes, in your chambers and warehouses, in the very streets, if you have only eyes to see it.

Stand no more gazing up into heaven; but return from the Mount of the Ascension to the city of your abode, to the duties of your vocation, to the struggles of your every-day life. There continue in prayer and supplication; there await in confidence that outpouring of the Spirit, which is never denied to those who do earnestly seek it: there live and there bear witness to Christ, that you may win yourselves, may win others, to God.

XII.

CHRISTIAN FORETHOUGHT AND UNCHRISTIAN ANXIETY.

Take therefore no thought for the morrow: for the morrow shall take thought for the things of itself.

S. MATTHEW vi. 34.

Fifteenth Sunday after Trinity, 1873.

I SUPPOSE that no passage in Holy Scripture has caused more real or more wide-spread perplexity than this. Here we have a precept which must mingle with the whole current of our lives, must affect the thoughts and the actions of every day and every hour. And yet it seems to set before us an ideal of life which is quite unattainable; and which, if attainable, would be destructive to human society. For it seems to tell us that in the affairs of this world we should be indifferent, reckless, improvident; that, if we would live rightly, we must live altogether for the moment; that it is culpable to look forward to the future, culpable to make provision for sickness and old age, culpable to lay by for wife and family.

I am not stating an imaginary difficulty. I speak of that which I know. I have met with cases, where a sincere believer has been sorely perplexed by this precept, as he has understood it. It has lain across his path of life, as a constant reproach to him. I have known cases also where the unbeliever has alleged it, and (I feel bound to say) has alleged it in all sincerity, as a triumphant argument against the perfect morality of the Lord's teaching. He has condemned it as contradicting the best experience of men, as conflicting with the first principles of political economy, as fatal to civilisation and subversive of society. And knowing this, as the passage occurs in the Gospel for this Sunday, I did not think that I could better occupy your attention this afternoon than by investigating its true meaning and import. It will not have been a useless task, if by God's grace I shall be able to meet some open objections, and remove some lurking scruples.

Now if the passage did mean what it has been supposed to mean, then the extremes in the scale of religious belief would be found to have met in an unexpected way. The recklessness of the Epicurean would be matched by the recklessness of the Christian. 'Let us eat and drink, for tomorrow we die' is the motto of the one; 'Dismiss all thought of the morrow; for the morrow will take care of itself' would be the echo of the other.

If it did mean this, then all those measures for preventing and alleviating human misery, which have engaged the attention of the statesman and the philanthropist and the parish-clergyman, are founded on an utterly vicious principle. Savings-banks and provident societies and superannuation funds and insurance companies—what are all these but direct and deliberate measures of forethought for the morrow, systematic organisations for setting at nought a Divine precept, if indeed that precept were rightly interpreted as enjoining a reckless neglect of the future?

No, assuredly no. Whatever else the text implies, it cannot at all events signify this. Forethought is the very bond of human society, the very earnest of human progress. Forethought is the very breath of the Christian life. Forethought is the very reflection of the Divine Wisdom.

It is the bond of society, and the earnest of progress. What is it that differentiates the child from the man, what is it that separates barbarism from civilisation, but the ability to realise the law of continuity in human affairs, and to make provision for the hereafter in accordance with this law? What is all education—the education of a nation, as well as the education of an individual—but an instrumentality for calculating consequences and a machinery for promoting forethought?

And, moreover, it is the very breath of Christian life. Again, I ask, what is it that distinguishes the Christian from the unbeliever, but that his horizon is immeasurably extended, and his forethought takes an infinitely wider sweep? The Christian is to the unbeliever what the civilised man is to the savage. The savage lives for the moment; he gathers the spontaneous fruits of the earth; he makes no provision against famine; he tills no ground, sows no seed, expects no harvest. As civilisation increases, forethought developes also. Its earliest efforts do not go beyond the wants of the year; it gathers in its harvests, and stores up its food for the winter. But gradually its range of vision expands. A great advance is made when a man drains a morass on which he may not hope to reap the grain, or plants an orchard from which he cannot live to pluck the fruit. The gain to society in this advance is clear. But what is its higher meaning? Why, it is another step forward towards the more extended foresight of the Christian; it is an unconscious tribute to the continuity of being, a stammering confession of an interest in the future, a recognition, however halting and imperfect, of a life after death. In this matter of forethought the civilised man stands midway between the barbarian savage and the Christian sage. Christianity is not the suppression of forethought; it is the education, the extension, the perfecting of it.

And once more: forethought is the reflection of the Divine Wisdom. Providence is another word for foresight: providence is prudence writ large: and thus Providence is instinctively used as a synonyme for God. With God indeed, strictly speaking, there can be no foresight and no forethought; for with Him is no before or after. The infinite past and the infinite future are all as a moment to Him. The eternal economy of the Universe is comprehended by Him at a glance. He is omnipresent in time, as He is omnipresent in space. But we call His eternal purpose providence, we call it foresight; because with our limited faculties we cannot otherwise conceive or speak of it. And human forethought is a reflection, however faint and feeble, of His glorious providence. For it is a realisation of the future as if present; it is an overleaping of intervening days and years and ages by the power of a reasonable faith; it is (so far as human capacities will permit) an annihilation of time.

'Be not deceived.' You cannot defy God's law with impunity. The invariable sequence, the inevitable rule, of cause and effect, is His eternal will alike in things natural and things spiritual. The law of seed-time and harvest pervades the whole economy of the Universe. Forethought is the recognition of this law. 'Whatsoever a man soweth, that shall he reap.' If you sow intemperance and profligacy now, you will reap disease and madness and a thousand nameless terrors hereafter. If you sow improvidence in youth, you will reap misery and want in old age. If you scatter the seed of recklessness, do not marvel when you gather in the harvest of despair. The seed is a hollow, empty, purposeless, indolent, vapid existence. You have sown the wind. The harvest is a beating, howling hurricane, which strips you of shelter and exposes you naked and defenceless to the elements. You have reaped the whirlwind. In vain will you shield yourself under the excuse that you are bidden to 'take no thought for the morrow.' In vain will you parley, when your voice is drowned in the raging storm. 'God is not mocked.' His law will vindicate itself at all hazards.

But, it will be said, whatever may be the consequences, as a matter of fact can any words more strong, and more explicit, be imagined, than the command to take no thought for the morrow? To the English ear this can only mean one thing; 'Be indifferent, be careless, be improvident, about what is to happen tomorrow.' To the English ear of today, yes; but how was it, when this translation was made? Words are the coins of the mind. They are the current medium of human thought. But coins, though at any given time they may be regarded as having a definite and fixed value, will rise or fall from age to age. The shilling of today has a purchasing power very different from the shilling of two or three centuries ago. So it has been with words. The phrase 'to take thought,' when it came into our English Bibles, expressed an idea quite different from that which it conveys now. Thus I read in one early writer that a certain person was 'put to trouble and died of thought.' I find it stated in another that an 'old man for very thought and grief of heart pined away.' So 'dying of thought' was equivalent to 'being killed with distress of mind,' 'dying of a broken heart.' I turn again to the Old Testament, and I find the very expression which we have here. Saul hastens the return of himself and his servant homeward, 'lest his father...take thought for them,' i.e. 'get anxious about them.' Thus, then, 'to take thought' in old English is 'to feel anxiety,' 'to be harassed with care;' and the precept assumes a wholly different meaning from that which is generally attached to it; 'Be not anxious about the morrow; for the morrow will have its own anxieties. Sufficient unto the day is the evil thereof.' And this corresponds exactly with the meaning of the original. The word translated 'thought' signifies not prudence, not forethought, but anxiety, harassing and distracting care. Thus the condemnation is hurled, not against a reasonable prudence about measures, but against a profitless solicitude about results. Thus it is a lesson not of recklessness, not of indifference, even in the affairs of this life, but of patience, of calmness, of firm faith in an Almighty power and love, which overrules all things for good.

But, though our Lord does not in this particular passage condemn forethought, still He certainly does throughout the Sermon on the Mount seek to guide and graduate it. In this, as in all practical matters, it is necessary to observe the due proportions of things. The character, the consequences, the duration, must be duly estimated: and our forethought must be meted out accordingly. It is this graduation of forethought which forms the leading idea of the context. We hold it culpable folly, if a man sacrifices the interest of after years to the enjoyment of tomorrow and the next day. It is only reasonable prudence, only common sense, we say, to make provision for after life. And yet, if men are asked to extend this principle, if they are told to enlarge the horizon of their forethought, if they are required to postpone the smaller interests of the life before death to the larger interests of the life after death, just as they have postponed the smaller interests of today and tomorrow to the larger interests of the years to come— at once this is unpractical, this is overstrained, this is fanatical. Yet only allow the premiss, and there is no escape from the conclusion. Only allow that man is destined to live an immortal life (and you do not seriously question this), and then the immortal life must be infinitely more important than the mortal by reason of its infinitely greater duration. Only allow (and you will not deny this) that truth and righteousness and love and purity are eternal principles, and then they must take an absolute precedence over meat and drink and clothing, over things which 'perish in the using.' Whenever there is a conflict between the two, the temporary must surrender unconditionally to the eternal.

And yet you demur, and you question, and you cavil, when you are told to seek first the kingdom of God and His righteousness, as if there were something unreal, something extravagant, in the demand. Nay, it is the truest, highest, rarest, most uncommon common sense, which is embodied in this precept.

Does not natural instinct bear witness to its reasonableness? When in the ever-memorable cavalry charge at Balaklava those six hundred horsemen bravely rode the length of the deadly valley amid the roaring of cannon on the right and on the left, facing certain destruction: or again, when on the decks of the 'Birkenhead' those brave soldiers, having first despatched the boats with the women and children in safety to the land, then themselves calmly awaited the end, as the vessel went slowly down, maintaining their ranks to the last with the same cool courage and the same steady bearing as if they were merely halting on the parade-ground; what was the instinctive, spontaneous, universal verdict, not of England only, but of all Europe, called forth by their heroism and self-devotion? Was there one dissentient voice amid this general chorus of praise, one murmur of disapprobation at the folly of these men in sacrificing their lives to duty, when they might have saved them? And what, I ask, was the meaning of this unquestioned and unquestionable judgment of mankind? Why, it was a confession that there is something better than food and raiment, something higher than this frail life with its paltry attractions and its transitory pleasures. It was a confession that true wisdom puts duty before life: and duty is a province, though only a single province, in that kingdom of God, which

Christ bids us seek first. Yes, the instinctive sense of mankind, when it is taken by surprise and speaks out of the fulness of the heart, when it is not warped by any consideration of self-interest, nor confused by any subtleties of a vain philosophy—the instinctive sense of mankind declares that it is good to 'seek first the kingdom of God and His righteousness.'

Our Lord then graduates forethought, but He condemns solicitude. He condemns it on two grounds. It is a practical mistake, and it is a religious mistrust.

1. It is a practical mistake. Be not anxious for the morrow. The morrow will bring its own anxieties. Do not anticipate them, but 'act in the living present.' Each day has its own cares, its own trials, its own struggles. They are enough, and more than enough, for that day. It is folly to accumulate upon these the anxieties of the morrow. It is folly to double your cares, incurring them first in the anticipation and then again in the reality. We hold that general both the happiest and the wisest man who, having carefully planned the strategy of the coming day, then dismisses it from his thoughts and lies down to rest, recruiting his powers of mind and body in the forgetfulness of sleep. So it is in the anxious warfare of life. The anticipation of care is as futile as it is unwise. It is futile; for it cannot change the unchangeable. If the trouble is to come, no previous

anxiety can avert it. If it is not to come, all previous anxiety is distress incurred in vain. It is unwise; for it is a waste of energy, a distraction of mind. Every moment spent on the possibilities of tomorrow is a moment abstracted from the realities of today. And these realities—the duties and the charities of the passing hour, the conflict of good and evil, the trouble, the temptation, the sin—these will need all the energies, and absorb all the thought, which we can bestow upon them. What might not be the effect on our moral and spiritual life, if we only gave to the education of the heart and the conscience one half of the time that is wasted in brooding over evils which will never arrive, and over troubles which we cannot avert!

2. But the religious error, involved in such anxiety, is graver still. It is nothing less than unfilial and churlish distrust of the love and power of our heavenly Father. The practical belief in the fatherhood of God constitutes the fundamental distinction between true and false religion. This portion of the Sermon on the Mount is wholly occupied in enforcing such a belief. The prayer of prayers begins with the enunciation of it. The words 'your Father,' 'thy Father,' 'My Father,' occur with astonishing frequency throughout the whole context. It appears as though our Lord would take hearts by storm, and lead us

captive by this endearing mode of address. He seems to say that this one word 'Father'—with all the ideas of love, and tenderness, and protection, and watchful care, which it involves—this word once lodged in the heart must quiet all anxieties, and crush all doubts, and quell all fears. If I can only realise the truth that He, the All-wise and All-powerful and Omnipresent, He Whom 'the heaven of heavens cannot contain,' He Who dwelleth in eternity, notwithstanding the infinitude of His Being, is not only *our* Father, but *my* Father—loves *me* with a Father's heart, watches over *me* with a Father's care—then I shall lack nothing, I shall dread nothing; for I shall know that all things—trouble and vexation and want and sorrow and pain—all things whatsoever will work together for my good. Just as the child, scared by some childish fear, or bursting with some childish grief, flees to its father's presence, clings to its father's knees, buries its face in its father's bosom, and all is well at once; so must it be with you. There is no trouble so special, and no grief so private, and no temptation so subtle, and no apprehension so vague, nothing so great and nothing so small, but that it will find a place in your Father's heart. Go to Him in childlike trust. Nurse no anxieties for tomorrow, but go to Him this very night. Open out to Him the grief which is breaking your heart;

carry before Him the trouble which is desolating your life; lay bare to Him the temptation which is gnawing at your conscience; fling down before Him the sin which has killed your soul. For He will console; He will alleviate; He will strengthen; He will make alive. Cast upon Him all your anxiety, without misgiving and without reserve, cast it upon Him, 'for He careth for you.'

XIII.

TRUE BLESSEDNESS.

But He said, Yea rather, blessed are they that hear the word of God, and keep it.

S. LUKE xi. 28.

Third Sunday after Easter, 1876.

THIS saying, to which I purpose directing your attention this afternoon, is eminently characteristic of the Gospel teaching. It is the rapid, unpremeditated reply to a voice from the crowd—a voice proceeding from an unknown person, and dictated by a sudden impulse. And yet it contains a lesson which is unexhausted and inexhaustible. It is the Master's standing protest against the misconception, the abuse, the degradation of His Gospel by the preference of the external and formal over the personal and spiritual, by the divorce of religion from morality.

The Saviour has been teaching after His wont. He has uttered words of rebuke, words of consolation, words of grace and of truth. The shaft has pierced home to the hearts of His hearers. The proud spirit of the Pharisee has quailed before that stern denunciation. The humble penitent has found refreshment and strength in those cheering tones. There is a directness, a depth, a life, a potency, in this new teacher's utterances, which contrasts strangely with the scholastic subtleties and the trivial distinctions and the moral subterfuges of the doctors whom they are accustomed to hear. One voice, breaking the silence, gives expression to the feeling which is upmost in the minds of all. It is (can we doubt it?) the utterance of a mother's voice, the outpouring of a mother's heart. Proud indeed might that woman be, who could boast of such a son. What mother would not pray that her child might grow up to be like Him, so gentle, so strong, so pure, so good, so great a rabbi, so wise a prophet? 'Blessed is the womb that bare thee, and the paps that gave thee suck.'

What more natural than this sudden outburst of admiration? It found a hearty response—we may venture to say—in all the assembled crowd. And it was not more natural than true. This title of 'blessedness' belongs in a very special sense to her, to whom it is here assigned, to the mother of the

Lord. It was conferred upon her by the voice of inspiration; it has passed from mouth to mouth throughout all succeeding ages. She herself declared in no faltering tones her conviction of the glory which awaited her; 'Behold, from henceforth all generations shall call me blessed.' Nor has time falsified her conviction. Here at all events Scripture and tradition—the Gospel and the Church—are at one. Her title has indeed been dishonoured, and her diadem tarnished, by the profane exaggeration, which confers on the human mother the attributes and the worship belonging to the Divine Son alone. But no foolishness, nor superstition, nor blasphemy of men, can recall the promise of God.

It was not therefore because the words were untrue, not even because they had overstated the truth, that the cry of this simple woman needed correction. But she saw only dimly and partially. Her utterance was an imperfect utterance. She had stated a lower truth, and she had ignored a higher.

In His reply, therefore, our Lord does not deny or question her statement—it was beyond the reach of question or denial—but He fastens on it, as an opportunity for imparting a higher lesson. To her first, and to us—to the Church in all ages—through her, He seems to address such language as this.

'Do you think it a blessing to be linked with Me

by ties of race or of kindred, to associate with Me outwardly, to eat and drink at the same table, to visit the same places, to gaze upon the same scenes? Ah! this is a poor and unworthy view of My Person, of My Gospel. Believe it, the true blessedness is not here; not in ties of relationship, even the closest, not in the communion of the senses—of the eye or the ear or the touch—not in any of these outward things; for these (even the best of them) are carnal, earthly, transitory, and I and Mine are eternal in the heavens. These may be blessings, if we use them aright; but they may also be curses—the most bitter and deadly curses. Here then is the blessing of which ye would speak: here in this inward communion with the Father through Me. Knit your hearts to My heart; think My thoughts; live My life. So shall ye be more to Me than all the ties of earthly kindred, even the most sacred; more than mother, more than sisters and brothers: for ye shall be one with Me— bone of My bone and flesh of My flesh, very members incorporate of My body—one in an indissoluble union, one eternally, one with the Father in Me.'

'Ye speak of the blessedness of My mother: ye speak rightly, for so it is. But know ye not, wherein her blessedness consists? Understand ye not, that it must be sought, where all true blessedness alone can be found, not in the sphere of the material world, not in the relations of outward things, not in a common blood, a common home, common sights and usages; but in the realm of spiritual verities, in a common heart and soul, in a common faith and love, in a common citizenship in the kingdom of heaven?' This was her blessedness, that by her purity and innocence, by her humble faith and unswerving trust in God, she was deemed the least unworthy among the daughters of men, to become the mother of the Redeemer. This was her blessedness; that when this unique privilege was announced to her, she believed the heavenly message; that hearing the story of the shepherds divinely guided to the manger in Bethlehem there to worship her babe, she pondered these things in her heart; that seeing the marvellous child grow from day to day—grow in wisdom, as in stature—and hearing Him speak as never child spake before, she kept all these sayings in her heart. This was her blessedness, despite all her sorrows—for her sorrows were beyond the common lot of motherhood—despite her sorrows, or rather by reason of her sorrows; for these were to her a mighty witness of God's favour, a gracious trial of her faith, a merciful discipline for the kingdom of heaven. In one sense her blessedness is unapproached and unapproachable: but in another, and this the highest sense of all, her blessedness may be thine and thine; for 'whosoever will do the will of

God, the same is My brother and My sister, yes, and My mother also.'

Such is the abiding lesson suggested by our Lord's reply. The truth, which it enforces, lies at the very root of the Gospel teaching—a truth even now but fitfully discerned in theory, and daily forgotten by us all in practice, yet a truth nevertheless which alone can give life to individuals and churches and nations. 'God is a Spirit: and they that worship Him must worship Him in spirit and in truth.' 'My kingdom is not of this world.' 'The kingdom of heaven cometh not with observation.' 'The kingdom of God is not meat and drink; but righteousness, and peace, and joy in the Holy Ghost.' 'God accepteth no man's person.' 'Henceforth know we no man after the flesh : yea, though we have known Christ after the flesh, yet now henceforth know we Him no more.'

Again and again do prophets and evangelists and apostles enforce this elementary truth. No frequency of reiteration is too wearisome, and no solemnity of warning is too grave, to emphasize its importance. Yet it is hardly too much to say that the whole history of the Church is one continued search after this truth, one unintermitted struggle against its opposing error. Do we need any explanation of this fact? We have only to ask our own hearts, to test our own experiences. Is it not a very real danger with all men—with all, at least, who have any religious feelings or aspirations—to repose on a doctrine or an ordinance or a privilege, on something good and true in itself, it may be; something desirable or even necessary as a means to an end; but something external to ourselves, something short of the purification of our hearts, and the renewal of our lives?

This spirit was never more rife than in the age and among the countrymen of our Lord. It is the special temptation indeed of a religious epoch and a religious people. It was this which the Baptist denounced, when he warned the assembled throng that God was able of those very stones which lay at their feet—yes, of those inert, senseless, worthless things which they spurned at every step—to raise up children unto Abraham. It was this which again and again called forth those stern rebukes and those hateful contrasts from the lips of our Lord Himself— how hateful, because how repugnant to all their cherished partialities and their sentiments of national pride, we at this distance of time can but dimly realise. They were told that crowds should gather from the east and from the west, from the north and from the south—the loathed Philistine, the hated Idumæan, Moab and Ammon, Asshur and Egypt, the hard, tyrannical Roman, the reckless, profane Greek, these unclean dogs of heathendom, these reprobate sinners of the Gentiles—and should throng into Messiah's kingdom: while they, the sons of Abraham, they, the heirs of the promise, they, the guardians of the Law, should be excluded and have their place in the outer darkness, where is the weeping and the gnashing of teeth. They were told—the proud, scrupulous, rigid Pharisees were told—that the very publicans and harlots should go in before them. What more bitter, what more humiliating, what more abhorrent, than such words as these? 'Blessed are they who have Abraham to their father: blessed are they who claim kindred with patriarchs and prophets and kings: blessed are they to whom is committed the keeping of the oracles of God: blessed are they to whom pertain the adoption and the glory, the covenant and the promises, for whom the Law was given amidst the thunders and the lightnings of Sinai, whose are the Aaronic priesthood, the temple-ritual, the daily sacrifice, the continual service of praise and thanksgiving.' But the voice of a higher inspiration breaking in disturbs this pride of patriotic self-complacency. 'Yea rather, blessed are they—sinners of the Gentiles though they be—blessed are they who hear the word of God, and keep it.'

And from the schools of the Pharisees this leaven spread into the Church of Christ. S. Paul's whole life was spent in combating this error, this preference of the outward and carnal over the moral and spiritual. For what was his position in relation to his antagonists? They refused to acknowledge his authority; they declined to listen to his teaching; because forsooth, unlike the Twelve, he had not attended the Lord during His earthly ministry, had not wandered with Him on the shores of the Galilean lake, had not worshipped with Him in the sanctuary at Jerusalem, had not received the last bread and wine from His sacred hands, had not entered the judgment-hall of Caiaphas, and stood beneath the cross on Calvary, and explored the solitude of the empty grave, and parted from the Master on the brow of Olivet. It was nothing at all to them that he had laboured more abundantly than any of the Twelve: nothing at all that he had preached Christ far and wide with a power and an energy far beyond the rest: nothing at all that the signs of an Apostle were everywhere visible with him: nothing at all that he was ready to spend, and be spent, in Christ's service, that he was 'in stripes, in imprisonments, in tumults, in labours,' 'in weariness and painfulness, in watchings often, in hunger and thirst, in fastings often, in cold and nakedness,' that for Christ's sake he died daily. None of these things moved them. One thing only they valued. To have known Christ after the flesh, this indeed was a privilege, which gave a title to hearing;

this was all in all. 'Blessed are the eyes that have seen Thy face, and the ears that have listened to Thy voice, and the hands that have pressed Thy hand. Blessed are they who have spoken with Thee, eaten with Thee, walked with Thee.' S. Paul's life and work were the crushing reply to all this. 'Yea rather, blessed is he, who has lived for Me, has laboured for Me, has died for Me; blessed are they who hear the word of God, and keep it.'

And as we descend the stream of time, the same tendency reappears again and again in different guises. One Church claims a paramount authority, because it was founded, or reputed to be founded, by a leading Apostle. Another attracts crowds of worshippers, because it possesses some imagined relic of the Life or Passion of Christ. Another is thronged by pilgrims from afar, because it is the real or supposed resting place of some devoted saint or martyr of old. A peculiar virtue is attributed to prayers uttered in such places; as if the favour of heaven were concentrated on them. We may find little resemblance at first sight between the grossest form of mediæval superstition, and the innocent, impulsive cry of admiration wrung from this humble hearer of our Lord. Yet it is the same feeling, exaggerated and caricatured. The underlying sentiment in both is the conception of Christ's blessing as something external and sensuous. And these very exaggerations enable us to understand more clearly how salutary, how wise, how full of meaning for all ages, is this simple saying of the Gospel. 'Blessed are they that can trace their lineage to that Apostle to whom Thou didst commit the keys of heaven; blessed are they among whom repose the bones of Thy faithful servants; blessed are they who possess but one shred of that garment without seam which clothed Thy sacred body, but one spine of that thorny crown which tore Thy sacred brow, but one splinter of that ever-blessed, because all-accursed, wood, to which Thy hands and feet were nailed for our redemption.' 'Nay rather, blessed are they who hear the word of God, and keep it.'

And let me add one memorable example of this false sentiment, as it stands out in the history of the Church. The pilgrimages to the Holy Land exhibited it with a force and a passion never equalled before or after. It became the one yearning of the pious mind, the one solace of the troubled spirit, the best preparation for a peaceful death, the truest assurance of a joyful immortality, to have set foot on that sacred shore, to have visited those hallowed scenes, to have washed in that stream where Christ was baptized, to have prayed at the manger of Bethlehem, on the mount of Beatitudes, in the garden of Gethsemane, at the cave of the Sepulchre, on the hill of the Ascension. They who had done this were invested with a special sanctity. They were the veneration and the envy of all. Such a pilgrimage was the one fit atonement of the darkest crime, the one true consummation of the saintliest life. Thus, year by year, crowds flocked to Palestine from all parts of Europe, till at length this sentiment culminated in the Crusades; and thousands upon thousands went forth—not to convert the souls, but to slay the bodies, of the unbelievers: not to rescue the brethren of Christ from ignorance and sin, but to rescue the manger and the tomb of Christ from a foreign domination. 'Blessed are they who go forth on this holy errand; who carry fire and sword into the houses and the temples of the Saracen; who wrest Thy sepulchre from the profane grasp of the infidel. Blessed are they who visit the scenes, which Thou didst visit, who tread the ground, which Thou hast trodden, who pray in the holy places, where Thou hast prayed. Blessed, thrice blessed, are they, who die in battle in that land, where Thou didst die on the cross.' So said the hermit preacher; so said the Christian bishop. And the listening crowds, we are told, responded with one voice; 'It is God's will: it is God's will.' We need not countenance that self-complacency of the present, which sees nothing to admire in the struggles, even in the errors, of the past. It may be that in God's sight a momentary outburst of honest, unselfish enthusiasm like this is far more beautiful than whole cycles of assiduous money-getting and luxurious civilisation, just because it is unselfish. Yet must we not confess that here at least the voice of the people was not the voice of God? In this passionate enthusiasm His voice, ever soft and low, was unheeded and unheard; 'Yea rather, blessed are they that hear the word of God, and keep it.'

And may it not be that among ourselves, in whatever religious school we may have been brought up, the same error is lurking still? Nay, must it not necessarily be so, while the human heart remains deceitful above all things? Are not we too tempted to place undue reliance on some external connexion; or, if not external, at least on some formal and superficial relations with Him; in any case, on something other than the life in Christ?

Do we lay stress on our position as members of an orthodox and Apostolic Church? Is it matter of self-congratulation to us, that the communion, to which we belong, preserves a just mean between superstition on the one hand, and anarchy on the other: that its ministry is duly ordained, that its services are decently performed, that its sacraments are faithfully celebrated? Is it a matter of the highest moment with us to observe rigidly the appointed seasons of the Church, to be diligent in our attendance on its ordinances? Do we think of this, and nothing more than this? 'Blessed are they that are baptized into Thy name, that frequent Thy churches, that keep Thy fasts and festivals; blessed are they that have the ministrations of an Apostolic priesthood.' 'Yea rather, blessed are they that hear the word of God, and keep it.'

Or again; do we hold by some religious watchword, do we emphasize some special doctrine as the keystone of our system? Do we, for instance, uphold the Apostolic teaching of justification by faith, urging it in season and out of season? Has this, as a formula, taken possession of our minds wholly? And have we nevertheless, while repeating S. Paul's words, forgotten S. Paul's meaning? Have we failed to realise, that faith with him was not an intellectual assent, not a barren conviction, not a religious formula, however enthusiastically maintained; but an entire belief, confidence, trust in God, a conformity of his own will to the will of God, an unreserved submission of himself to the commands of God, a prompt, unquestioning dedication of strength, abilities, wealth, comfort, honour, everything, to the service of Christ, a readiness to live and to die for Christ? 'Blessed are they who adhere to the teaching of Thine Apostle Paul; blessed are they who have truly apprehended the plan of salvation; who know that human merit is as filthy rags, that saving faith is all in all.' And still the Divine caution is whispered in our ears; 'Yea rather, blessed are they who are followers of Paul, as Paul also was of Christ; blessed are they who hear the word of God, and keep it.'

This then is the lesson of the text, so simple in statement, so difficult in practice. This is the one absolute condition of spiritual blessing, the one ultimate test of true discipleship; 'By their fruits ye shall know them.'

XIV.

HASTY JUDGMENT.

Judge nothing before the time, until the Lord come.

1 CORINTHIANS iv. 5.

Second Sunday after Epiphany, 1873.

THESE words speak to us with singular directness at the present time. Four days ago the grave closed over the mortal remains of one, who not long since was the most powerful ruler, and the foremost man, of his generation[1]. Even, if the approach of death had been slower and the warning more explicit, we should still have received it as a startling announcement, that the lips, on whose oracular utterances the fate of Europe hung for long years, were silenced, and the hand, which had dictated peace and

[1] The Emperor Napoleon III.

war to the nations, was stiffened in death. And the strange vicissitudes of his life invested its close with a still more tragic interest. Exile, emperor, victor, vanquished, he had passed and repassed from one extreme to the other in the scale of fortune. Brilliant triumphs and unequalled disasters in war, an empire rapidly consolidated and still more rapidly lost, the intoxication of popular idolatry and the bitterness of popular hatred, the gaiety of a magnificent court and the agony of intense bodily suffering—such were the sharp contrasts of this eventful career. All those tremendous common-places of human experience— the instability of fortune, and the irony of life, and the rude irreverence of pain and disaster, and the stern republicanism of death—received a new and striking illustration in the fate of their most recent victim.

And in the ten days just elapsed the dead man has lived his life over again. The world has been sitting in judgment on his character. All his past actions have been summoned as witnesses for or against him. All his real or supposed motives have been scrutinised and dissected with a pitiless minuteness. In every social gathering, and in every public print, this has been the one absorbing topic of discussion. It has passed from mouth to mouth, and it has flashed from wire to wire; till the remotest hamlets have been impanelled to assist in the verdict.

It would be futile, even if it were right, to object to the rigid scrutiny which awaits the lives of famous rulers after death. As a warning and as an example, it is well that they should feel the glare of publicity upon all their actions. But I ask (for with this aspect of the matter alone I am concerned) what is the value of the verdict, when given? Is it adequate? Is it complete? Even though it may form a fairly comprehensive estimate of the statesman, the general, the ruler, what does it know of the man—the man with his drawbacks or advantages of education and position, his motives, his temptations, his whole complex inner life; the man in himself, stripped of all external circumstances; the man, as he will appear one day before the tribunal of Christ, when the hidden things of darkness will be brought to light, and the counsels of all hearts made manifest?

And even in its own limited sphere is this verdict so clear, so precise, so unanimous, that it at once commands our unquestioning acquiescence? Did not his own countrymen within a very few months give and revoke a most deliberate judgment, passing from almost unanimous applause to almost unanimous execration? Are we not warned that the judgment of posterity will not be the judgment of his contemporaries; that his name must be added to the long list of those, whom history hereafter will be called to rehabilitate? Has not his character been described as an insoluble enigma, a conflicting result of antagonistic qualities, of boldness and hesitation, of enthusiasm and caution, of affectionate warmth and remorseless calculation, a mixture of the sceptic and fatalist? And what is all this, I ask, this vacillation, this self-contradiction, this futility, in men's estimate, but a confession, that it is not given to man to fathom the heart of man, a warning that in the Apostle's language we should 'judge nothing before the time, until the Lord come'?

And yet, here, if anywhere, the materials exist, which might be thought to have secured an adequate and final verdict; for he of all men lived and died in the full blaze of publicity. During his long term of power, hardly a day passed when some record of his doings was not flashed to all the capitals of Europe. His movements, his looks, his words, his silence, all were duly chronicled. Despite himself, the world was taken into his confidence; and yet the world confessed that it did not understand him. It is the penalty, which royalty must pay, that even the privacy of the sick-chamber and the sanctities of the house of mourning are ruthlessly invaded. The minute details of a painful malady, the worn expression of the lifeless countenance, the very looks and the tears of the survivors, all are noted down, as if with the design that no single fact might escape, which could bear directly, or indirectly, on the estimate of his character. And yet this is the result.

'Judge nothing before the time.' Certain it is, that the elements of the final judgment in his case, as in ours, will be very different from those on which any anticipatory verdict of men could be based; that much, both of good and of evil, which assumes vast proportions in our estimate, will sink into littleness, when weighed in the scales of the Eternal Justice; that much, whether of good or of evil, which we do not know and cannot suspect, will start forth from the abysses of the soul, when the light of the Eternal Presence is turned full upon it. Certain it is, that at that great assize the principles, which will rule the verdict, are not the principles, which have dictated the comments of to-day; that the standard of praise or blame will not be success or failure ; that Mexico and Sedan will not be the darkest counts in the arraignment, nor Sebastopol and Solferino the most telling pleas for the defence. Certain it is, that neither the partiality of friend nor the prejudice of foe will interpose, as now, to distort and darken the sentence: Italian, Austrian, Imperialist, Democrat—the conflicting interests of nations and the antagonistic sentiments of parties—will be voiceless then. Certain it is, that the judgment in the High Court of Heaven will be at once more strict, and more merciful far, than the trial before the bar of public opinion; more strict, for it will scan motives, desires, intentions, the abandoned project, the abortive counsel, which are concealed from the keenest glances and the liveliest suspicions of men; more merciful, for Omniscience alone can duly weigh and estimate the unique difficulties of temperament and education, and the thousand unsuspected temptations that crowd about the path of him who commands the resources of an almost unlimited power. Certain it is, that one rule will be applied to all alike, to prince and to peasant, to him and to us; that in that final award our opportunities will be weighed against our impediments, our gifts against our temptations; and, this adjustment made, the principle will then be applied, 'Unto whomsoever much is given, of him will much be required.' Certain it is, that just those features will be most acceptable in God's sight in his case, which would be in ours— not the triumphs of diplomacy nor the feats of war; but the unswerving constancy, which never deserted a friend however humble, the lively gratitude (rare in common men, rarer still in princes) which in prosperous days never overlooked the services rendered in adversity; the heroism of physical endurance, which fought with the agony of a painful malady, pursuing the daily task in silent suffering; the still nobler heroism of moral endurance, which bore alone without a sign of impatience or a syllable of reproach the burden of an unparalleled disaster and the execrations of an indignant people, grandly disdaining to shift or to divide the blame, which assuredly was not his alone. All these things are certain. But most certain is this, that, whosoever—whether emperor or artisan you or I—may be accepted in the great and final day, he will owe his acceptance, not to his merits nor to his character nor to his achievements, but to that vast reserve of God's mercy, which He has revealed to us in Jesus Christ our Lord.

Such are the reflections suggested by the text. S. Paul had received cruel treatment at the hands of the Corinthians. For two years he had devoted himself wholly to their spiritual needs. He had taken nothing from them; he had given everything to them. His thoughts, his energies, the labours of his hands, the anxieties of his heart, all were theirs. He was ready to spend and be spent for their sakes. But they had returned his affection with coldness, and they had met his efforts with scorn. He had not the prestige of primitive apostleship. He was not eloquent enough, or learned enough, for their fastidious demands. Other teachers were courted and extolled. He only was neglected and despised.

To all this cruel ingratitude, this unworthy depreciation, he had one reply. He refused to submit his character and his ministrations to these self-constituted judges. He denied the competency of the court to deal with the matter at all. Strong in the conviction of his own sincerity, he appealed to a higher tribunal, before which alone he would suffer his cause to be tried. He would accept no anticipatory verdict from men; for the evidence was partial, the witnesses were biassed, the jury was packed. At the bar of the Eternal Justice alone he would stand. There only the verdict could be final, for there only the court was supreme. To him therefore it is an infinitely small matter, that he should be acquitted or condemned, whether by his Corinthian censors or by any other human tribunal.

What knowledge has one man of another, that he should constitute himself his judge? What knowledge of another, do we ask? Nay, what knowledge has he of himself? Grant for a moment, that I am not aware of any fault, that I can bring no accusation against myself. What then? Am I competent? Am I impartial? Am I omniscient?

This, I suppose, is S. Paul's meaning, when he closes his argument with the words, 'Yea, I judge not mine own self; for I know nothing by myself, that is, I am conscious of no wrong in myself; yet am I not hereby justified.' These words, as I suppose, give not S. Paul's opinion of his own actual condition, but his statement of a hypothetical and (from its very nature) an impossible case. For, unless I am much mistaken, it would have seemed infinitely shocking to S. Paul to use such language of himself. How could he, who counted himself not to have apprehended, he, who prayed that he might not be found a castaway, be conceived to say that his conscience charged him with nothing? Charged him with nothing? Think you that the memory of the blood streaming from those mangled limbs, and the glow lighting that saintly countenance, and the prayer of forgiveness rising to heaven from those martyr lips, had passed away and left no sting behind? God might have forgiven him; but he could never forgive himself—the man, who had hounded on those religious assassins to their fatal deed. Or do you imagine that during those long years of ministerial labours, despite all his energy and all his love, he saw in the retrospect no error or short-coming, nothing to blame and nothing to amend? Nay, the best and saintliest of men must always be the most severe judges of themselves; for their moral standard is the loftiest, and their moral sensibilities are the most keen. The trivial omissions, the unguarded words, the rebellious thoughts, the subterfuges, the self-deceptions, all the unobtrusive sins of the passing hour, which escape the meshes of a coarser conscience, are duly arrested by theirs. They know most against themselves, for they note and record most.

Grant that you acquit yourself at the bar of conscience, that the acquittal is impartial, is sincere. Are you competent, as a judge? Have you all the data before you, on which the verdict must be founded? How much do you know of yourself? At this very moment your friends, your neighbours, even casual strangers, discern faults in you, which you do not actually and perhaps may not ever suspect. They see one side of you; you yourself, another. Yours is the larger fraction, but it is only a fraction still. There are intricate complications in the heart of every man, which far transcend his powers to unravel. At times we may almost realise—not indeed the knowledge of ourselves, but the knowledge of our ignorance of self. A shock is given to the moral system by some unwonted occurrence—a disappointment, a loss, a sickness, a bereavement, a desertion, a surprise of temptation, a victory of sin. A momentary light is flashed in upon the man's heart, and reveals to him his inability, his meanness, his inconsistency, his degradation. Then he begins to suspect how little he has known of his true self. But the flash is gone, and the old darkness gathers about him. What do you remember now of the eventful history of some one sin which has long become a habit—the warnings, the compunctions, the counteracting influences, the growing attractions, the faint resistance, becoming feebler and feebler as the allurement became stronger and stronger? How little do you scrutinise, record, realise the motives, which urge you to the conduct of to-day or to-morrow, too absorbed in the energy of the processes, and too eager about the success of the results! Yet just here, in this past history, here, in these directing motives, are the main elements in which your responsibility consists, the chief data on which your final sentence must be based.

And if you are not competent to judge yourself, how will you dare to judge another? While you cannot track the windings of your own heart, to which you have free admission, how can you fathom the secrets of your neighbour's, where entrance is absolutely barred to you? Of his motives you can *know* nothing. You can only hazard a conjecture. Your conjecture will be wrong in numberless cases; it must be inadequate in all. Yet on the motive the true character of the action depends. And how, again, can you strip off the mask, which men assume to disguise their real selves? Here is one man, who has been guilty of a crime, punishable by law. He is suspected. By bold and consistent lying he repels the charge. Society takes him at his word, receives him back into favour, perhaps regards him as an injured man. Here is another, who has committed the same crime. A single falsehood would save him from the consequence of his guilt. But conscience asserts herself. He has fallen carelessly into the sin, but he cannot deliberately tell the lie. He will face the loss of liberty, the brand of infamy, the forfeiture of all that makes life worth having, rather than do violence to his supreme convictions. He confesses, and is condemned. The world howls in execration over the deed. Need I ask whether the verdict of the world in these cases will be ratified at the bar of Eternal Justice?

And still less can you estimate those manifold influences of external circumstance, which separate class from class and man from man, and which in the eye of the Omniscient Judge must constitute infinite gradations in the heinousness of the same sin. I have alluded already to the special temptations of exalted rank, of boundless resources, of absolute power. It is quite impossible for us common men to realise them. An impenetrable barrier interposes, and shuts off our sympathies. Let us turn now to the other extreme of the social scale. You are shocked with some exposure of degraded vice, which appears in our police reports. Have you thought of the infected moral atmosphere which that offender has breathed from infancy? Have you realised the squalid court, the crowded room, the want, the blasphemy, the depravity? Has it occurred to you to ask yourself, whether you could have withstood all these influences for evil? Spare not the sin. Hate it; for it is hateful; but do not steel your heart against the sinner. Remember the infinite tenderness of the Son of Man, Whose disciple you are; and do not withhold the sympathy of your pity or the charity of your hope, as you yourself trust to be forgiven through God's infinite mercy in the last day.

For there will be manifold surprises, strange reversals of our human verdicts, in that final Court of Appeal; strange reversals, when the respectable citizen shall be condemned, and the convicted felon acquitted; strange reversals, when the preacher of righteousness shall be shut out, and the outcast of the streets welcomed into the everlasting abodes. These things must be. The voice of Christ has said it; the claims of justice demand it. Ponder over these things, and judge nothing before the time. Judge not, lest you judge wrongfully; judge not, lest ye yourselves be judged.

XV.

THE SPIRIT AND THE LETTER.

The letter killeth, but the spirit giveth life.

2 CORINTHIANS iii. 6.

Septuagesima Sunday, 1877.

I SUPPOSE that we do not at all realise the extent to which even in the common things of life we are indebted to the teaching of S. Paul. No idea is more familiar to us than the distinction between the spirit and the letter. We talk of the spirit of a promise, of the letter of the law; we speak in condemnation of one person who observes an engagement in the letter but breaks it in the spirit, and in approval of another who disregards a pledge in the letter only that he may fulfil it in the spirit. But we do not connect this idea especially with S. Paul. If we chance to think of him, it probably occurs to us that he used this distinction, just as we should use it, because it was natural, because it was familiar, because it was on every one's lips in his day, as it is in ours.

Yet, so far as I am aware, it occurs in S. Paul for the first time. No doubt the idea was floating in the air before. But he fixed it; he wedded the thought to the words; he made it current coin. And from him it has penetrated to every province of human life. For S. Paul's words, as Luther truly said, 'are not words; they are live things, they have hands and feet.' Yes, feet to go everywhere, and hands to grasp everything.

I propose therefore this afternoon to enquire, what this distinction means in itself, how S. Paul applies it in the first instance, and of what further application it admits.

Now the idea of a 'letter' is something definite, fixed, immoveable. It implies a hard and fast line. It cannot be modified according to times or places or persons. It is inexorable; it is irreversible. When Pilate says, 'What I have written, I have written,' he means that the matter has gone beyond the point when discussion is possible. By the maxim *Litera scripta manet* ' the written letter abides,' we mean that the thing cannot be hidden, cannot be questioned, cannot be slurred over, cannot be recalled. It is there, as we say, in black and white. It has taken its place among the permanent things of the world.

On the other hand 'spirit' means the direct opposite to all this. Spirit is properly a synonym for breath, a pulsation of air, a gust of wind. The Divine Influence, the Divine Person, is called the Holy Spirit. The name is given, because no other symbol would so fitly describe the operations of the spirit. These operations are silent and imperceptible; they are seen only by the results. The spirit moves invisibly, as the air moves. And, like the air too, it quickens and sustains; it is the one indispensable condition of life for man. Withdraw the spirit, and the movements of the soul languish, the respiration of the soul ceases, the life of the soul is extinguished. Like the air too, its operations are various. Sometimes it resembles a gentle breeze, fanning the earth, giving health and vigour and joy to all things around; sometimes it is a mighty rushing wind, a fierce hurricane tearing up ancient forests, and hurling down strong cities, deafening with the crash of falling ruins, but itself unseen, intangible, imperceptible, mysterious still. 'The wind bloweth where it listeth, and thou hearest the sound thereof, but canst not tell whence it cometh, and whither it goeth: so is every one that is born of the Spirit.' Measure it you cannot; weigh it you cannot; grasp it you cannot. It plays about you; it buffets you; it makes you reel and stagger; it sweeps you onward. And yet you cannot so much as see it.

But the characteristic in which the spirit especially resembles the stirring air, and with which we are most closely concerned, is its adaptability. However small or however great is the space which it is called to fill, it contracts or it expands accordingly. The spirit, as we should say in the language of natural philosophy, is perfectly elastic. A breath of air will make its way through any crevice, however narrow; it will diffuse itself over any room, however large. It adapts itself to every irregularity; it fills every interstice. It is this elasticity which makes it so fit a symbol of the spirit.

This antithesis of the letter and the spirit occurs three times in S. Paul. In the first passage, in the second chapter of the Epistle to the Romans, the Apostle is contrasting the true Jew with the false. The true Jew is that man—of what nation soever he may be—who acts up to the light which is given him. He may be no descendant of Abraham; he may not have been initiated into the covenant; he may keep no passovers, observe no sabbaths, offer no sacrifices; he may never have heard of the tables of the law. He is a heathen dog in the eyes of yonder Pharisee. But he is just, he is honest, he is pure, he is merciful and loving, he is reverential. Therefore he is the true Jew; therefore his is the true circumcision; for it is, says the Apostle, 'of the heart, in the spirit, not in the letter; whose praise is not of men, but of God.'

No, not of men. The tendency of men is always to prefer the letter to the spirit. An incident, recorded in the history of the earliest conversion of that country, on which the attention of Europe has of late been fixed, is a painful illustration of this. The Bulgarians, when first brought to a knowledge of the Gospel, put to the then Bishop of Rome—one of the most famous of the Popes—a question relating to the state of their deceased heathen forefathers. He sternly excluded all hope of salvation for them. He pointed to the passage which speaks of a sin unto death, a sin past praying for. Do you wonder, that he drove them to look elsewhere for more humane, more righteous teachers? And indeed this was not the first, as it has not been the last time, when such cruel language has been held. Christian fathers before him, Protestant missionaries after him, have sinned in the same way. Did they need this fierce thought to stimulate their missionary zeal? Nay, might they not have drawn a truer lesson from that chief of missionaries, who laboured more abundantly than all? Was it not enough, that the love of Christ should constrain them, as it constrained him? Was not the sense of God's infinite gift in the death and passion of His only Son, was not the consciousness that He had called them from death to life, that they owed everything which was noblest, best, truest, in themselves to His Gospel, was not the sight of a world steeped in ignorance and sin, was not the obligation of Christ's express command to teach all nations, were not all these combined a sufficient motive to exertion; that they must forge this terrible weapon to wield in their spiritual warfare? Is not this indeed to make sad hearts that God hath not made sad? And yet all the while the Apostle's own language is clear and explicit, declaring that the Gentiles, not having the law of Moses, had yet a law in themselves, and that by this law they would be judged. And if there were Jews who were Jews in the spirit, though not in the letter, so also must there be Christians. Many heathen shall come from East and West—Zoroaster and Buddha, it may be, Socrates and Epictetus and Marcus Aurelius; while the children of the kingdom—the ministering priest and the learned apologist and the eloquent preacher and the rigid devotee—shall be cast out. By the spirit, not by the letter, shall men be judged.

The second passage, in which this distinction occurs, is likewise in the Epistle to the Romans. In the seventh chapter of that Epistle, the Apostle contrasts the Christian dispensation with the Mosaic, the Gospel with the Law, as the newness of the spirit with the oldness of the letter. In the context he describes the fatal effects of the Law. It wakes up the consciousness of guilt in the man. So sin starts into life, and it kills the man.

The same is the idea in the third passage, from which my text is taken. Here too the contrast is between the Law and the Gospel. The one was written on tables of stone, graven in hard and fast lines. The other is altogether different. Here everything is elastic, mobile, flexible, ready of adaptation, full of life. The material, on which it is written, is not the hard slab of stone, but the fleshy tablet of the human heart. The pen, which traces the characters, is not a pen of iron, but the Spirit of the living God. And, corresponding to this difference, is the contrast in the effects. The one was a ministration of death, a ministration of condemnation; the other, a ministration of righteousness. 'We are ministers,' says the Apostle here, 'of a new covenant, not of the letter, but of the spirit; for the letter killeth, but the spirit giveth life.'

This then is the primary meaning of the text. The letter is a synonym for the Law; the spirit for the Gospel. The Law was holy and just and good; but the Law could never make perfect. Law may restrain, may educate, may direct, but it cannot give life. On the contrary its effect is, in the Apostle's language, to kill. By giving edge to the conscience, it intensifies the sense of remorse, it wounds, it prostrates, it slays. A child will go on doing a certain wrong act thoughtlessly and ignorantly, till it has become a habit, without any sense of inward dissatisfaction; till at length some authoritative voice (of a father or of a mother, it may be), which is a law to that child, says, 'That is a wicked act; you must not do that.' Then everything is changed. From that time forward each recurrence of the evil habit brings misery to the child; each fresh outbreak of temptation costs it a cruel struggle. The child's conscience has been awakened by the commandment. The child has been taught the sinfulness of the sin. The child is far better than it was before; but it is far less happy. It has the sentence of condemnation in itself. To use S. Paul's language, the commandment has slain the child.

So it was with the Mosaic law. The Mosaic law was given to educate the conscience of the Jews, and, through the Jews, of the whole human race. It issued prohibitions; it imposed penalties; it prescribed rites. Thus by a system of obligations and restraints it taught effectually the heinousness of sin. Every day and every hour, by some rite enjoined or some commandment contravened, it reminded the Jew of his guilt. But all this in itself could only kill; it could not make alive. The Law said, 'Do not this; for, if thou doest it, thou shalt surely die.' The principle of life, under the old dispensation, was not the Law, but something behind the Law—the fact of a merciful and loving Father, realised in the heart and conscience of the faithful. But this realisation was still only shadowy and incomplete. It was then at length in the Incarnation of the Son of God that this love was perfectly manifested, then at length in the atoning blood of Christ that the pardon for sin was fully assured, then at length in the dispensation of the Spirit that the sympathetic union of man with God was completely established, the filial relation was realised and the pardoned one—now no more a slave, but a son—had courage to look upward and cry, 'Abba, Father.'

This is the primary sense, in which the Apostle speaks of the letter killing and the spirit giving life. But, like many another maxim of S. Paul, the saying is far too full to be exhausted by its primary meaning. It has application as wide as human life is wide, as human thought is wide.

On one such application—perhaps the most important of all—I shall venture to dwell for a few moments. There is probably no serious Christian, who has not at some time or other felt inwardly pained, to think that he does not fulfil, that he makes no earnest attempt to fulfil, that the circumstances of life will not allow him to fulfil, certain precepts of our Lord to the letter. If a man should sue him at law and take away his coat, would he let him have his cloak also? If a man should compel him to go one mile with him, would he go with him twain? Were he to fulfil these precepts literally, what injustice, what misery, what confusion might not ensue? The words of Christ are the most sacred of all words. Yet even here, even in the words of the Divine Word Himself, it may be said, in some sense, that the letter killeth, but the spirit giveth life. And this, because human language necessarily confines the expression of the Divine thought. Human language is limited, and the thought is unlimited. In this particular case the spirit of the precept is the condemnation of a litigious, self-assertion. The spirit cannot be too promptly or too absolutely obeyed. One principle is here laid down in a concrete form, as it were in a parable. Human language cannot compass more than this. This principle is inviolate in itself. But right conduct is a very complex affair. Right conduct consists in taking into account many principles at once. In the case before us, by obeying the precept to the letter we might violate some other principle. We might, for instance, encourage a temper of lawlessness and violence in action; we might lead to the moral deterioration of another.

Or again, take the precept, 'Give to him that asketh thee.' The letter would lead to what is called indiscriminate charity; and indiscriminate charity is productive of the greatest evil. But here again the spirit of the precept is plain, and it is imperative. We cannot be too ready to impart to others the best gifts—whatever those gifts may be—with which God has endowed us. We cannot be too merciful, too self-denying, too sympathetic. But the form, which alms-giving more especially should take, must vary with the varying ages. In our own time, when there are poor laws, and workhouses and hospitals and dispensaries, when there is organized hypocrisy and professional begging, it is quite clear that we cannot follow in exactly the same lines which were the best in Palestine eighteen centuries ago, when none of these things existed. The question we have to ask, and answer for ourselves, is not only what Christ did or commanded then, but also what He would do or command us to do in this altered state of society now. In short, we must endeavour to ascertain the mind of Christ through the recorded words and works of Christ—to ascertain it, and to follow it absolutely, without any reservation or afterthought.

And our teacher here must be the Holy Spirit of God, 'the Spirit which searcheth all things.' He is the only safe interpreter of Christ's words and works.

He alone can translate them for us into modern language, and adapt them to modern life. This is the promise vouchsafed in His name. 'He shall take of Mine, and shall show it unto you.' If we go to any other teacher, then our attempts to evolve the spirit from the letter will be a hopeless failure. 'The natural man receiveth not the things of the Spirit of God, for they are foolishness to him.' But, if we approach Him with a single eye and a single heart, not wishing to spare ourselves, not seeking to excuse ourselves from irksome duties, but desiring only to learn, and prompt, when we have learned, to obey, then He will not fail us. 'If any man will do His will,'—'is ready to do His will,'—'he shall know of the doctrine, whether it be of God.'

XVI.

S. PAUL OUR EXAMPLE.

If I be not an Apostle unto others, yet doubtless I am to you.

1 CORINTHIANS ix. 2.

Feast of the Conversion of S. Paul, 1874.

IN this place, on this day, the preacher cannot hesitate about his theme. Speaking on this great festival which commemorates the Conversion of S. Paul, speaking in this famous church which bears the name of S. Paul, the great Apostle of the Gentiles must be, this afternoon, our example, our teacher, our guide.

S. Paul, in the words of the text, claims to stand in a very intricate and very sacred relation to the Corinthian Church. He had planted the first seeds of the Gospel among them. He had preached to them, had toiled among them, had suffered for them. Corinth was written on his heart. Others might question his authority: others might disdain his teaching. But Corinth—his own Corinth—was the last place, where such feelings should be entertained. Corinth was a witness against herself. 'If I am not an Apostle to others, yet indeed I am to you.'

And to-day we may well imagine the Apostle addressing the same words of remonstrance to ourselves, to the congregation which gathers from time to time within these walls, to the clergy and the laymen of all degrees whose privilege it is to minister daily in this sanctuary: 'Whatever may be the influence of my teaching on others, yet with you it should be paramount. My name, my authority, my work, are ever before you. With you my relations are most sacred and quite unique. To you I am an Apostle, if to any congregation in this metropolis, in England, in Christendom.'

For indeed the dedication of this great church in the name of S. Paul is a much more striking fact than at first sight appears. We ourselves are very familiar with sacred buildings commemorating the Apostle of the Gentiles. It is almost the first name, which could occur to us when dedicating a church in any town or neighbourhood, where it was not already forestalled. The case was far otherwise, when in the sixth century of the Christian era Ethelbert king of Kent founded on the very spot, where we are now assembled, a cathedral dedicated to S. Paul. The selection then was very singular, almost unique. Despite the great and unparalleled labours of this Apostle in the first diffusion of the Christian Church, despite the exceptionally large space occupied by his writings in the volume of the New Testament, it is a strange fact that in Western Christendom during the early and middle ages the name of S. Paul was very rarely given to any church. Besides the building, in which we are met, there is indeed one other instance among the more famous churches of Western Europe: but this one exception may be said to strengthen the rule. It is the church built on the traditional site of the Apostle's martyrdom and burial, the church of S. Paul without the walls of Rome. Of our English cathedrals not one, I believe, besides our own, is dedicated solely to the Apostle who laboured more abundantly than all, whom tradition especially associated with England. Some of the noblest, such as York and Westminster, bear the name of S. Peter—the most favourite dedication of all. Others, and these not a few, are designated after the mother of our blessed Lord. Others, again, bear the name of local saints. In the midst of all this strange neglect, it is surely a notable fact, that our own great church—the cathedral of this metropolis, the cathedral of the greatest city in the modern world—bears the appropriate name of the Apostle of the Nations. May we not take this unique fact, as our watchword and our beacon, a sign of our special calling here, and a token of the spirit which should animate us in our work? More than seven centuries ago, when the Cathedral of S. Paul was laid in ruins by a fire—not the first nor the last of those fierce conflagrations which have raged on this site—a neighbouring bishop pleaded in his diocese for contributions to the rebuilding, on the ground that, though S. Paul had planted Churches throughout the world and shed the light of the faith in all lands, yet this was the only episcopal see on earth which bore the Apostle's name. On the same grounds I press upon you an appeal of another kind to-day. As the memory of S. Paul is our special privilege here, so his example is our special inheritance and his doctrine our special obligation; 'If I am not an Apostle to others, yet indeed I am to you.'

As year after year the Festival of the Apostle's Conversion comes round, we cannot fail to be impressed with the long *continuity* of the history, which connects this site with the name of S. Paul. Before the earliest dawn of all those great intellectual and social and political influences, which have moulded the character of England, before, long before, the birth of the English literature, the English constitution, the English empire, we might almost say before the birth of the English language and the English nation, the Apostle of the Gentiles was commemorated on this spot. Invasion has followed invasion; dynasties have risen and fallen; all things around and about have changed; but this one name has remained throughout fastened upon this one site. From age to age fire has done its worst; building after building has fallen a victim to its rage; but each successive fabric as it rose, amidst every vicissitude of time, with every divergence of style, has handed down to the next the name of Paul, Paul the servant of Jesus Christ, as our special inheritance in these latest times. And S. Paul's has ever been the familiar name of this building. Other great churches are commonly described by their locality: we speak of Lincoln, of Canterbury, of Durham, of York, of Westminster; but London Cathedral is an unused and almost unknown designation. We recognise it only as S. Paul's. Thus he has 'been with us at all seasons,' through his name and his example he has 'gone among us preaching the kingdom of God;' 'for the space of' thirteen centuries at the least 'he has ceased not warning every one night and day.' 'Be ye followers,' or rather, as it should be rendered, 'Be ye imitators of me, even as I also am of Christ.'

But what need—it may be said—what need have we of any secondary example to follow? Have we not our perfect pattern, exemplar, ideal, in Christ? Why should we descend to a lower level? What is this but to substitute the *Imitatio Pauli* for the *Imitatio Christi?* Nay, I reply, if there should ever be found any conflict between the two, we cannot hesitate whom to follow. If Paul should break out in impatient remonstrance before an unrighteous judge, 'God shall smite thee, thou whitened wall,' then we turn away to a greater than Paul, 'Who suffered for us, leaving us an example,' 'Who when He was reviled reviled not again, when He suffered, threatened not.' Indeed it were sheer blasphemy to put Paul in the place of Christ, or to seek union with God through Paul. But this very point—the union with God in Christ, this realisation of Christ's presence, this most difficult of all lessons to master—is just the lesson which Christ Himself cannot illustrate, cannot teach by His example, because He is Himself the Lesson. Now it is an unspeakable help to us to have before our eyes a vivid exemplification of it; to trace in the manifold and complicated relations of daily life the working of this one principle, as the mainspring of thought, of feeling, of conduct—the realisation of Christ's presence, the mind of Christ appropriated (as it were) and absorbed in the mind of the believer. We need not only the Great Example Himself, but we need also an example of the following of the Great Example. Such an end (can we doubt that it was a providential end?) is served by the biography and letters of S. Paul. The position, which he holds in the Scriptures, is quite unique in its prominence. It is the explanation, it is the seal, it is the indication of his own bold, but not over-bold, appeal to the Corinthians, uttered in no access of self-glorification, but dictated by the guidance of a higher Spirit and approved by the Christian conscience in all ages, 'Be ye followers, be ye imitators, of me, even as I also am of Christ.'

For observe, how all the requisite conditions of such an example meet in the person of S. Paul.

First; in such a man the one principle of action must be illustrated in manifold capacities and relations of life. Now, in the older history of the human race, it would be difficult to point to any man, who fulfilled this condition more completely than S. Paul. No biography is more fertile in incident; none more complex and varied in its manifestations. With Greeks and barbarians, with Romans and Jews, in Europe and in Asia, among friends and among foes, with rich and poor, with weak and strong, now defending himself against a powerful conspiracy, now animating a demoralised ship's crew amidst the perils of the tempest, now rapt in beatific visions, now toiling hard with his own hands for his daily bread; in almost every conceivable relation of life—working, preaching, acting, suffering, hoping, fearing, living, dying—he is seen. And still the motive power is the same, 'Not I, but Christ that liveth in me.'

And again; in such an example as we have supposed, it is necessary that he should be his own spokesman. We want to know the exact expression of his feelings, the inmost working of his mind. This is just what S. Paul's own letters give; and what no report of others could have given. In the whole range of literature there is nothing like them. Other correspondence may be more voluminous, more elaborate, more studiously demonstrative. But none is so faithful a mirror of the writer. In none does the man's personality, the man's character, stand out so distinctly, so naturally, so unreservedly, in all its varying moods, and all its manifold interests. And what do we suppose was the providential design in all this? What, but that we might trace the intricate workings of a mind which conformed itself to the mind of Christ, might imitate the manifold energies of a life in which Christ lived again.

Once more; in such an example, it is requisite that he should be situated like ourselves with regard to Christ. Like ourselves, he must not have been a personal disciple of Christ. Like ourselves, he must have been denied the support of daily intercourse with the Saviour in the flesh. In his case, as in ours, faith must not have had an ally in memory. By him, as by us, Christ must have been realised only spiritually. This Paul is to us. This Peter and John never could have been—Peter with all his fervour and John with all his love. We might have evaded their example. It would have seemed hardly to touch our case. Had not they both gone in and out with Him for well-nigh three whole years? Was not Peter's confession of faith wrung from him at the Saviour's very feet, and had not John at that last sad solemn meal leaned on the Saviour's own bosom? Yes, here—we might have said—here was the explanation of their stedfastness; here in these external aids, in this visible, tangible communion, was the secret of their vivid realisation of Christ's presence in after-life. So we are tempted to argue. We forget that this external communion was accorded not to a Peter and a John only, but to a Thomas who doubted and to a Judas who betrayed. S. Paul is God's protest against this self-delusion: S. Paul is God's witness that this realisation of Christ may be attained, and attained in the highest degree, by one who like ourselves has never known Christ after the flesh.

And this appropriation of Christ, this union with God in Christ, is the very soul of S. Paul's teaching. Ask different persons what is the leading, the characteristic doctrine of the Apostle of the Gentiles, and you will get different answers. Some, and these the larger number, will reply, justification by faith. Others, and these not a few, will say, the liberty of the Gospel. But read his Epistles for yourself, and you will find that for once when either of these doctrines is referred to, union with Christ will be mentioned ten times. They are indeed prominent; they are discussed, are argued, because they were impugned. But it underlies the whole. It appears under every variety of circumstances, and in every form of language. Now it is the 'putting on Christ;' now it is the 'being transformed into Christ's image;' now it is 'being crucified with Christ;' now it is the 'bearing about in the body the dying of the Lord Jesus:' now it is the 'rising with Christ,' the 'living with Christ.' Now, conversely, it is Christ 'being formed' in us, Christ 'living in' us.

And just this it is, which interprets the Apostle's appeal, 'Be ye imitators of me, even as I also am of Christ.'

'Not Paul, but Jesus' has been the cry of more than one sceptical writer, who has impugned the accredited views of Christian doctrine and Apostolic history. 'Not Paul, but Jesus'—a thousand times. 'Not Paul, but Jesus,' the Apostle himself would have said. 'Not Paul, but Jesus,' the devout believer will say to the end of all time. 'Not Paul, but Jesus:' yes, but Jesus was manifested in Paul; Jesus worked in Paul; Jesus lived in Paul; Jesus died in Paul. S. Paul's life was the great example to all time of union with God in Christ. Such is his appeal to us to-day: 'I have striven to grow into Christ, to put on Christ, to live with Christ, to die with Christ. This was the one guiding principle of my life. So strive ye. Be ye followers of me.'

And this is also the soul of Christian ethics Are there any here, on whose ears such words fall altogether dead, who can attach to them just no meaning at all? Then, however respectable they may be in their lives, they know no more of the higher graces and gifts of the Christian character— the absolute self-renunciation, the perfect trust, the absorbing love, the willingness to dare and to suffer anything—than the idle loiterers in the plains know of the glories of a sunrise amidst the Alpine heights. Are there any, who have apprehended however feebly their meaning, who have caught, it may be, from far below a passing glimpse of the rosy light which tips the snowy peaks, who are filled with yearning at the sight? Let them take courage from S. Paul, and struggle upward, and thank God for this bright example thus vouchsafed to them.

Only imagine for a moment S. Paul's Epistles blotted out at once from our Bible and our memories. Only reflect what history would have been, what human life would have been, if they had not been written, or, being written, had not been preserved—how impoverished, how dwarfed, how blighted. Try to realise, if you can, the extent of the loss to yourself each day. Think of the void which would have been left in your heart, and in your mind. And let the extent of this imagined loss be the measure of your thanksgiving to-day; while you determine henceforward to understand more fully the great lesson of his life, and thus to give a practical answer to his appeal, 'If I be not an Apostle to others, yet indeed I am to you.'

XVII.

THE PHILIPPIAN GAOLER.

Sirs, what must I do to be saved?

ACTS xvi. 30.

Second Sunday after Christmas, 1879.

IT was a strange question to come from such a person. Of all employments and positions in life, the office of a gaoler in S. Paul's time would seem to hold out the least promise to a Christian preacher. The Christian preacher looks for some impressibility in his hearers. If he cannot reckon on high spiritual insight, he will at least approach his audience through their sympathies and affections. He will knock at the door of their humanity; and in this way he will obtain an entrance for his divine message. But what can he hope for here? Humanity has no place in a gaoler's language. Humanity is excluded by his very functions as a gaoler. A gaoler lives in hourly intercourse with criminals. He sees human nature in its most brutal and degraded forms. He becomes familiarised with crime. He gets to regard vice, as the rule, not the exception, in mankind. He ceases to believe in human virtue, at least in its higher and nobler types. He sinks into a hard cynicism. Has he not had too wide an experience to put any faith in the illusions of philanthropists and preachers? Virtue is a mere pretence, and repentance is an elaborate hypocrisy.

And he becomes hardened also in another way. Whatever feelings of compassion he may have naturally, he is forced to thrust them aside. If he were too gentle, or too sensitive, or too merciful, he would be unfit for his trade. He must steel his heart to the inroads of pity. He must ply his task in a stern, relentless, mechanical way. To lock those chains, to bar that door, to shut out the face of heaven, perhaps for ever, on this victim, to drag out that other half-blinded once more into the light of day, only that he may lay his head on the block or stretch his limbs on the cross—this is the cruel routine of his daily life. What room is there here for sympathy, for love, for tenderness, for any of those humane emotions on which the Christian preacher reckons as his most powerful allies?

The gaoler at Philippi is introduced to us first,

performing his gaoler's task. Here are two new prisoners to be looked after. They are far more dangerous than the ordinary run of prisoners. They are disturbers of the public peace; they are revolutionary agents; they are foreign emissaries; they would subvert the social and political institutions of the place. 'These men, being Jews, do exceedingly trouble our city.' 'They teach customs which are not lawful for us to receive, neither to observe, being Romans.' Accordingly they have been scourged first, and they have been cast into prison afterwards. Special injunctions are given to the gaoler. The prisoners must on no account be allowed to escape. He is not wanting on his part. He obeys his orders to the letter, and beyond the letter. He thrusts them into the inner dungeon, a dark underground vault, as would appear from the sequel. He is not content with this. He has made their feet fast in the stocks. Even the slight liberty of movement, which heavy chains would have allowed them, is rendered impossible. He has not suffered himself to be betrayed into any weakness. He has performed his grim task with relentless rigour. He has done his gaoler's work in a true gaoler's spirit. What hope more hopeless, than the conversion of such a man as this? The poor itinerant divining girl—half impostor, half demoniac—was a far more promising subject than he. It was not in a heart like this, that any profound spiritual emotions could be looked for. It was not on lips like his, that we should expect the question to arise, 'Sirs, what must I do to be saved?'

But the man, though a gaoler, was a man still. He had his human emotions, his human fears, aye and—as the sequel shows—his human compassions also, which his grim trade had been powerless to crush out. We must not imagine that, when he asked the question, he asked it with any very distinct conception of its bearing. He spoke of saving himself. What did he mean by this? His soul was convulsed by a tumult of conflicting passions. Only the moment before he would have done the very reverse of saving himself; he would have committed suicide. The first instantaneous terror was past. His prisoners were safe. His own life was safe—safe from his own murderous hand, and safe from the displeasure of his masters. But a vague, bewildering awe had seized him. He was in imminent peril, he knew not whence and how. Hence his imploring cry, 'What must I do to be saved?' And God took him at his word. God accepted his confused yearning; God heard his inarticulate utterance. He asked for salvation. And God taught him salvation; God gave him salvation, a gift far higher, far nobler, far more beneficent, than it had entered into his heart to conceive.

It is instructive to observe the instrumentality, which laid the gaoler prostrate at the Apostle's feet. This instrumentality is two-fold, partly external and partly moral. There is the physical catastrophe, and there is the spiritual influence.

1. There is the physical catastrophe. Suddenly, we are told, there was a great earthquake. The prison was shaken to its foundations. The doors flew open. The fetters were loosed. It is so that God works not uncommonly in His regenerative processes. Through the avenue of the senses He forces His way to the spirit. It may be that the Lord Himself is not in the great and strong wind, nor in the earthquake, nor in the fire; but the fire and the earthquake and the strong wind are His precursors, are His pioneers. They are as the voice of one crying in the wilderness of the man's heart, 'Prepare ye the way.' They arrest the eye and the ear; they overawe and subdue the spirit; they hold the man spell-bound; and in the supervening silence the still small voice is heard.

So it was here. Shaking the foundations of the prison, this earthquake had shaken the foundations of this man's self-sufficiency too. Opening the doors of the cells, it had opened the doors of his spiritual capacity also. Shaking off the chains of the prisoners, it had shaken off the fetters of obdurate routine from his heart likewise. Awakening him out of his bodily slumbers, it had awakened him at the same time from the torpor of his spiritual apathy. And so agitated and bewildered—his whole moral nature reeling and staggering with the shock—he flings himself at the Apostle's feet.

2. But this was not sufficient. The physical shock might arrest, but it could not instruct. It might overawe, but it could not inspire. The rumbling and the crash of the earthquake is not the only voice which breaks the midnight silence. There is the voice of prayer and praise, borne aloft to the Throne of Grace from those subterranean dungeons. We may well imagine that this voice also, so strange, so unearthly, so unlike the gibes and the curses and the blasphemies which were wont to issue from the prisoners' cells, had arrested the gaoler's ear; that they had suggested hopes and fears, which he could but vaguely understand; that they held out to him a new ideal of life, at which he blindly clutched; that, mingling with his dreams, they had moulded his awakening thoughts; and thus insensibly they had shaped the cry which rose to his lips, 'Sirs, what must I do to be saved?'

This is a type of God's dealing with our own hearts. It may be that during the year, which has just run out its course, God has spoken to one and another in this congregation with this two-fold voice.

Some unwonted catastrophe has convulsed our lives. The sudden bereavement has stunned our senses. The crash of our fortunes has stricken us down. The failure of our plans in life has crushed us in its ruin. The hairbreadth escape from some ghastly accident, or the unexpected recovery from some deadly sickness, has awed us in the retrospect. Here is the earthquake, which has awakened us from our slumbers, which has subdued and terrified us, which has sent us trembling and staggering to the Apostle's feet. And meanwhile for us, as for the Philippian gaoler, the voice of the earthquake has been supplemented by the voice of prayer and praise. The fresh memory, it may be, of some dear companionship, severed by death, has borne our spirits upward on its wings. The present blessing of some hallowed friendship has purified and elevated our thoughts. The stimulating example of some heroic, saintly life, whose record is enshrined in history, has nerved and inspired us. The reading of the Bible, or the services of the Church, or perchance the voice of the preacher has struck some chord which has vibrated through our spiritual being. In one way or another the voice of prayer and praise has found its way to our heart of hearts—in the midnight silence, amidst the crash of the earthquake and the trembling of the prison cells; and in our awe, in our bewilderment, in our vague unsatisfied, tumultuous yearning, we have uttered the imploring cry, 'What must I do to be saved—to be saved from hardness, to be saved from sin, to be saved from self, to shake off this torpor of death, to awake to God and to life?'

Since we met in church last Sunday, another year has drawn to a close—a year eventful in many ways, a year of striking inventions, of appalling catastrophes, of desolating famines, of vast political disintegrations and reconstructions, of wars and rumours of wars. And Death, our stern monitor, has enforced his solemn lessons with more than his wonted emphasis. His strict impartiality has rarely received more impressive illustrations than in the twelve months past. Here he has mowed down the obscure and unknown in countless multitudes at a single stroke: there he has lopped off one by one with fatal precision of aim the heads that towered above the rest. In his wholesale sacrifices he has shown his wonted indifference to circumstances and to means. He slew his thousands in battle here in Europe, and his tens of thousands by famine there in Asia. He plunged a whole cargo of human victims without a moment's notice in the midst of their holiday making, here at our very doors in a river grave; and within a few days he smothered another heavy freight of sufferers, surprised while plying their daily toil there in a distant colliery deep under ground, summoning earth and fire as his executioners in this case, as in the other he had impressed water to do his behest. And in singling out his conspicuous victims too he has dealt with an even hand. He began the year by striking down in rapid succession the two sovereigns who represented, as no other men could represent, not to their own country only, but to the whole civilised and thinking world, the two seemingly antagonistic principles whose reconciliation must be the great work of the coming age—the religious inheritance of the past, and the political aspirations of the future. At the beckoning of his stern hand the two rival potentates of the Vatican and the Quirinal, who for long years had dwelt apart, though inmates of the same city, each in his palace fortress—the one frowning on the other, stubborn and irreconcilable—were brought together in the silent, lowly chambers of the grave. And his year's work, which he thus inaugurated, he has carried out in the same impartial spirit. He has laid his grip on the crowned king, but he has not spared the discrowned king. He has summoned this royal lady in widowed age, and that other a bride of yesterday, and that other again a matron in her prime, the mother of a youthful family. This—the latest of his royal victims, the mourned of two great nations—he has reserved, as it were, to crown with a peculiar solemnity the warnings of the year at its close; for this latest loss appeals to the heart of our common humanity, recalling, as it does, not some intellectual movement or world-wide political aspiration, not any partial or narrow interest, but the silent, unobtrusive, homely duties of the woman, of the daughter, of the sister, of the wife, of the mother, of the nurse. And we too, it may be, in our own circles, in our own homes, have felt the chill presence of death. There is a vacant chair by our fireside; there is a vacant place in our hearts. If we are men, there is a painful memory of the past. If we are Christians, there is a joyful hope for the future. But the present is a blank void, a darkness only the more dark because it is visible, an aching pain which we bear as best we may. The wife, the parent, the child, the brother, the friend that was more than a brother, is gone. The ruthless reaper has put in the sickle. He has gathered in the ripe grain. 'The harvest'—the harvest of our affections—'is past; the summer'—our summer of life—'is ended. And we'—are we saved?

'What must I do to be saved?' This is no worn-out, obsolete question. It is as real now, as it was eighteen centuries ago; as pertinent here in the heart of Christendom, as it was there amidst the surroundings of paganism; as vital to you and to me—to us baptized Christians—as it was to that poor, bewildered, terror-stricken, heathen gaoler in that far-off Roman colony.

But it matters much—it matters everything—in what sense we ask the question. What do we mean by this saying? From what evil do we desire to be rescued?

There are three distinct senses, in which this question may be asked.

First of all; we may ask it with reference to our temporal affairs. What shall I do to save myself from the impending ruin of my fortunes? To save myself from this threatened forfeiture of my good name? To save myself from the vengeance of the law, which my carelessness or my dishonesty is bringing upon me? To save myself from the social entanglements, which my profligacy and my selfishness have woven about me? To the question, so asked, the text furnishes no answer. Of salvation in this sense it has nothing to say.

Or secondly; we may ask it of our eternal welfare, and yet not ask it in the best way. Our motive may be sheer terror—nothing else. The dread hereafter absorbs our thoughts wholly. Of God's Fatherly love outraged and wounded, of the Temple of the Holy Spirit sullied and profaned, of Christ's transcendent sacrifice despised and set at nought—of these we reck nothing. But the worm that dieth not, the fire that is not quenched—this is the terrible apprehension, which haunts our dreams, and dogs our steps in our waking hours. In short, it is not the wrongdoing itself, but the punishment of the wrongdoing which troubles us. Salvation to us is not salvation from sin, but salvation from the consequences of sin.

Thirdly and lastly. Would we ask the question, as it should be asked? Would we ask it in such a way, that it will receive its full and effective answer? Then our petition will run thus. What must I do, that I may be delivered from this my sin? What must I do, that I may cleanse myself from this impurity, which sullies my soul? What must I do, that I may rid me of this untruthfulness, this dishonesty, this insincerity, which mars my life? What must I do, that I may expel this avarice, which cramps my heart? What must I do, that I may shake off this lethargy, which numbs my spirit? What must I do, that I may cast out this demon of worldliness, of self, which shuts out Thee and Thy presence, O God? For Thou, Lord, and Thou only, art salvation, Thou only art heaven, Thou only art eternal life.

And to the question so asked the answer is still the same to us, as it was to this heathen gaoler eighteen centuries ago; 'Believe on the Lord Jesus Christ, and thou shalt be saved.' Believe on Him, not as a traditional heirloom, not as a formal creed, not as a sentimental aspiration, but believe with that direct, personal, living faith, with that practical trust and confidence, which will draw you to Him, as the truest of friends, for advice, for consolation, for strength, for renewal, in all your sorrows and in all your trials.

And, above all, believe that He has power to save you from your sins. What were the terms of the angelic message, of which the season reminds us? 'Thou shalt call His name Jesus: for He shall save His people'—not from the wrath to come, not from the fire that is not quenched, not from future retribution in any form (though this also He shall do), but first and chiefest—'from their sins.' Yes; it is this actual weight of sin, under which at this moment you are staggering, that He undertakes to remove. It is a present strength, a present cleansing, a present renewal, a present salvation, that He promises to you. This faith—the highest form of faith—will indeed remove mountains. 'I can do all things through Christ which strengtheneth me.' 'Only believe,' and thou shalt be saved. 'Lord, I believe; help Thou mine unbelief.'

XVIII.

THE CONSTRAINING LOVE OF CHRIST.

The love of Christ constraineth us.
2 CORINTHIANS v. 14.

Twelfth Sunday after Trinity, 1876.

WHO is this Paul that writes these strange words? Who is this Christ to whom he ascribes such marvellous power? What had been their past connexion? What were their present relations? How can we explain this tyrannous influence, this complete absorption of self in another, to which the writer confesses? Is he speaking of some devoted parent, to whose fostering care and patient self-denial he feels that he owed everything? Or of some loved brother, with whom all his fondest memories of life—in infancy, in childhood, in youth, in manhood—are bound up? Or of some friend, who has been more to him than a brother, from whose large heart and commanding intellect he has learnt lessons that were more precious than life itself, in whose purity, in whose nobleness, in whose entire self-forgetfulness, he has seen a standing protest against all that was base and mean in himself? Nay; he was none of these. He was not a parent, not a brother, not a friend, as men count friendship. He was an entire stranger, whom Paul had probably never seen on earth, whom certainly he had never cared for, never loved. And he was dead too; had been dead now more than a quarter of a century. So that there was nothing, absolutely nothing, in their human relationships to account for this strange, this extravagant, this passionate language.

And the more we examine the facts of their past history, the more hopelessly bewildering do we find them, as tested by the ordinary standard of human occurrences and human motives.

It is now the year 57 or 58 of our era, when S. Paul writes these words. Place yourself in imagination some twenty-five or thirty years earlier than this date. What do you see then? Here is a Jew of humble rank, a carpenter's son, sentenced to suffer as a criminal, executed by a most ignominious death, put out of the world with the emphatic approval of all classes, the haughty Pharisees, the scornful Romans, the mocking soldiery, the hooting populace What was there to attract, to subdue, to dominate, in this most painful, most repulsive of all scenes? And yet this is the Christ—this humble peasant, this despised outcast, this hated criminal—whose constraining power the writer confesses to be absolute over all his thoughts and feelings and actions.

And next, what does past history tell us about the writer himself? Is there any key here which will unlock the secret? Place yourself again in imagination a few years later—some twenty years before the words were written. What do you find then? Why, just what the previous scene would lead you to expect. This Paul, the writer, is devoting all the energies of his sincere and passionate nature to the extermination of an infatuated sect that has gathered round the name of this dead man, this criminal whom all classes alike had agreed to execrate. He spares no pains; he shrinks from no severities. Men and women, young and old, falling into his hands, are treated alike. Imprisonment, torture, death—such is the fate that awaits his victims. No sincerity, no innocence, no patience or meekness in the sufferers touches his heart. Even the spotless purity and the transparent holiness of a Stephen only adds fuel to his indignation.

The name of Christ is an abomination to him. The followers of Christ are outside the pale of our common humanity.

I have asked you to turn yourselves back in imagination some twenty-five years, and again some twenty years before these words were written. It is not a wide space of time for the memory to range over. About the same interval separates us from the Crimean War and from the Indian Mutiny. And yet it seems to us who were grown up at the time, as if these things had happened only the other day. How vividly do we picture to ourselves the struggles, the perils, the triumphs of Alma and of Inkerman! With what painful distinctness do we recall the horrors and the suspenses of Delhi and Lucknow and Cawnpore! And can we suppose that S. Paul remembered less distinctly the incidents in his own personal career, so striking, so unique, so fraught with the most acute pain and the intensest ecstasy? Nay, we may be assured that each momentous crisis, each signal event, stood out in his recollection with a sharpness of outline and a fulness of detail, which would shame the average memory of the average man. For he was after all the same Paul, who had hounded on the savage executioners to the stoning of Stephen; the same Paul who 'breathed out threatenings and slaughter against the disciples of the

Lord;' the same Paul who (it is his own metaphor) had harried and devastated the Church of God. His step is not quite so elastic; his face is not quite so free from furrows; his spirits are not quite so buoyant. But there is the same fire, the same zeal, the same intensity of passion and of action now as then.

The same, and yet how changed! 'The love of Christ constraineth me.' The love of Christ! What did he know *then* of the love of Christ? Had he not loathed and execrated the very name of Christ, hated it with all the hatred of which his intense nature was capable? 'I can do all things through Christ that strengtheneth me.' 'All things *through* Christ'? Nay, surely, '*in spite of* Christ, *against* Christ.' Had he not 'thought that' he 'ought to do many things contrary to the name of Jesus of Nazareth'? And he had acted upon this conviction with a persecuting energy which has rarely been surpassed before or after. But now—he was changed, shall we say? Nay rather, let us use his own language; he was 'born again,' he was 'created anew,' he was called into being from not being. Hitherto he was not, and now he *is*. In Jesus Christ he is a new creature, a new creation. In Jesus Christ old things have passed away—for ever away. All things, yes, all things have become new. In Jesus Christ the prophetic anticipation is already realised. There is a new heaven overhead; there is a new earth beneath his feet. All things human and divine are changed to him now. The objects, on which his eye rests, though still the same, are not the same. They are invested with a new power and meaning. The external world has undergone a change corresponding to the inward man. His thoughts are new; his associations are new; his hopes and aspirations are new; his motive is new.

Yes, his motive is new. This is the grand central fact, the prime secret of the change. There is a new mainspring to the machinery of his moral and spiritual being. Hitherto he had acted from various considerations and impulses. He had been influenced by self-assertion or self-indulgence; he had been led by party spirit; he had been the slave of convention or of habit; he had been impelled by a desire of popularity or of fame; he had been stimulated by rivalry; he had been driven forward by fear, or held back by shame; he had been moved by higher motives than these, though not by the highest, by a spirit of patriotism, by a fire of orthodoxy, by an enthusiasm of religion, a zeal of God, though not according to knowledge. But now all these lower motives were neutralised, were crushed, were transformed, were absorbed, were glorified, in the one transcendent, overwhelming, all-pervading thought of the constraining love of Christ.

The love of Christ. The Apostle does not mean, as at a first glance we might suppose, his own affection for Christ, his own devotion to Christ. This affection, this devotion, was indeed a constraining power. But it was only second in the chain of causes and consequences. It was not the source and origin of his energy. The source must be sought farther back than this. The source must be sought outside himself. The source must be found in God, not in man. Not his love for Christ, but Christ's love for him, for others, for all mankind, for a world steeped in ignorance and sin and misery—this was the prime cause of all his moral activity, the paramount motive which started and directed all the energies of this most magnificent of all magnificent lives. His own love for Christ was only the response, only the sequel—as he himself would have confessed, the necessary, the inevitable sequel—to Christ's love for him once impressed upon his being. Christ first loved him, and he (how could he help himself?) was fain to love Christ. It was not he, Paul, that lived any longer; it was Christ that lived in him. It was not he, Paul, that planned, that felt, that toiled, that suffered for Christ, that traversed the world with his life in his hand for Christ, that was instant in season and out of season for Christ, that died daily for Christ; but it was Christ's own love, fermenting like leaven in his inmost being, stirring and animating his sluggishness. This unspeakable love rises up before him, as the one great fact, which will not be thrust aside, the one clear voice which will not be silenced. It haunts him sleeping and waking. It occupies the whole background of his thoughts. Forget it? How can he forget it? Others may forget, but he can never forget.

For what had this love of Christ been to him, Paul, individually? Could he forget that he had been the chief of sinners, because the chief of rebels; that his ingratitude had far exceeded the ingratitude of that excited Jewish mob, of that flippant Roman soldiery, because he had persecuted intelligently, deliberately, persistently; giving his whole mind, as well as his whole heart, to the work? And yet Christ singled out *him* of all men; rebuked him, caressed him, subdued him, won him; held him up to an astonished world as a signal token of God's long-suffering and mercy. Can we wonder that in his own emphatic language it 'constrained' him, that is, held him tight in its grip; that it bound him hand and foot; carried him whither it would and stayed him when it would; that it fettered all his movements and forced all his actions? Aye, he was more than a conqueror through Christ, but he was less than a captive through Christ. He was Christ's freedman, but he was Christ's very slave also. It was this love of Christ, this stern, imperious, relentless master, which dragged him from city to city; which exposed him to heat and cold, to famine and nakedness, to perils on all sides; which drove him to prison and to death.

The bearing of these facts on Christian evidences is obvious. They have forced an acquiescence from many a suspicious and reluctant spirit. Many, who have seen their way to setting aside all other external evidence, have found this an insuperable barrier in their path. Many, who have held themselves entitled to doubt the early date and the historical credibility of the Gospels, have been convinced by S. Paul's conversion and life, as an evidence of S. Paul's belief. Such a conversion, followed by such a life, would have no basis to rest upon, unless the main incidents of the Gospel, as we have them, were accredited facts at the time. But it was not for this purpose that I have offered the subject for your consideration this afternoon. I had a directly practical aim in view. We have dwelt thus long, with little effect, on S. Paul's resistance to Christ's love, overcome at length by its persistent force, unless we have seen—each one of us—in this strange story, a type, a parable, of that which is, and of that which may be, with ourselves individually. His stubbornness, his ingratitude, his defiance of God, is but ours written out large. The form may be different, but the essence is the same. We too have seen the love of Christ as manifested in the narrative of the Gospels and the career of the Church; we too have experienced the goodness of God in the thousand blessings and opportunities of our daily life. Well for us, if we too are acting ignorantly, as he acted. Well for us, if we have shown the same zeal, the same vigour, the same self-devotion, the same sincerity, which he showed, even when most mistaken. His resistance was active, intensely active; ours may be passive, most probably it is, but it is a fighting against God all the same.

And if his sin is a type of our sin, may not his victory be a type of our victory also? Do we suppose that the love of Christ, as a motive of action, has lost any of its force by the lapse of eighteen centuries? Have we ever given it a fair trial? We have perhaps cast a passing glance at it, grudgingly stolen from the occupations of business or the attractions of pleasure. But what is this? Have we contemplated it, studied it, appropriated it, absorbed it? Has that life, that work, that character, that Person—all those elements which combine to present the complete picture of that love—have these, I say, been the one great object of our contemplation, filling all the interstices of our work and our recreation alike, till they have become the daily food of our moral life? And, if it is not so, can we wonder that our hearts are cold, that our lives are listless, that our allegiance is divided between God and the world—the world getting far the larger share? I say to you, and I say to myself, Give it a fair trial. I cannot pretend that the task is easy. It will cost no common effort. But the result is certain. The love of Christ worked miracles in S. Paul. It has worked miracles in all who have followed in S. Paul's footsteps.

How can it be otherwise? What is it that determines the character of the man? It is not the results of his actions. A cruel, ambitious, profligate conqueror has more than once proved a benefactor to mankind. Yet no one with any moral sense will call such a man a good man. It is not in the deeds themselves. These may be beneficent and useful. But they may be done, not because they are beneficent and useful, but to procure popularity or fame. It may be a question of barter in some form or other after all. But, if the character of the man is not determined by the results of his actions, nor by the actions themselves, it must be by his *motives*. And here you have the purest motive of all. A motive to be pure must be unselfish. And this is altogether outside self. It is the study of another's character;

it is the admiration of another's goodness; it is the awe, the gratitude, the loyalty, the reciprocation, the love, the exaltation, because the abasement, which comes from the contemplation of a perfect ideal in One, Who is at once a Brother, a Friend, a Saviour, a Master, a King.

And, being the purest, it is also the most efficient of all motives. Love—I speak not of passion—is proverbially the most potent of moral influences, the love of husband and wife, the love of brother and brother, the love of friend and friend, the love of parent and child. And here is love in its highest form, love in its ideal perfection, love without any alloy of earthly passion, love most human, because most divine, love kindly inspiring, energizing your whole heart and your whole life. Only realise this love, and you also will be more than conquerors; conquerors, while you are dragged helpless in the triumph of the Omnipotent Captain at His chariot wheels; conquerors, because captives; conquerors of the world, because conquerors of self.

XIX.

MADNESS AND SANITY.

I am not mad, most noble Festus; but speak forth the words of truth and soberness.
ACTS xxvi. 25.

First Sunday after Trinity, 1875.

IT was no even-handed contest in which the Apostle found himself engaged, when he appeared in the presence-chamber at Cæsarea. The place, the season, the persons, the surroundings of the scene might well have appalled a man of less conspicuous courage or of feebler convictions.

It was the occasion of a great state ceremonial, a durbar (we might almost call it), when the imperial viceroy, the representative of the law and majesty of Rome, newly arrived in his province, received the welcome and the homage of the most powerful of native princes. King Agrippa, we are told, had come with great pomp to Cæsarea to salute Festus. We happen to know from other sources that he had reasons of his own for wishing to conciliate the favour of the new governor. Just at this time he had a quarrel with the Jews, and he was anxious to secure the powerful support of Festus. He had recently added to the palace of the Herods a lofty dining-hall, from which his guests could look down upon the Temple area. The priests and guardians of the sacred precincts resented this intrusive curiosity. It was indecent, and it was contrary to all precedent, that the most sacred rites should thus be exposed to the profane gaze of idle revellers. They therefore built up a high wall, which shut out the king's view. Agrippa resented the indignity, and endeavoured to get the obstruction removed. He applied to Festus for aid, and Festus warmly espoused his cause.

All this we have on the authority of the Jewish historian. And I mention the fact for two reasons. In the first place, it illustrates the truthfulness of the narrative. Where we are able to test the incidents in the Acts by contemporary history and archæology, we cannot fail to be struck with the correspondences. There is a coincidence sometimes in the actual events, sometimes (as here) in the historical position, which affords the highest guarantee of truthfulness. The officious welcome given by Agrippa to Festus on his

arrival, the cordial relations existing between the
Jewish king and the Roman governor, as here related,
receive a flood of light from the account of the Jewish
historian. The narrative of S. Luke and the narrative
of Josephus fit together, as complementary pieces of
a historical whole. In the second place, a reflection
is suggested by what is said, and what is left unsaid,
in the secular historian of the day. His account
illustrates the false estimate of the relative proportions
of events, which men inevitably take who are mixed
up in them. This aggressive insolence of Agrippa
was the one topic of general interest at the time.
It was eagerly discussed, we cannot doubt, by high
and low, among priests and people, at every public
concourse and in every domestic circle. It alone has
obtained a place in the record of Josephus. When
the rumour got abroad that the king had hastened to
Cæsarea with a splendid retinue to welcome the new
governor on his arrival, all tongues would be eager
to tell, all ears open to hear, how Festus had received
his visitor, and what line he was likely to take on the
burning question of the day. But this interview with
Paul—who cared for it? Who talked about it? It
was a wholly unimportant episode in a conjuncture
of the highest public moment. The historian says
nothing about it. Why should he? The name of
Paul is not once mentioned throughout his narrative.

Yet time has wholly reversed the verdict of contemporary history. Of the magnificent palace of the Herods, of the goodly buildings of the Temple, not one stone is left standing upon another. For eighteen centuries they have been a ruin and a desolation. The aggressiveness of Agrippa and the policy of Festus have alike passed away, leaving not a trace behind. But the words of Paul are living, germinating, fructifying still. Still his outspoken reply to the blunt taunt of the Roman governor appeals to the latest generations as a mighty witness to the Gospel; 'I am not mad, most noble Festus; but speak forth the words of truth and soberness.' Still his pathetic rejoinder to the flippant sarcasm of the Jewish king stands out as a model of Christian courtesy and largeness of heart; 'I would to God, that not only thou, but also all that hear me this day, were such as I am, except these bonds.' The quarrel of Agrippa has vanished out of sight. The pleading of Paul is the inheritance of all the ages.

Never probably had the Apostle found himself before a more uncongenial audience. The imperial governor, the native sovereign, their splendid retinues, Roman officials, Jewish priests, soldiers and civilians, courtiers and holiday makers—some cold and indifferent, others bitterly hostile—were all alike devoid of sympathy.

In this unfriendly concourse the attitude of Festus more especially demands our attention. Festus was not a man whose opinion could be lightly disregarded. We have not to do here with a sceptical and cynical worldling like Pilate, or a cruel and reckless profligate like Felix. He is eminently just. He is transparently sincere and outspoken. He is a prompt and vigorous ruler. He is the very man to whom in the common affairs of life we should entrust our cause with confidence. Nothing could be more upright than his treatment of the prisoner from first to last. His predecessor had cruelly detained this Paul bound for two whole years; Festus brings on his cause at once. The Jews ask him to send Paul to Jerusalem; he declines to take this unusual course. They press him to give judgment against the prisoner; he flatly refuses. 'It is not the manner of the Romans,' he says bluntly, almost rudely, 'to condemn any man without a fair trial.' Accordingly the prisoner is confronted with his accusers. The governor hears the complaints; they are many and serious; but he judges them to be altogether vexatious and irrelevant; they do not come under the cognisance of the Roman law. He is ready to release the prisoner; but the prisoner appeals to Cæsar; and so the cause is taken out of his hands. Yet even then he is not satisfied. He wishes at all events to understand the rights of the case; 'It seemeth to me unreasonable,' he says, 'to send a prisoner, and not withal to signify the crimes laid against him.'

The whole narrative thus sets Festus before us, as a man of strict integrity, worthy of the highest respect in the ordinary business of life. This is the bright side of his character. But he has no ideas or aspirations beyond. His view is strictly limited to the affairs of this world. When the future and the unseen are mentioned, he is lost in confusion. He is as helpless in dealing with such topics, as one colour-blind in discriminating the hues of the rainbow. His outspoken sincerity only betrays the extent of his helplessness. He is blunt even to contempt, when he refers to 'one Jesus, Which was dead, Whom Paul affirmed to be alive.' 'Affirmed to be alive!' This was decisive. Could any sane man maintain an absurdity like this? He listens for a time with patience, while S. Paul pleads his cause; but at length he can no longer restrain himself. He is confirmed now in his surmise. He interrupts the prisoner, shouting rather than speaking, 'Thou art mad, Paul.' What is this but the incoherent rambling of a maniac—all this talk about sin, and repentance, and forgiveness, and salvation? What is this but the very phantom of a diseased brain—this story of the apparition on the way to Damascus, with the light and the voice, notwithstanding the many circumstantial details which invest it with the air of sober history? 'Thou art mad, Paul.' All this has just nothing in common with the solid experiences, the stern matter-of-fact duties of the Roman magistrate and the Roman citizen— in short, with the acknowledged realities of human life.

'Thou art mad, Paul.' Yes; it was madness, sheer madness, to commit social suicide, as this Paul had done. For indeed his conduct deserved no other name. He had given up a high and honourable position among his fellow-countrymen; he was learned after the manner of their learning; he was orthodox according to their standard of orthodoxy; he was able and energetic; he stood well with the chiefs of his nation; he was on the high road to promotion. And yet he suddenly gave up all—and for what? To become an outcast and a wanderer on the earth; to be hated by the Jews and scorned by the Greeks; to drag out a miserable career of penury, of suffering, of toil and danger; to carry his life in his hand from hour to hour; to be shipwrecked, imprisoned, scourged, stoned, left for dead; to be spurned by all men as the very filth, the offscouring of society, the scum of the world. Who has put the case more strongly than the Apostle himself? Aye, he knew (no one could know better) that he was mad, irretrievably mad, as the world counts madness. 'We are fools,' he says of himself, 'we are fools for Christ's sake.'

'Thou art mad, Paul.' It was not only that his practical conduct betrayed his insanity; his religious creed also was nothing better than the raving of a maniac. Who ever heard before of one claiming the allegiance and the worship—yes, the worship—of the whole world for a Crucified Malefactor, this Jesus, this dead Man, 'Whom Paul affirmed to be alive?' There was no difference of opinion here between Jew and Greek. On most questions affecting religion the one spoke a language quite unintelligible to the other. But here there was absolute unanimity of sentiment. Festus and Agrippa, the Roman soldier and the Hebrew priest, alike must join in condemning it. This doctrine of Christ crucified, nay, Christ risen again—it was a scandal to the Jew, and it was folly to the Greek. Here again no one knew better than the Apostle, how his teaching was regarded by the learning and the intelligence and the sagacity of his age. He knew it; he repeated it; he gloried in it. He invited all men to become mad, as he was mad. This madness, he maintained, was the indispensable condition of all higher knowledge. 'If any man thinketh to be wise in this world, let him become a fool, that he may be wise.'

So then two wholly irreconcilable views of life

confronted each other in Festus and Paul. Paul was sincere; had he not given the amplest proof of this? Festus also was sincere. His whole conduct breathes the air of sincerity. And yet between the two there is a yawning, impassable gulf. If Festus is right, Paul is mad, hopelessly mad; if Paul is right, Festus is blind, stone-blind.

It is not my purpose now to treat this scene in its bearing on Christian evidences. From this point of view it would suggest not a few important reflections. I might point for instance to the calmness and sobriety of the Apostle's statement; to the perfect assurance with which he details the history of his conversion and the grounds of his belief; to the manly and courteous simplicity with which he replies to the rebuke of Festus and the sarcasm of Agrippa. Certainly nothing is more unlike the delusions of an enthusiast, or the ravings of a maniac, than the whole tone and manner of S. Paul on this occasion. Or again, I might turn away from the scene itself to its results. I might remind you that the civilised world after long wavering did ultimately prefer the madness of Paul to the sanity of Festus. I might ask you to reflect how enormous has been the gain to mankind from this preference, and how terrible would have been the loss, if it had taken Festus as its teacher and condemned Paul as a lunatic. I might point out how

Christianity rescued a helpless world, hastening to its ruin, seething in its own corruption; how it endowed human society, thus rescued from premature moral decay, with fresh youth and health, by infusing into it new convictions and new hopes; how this re-creating, renewing, reinvigorating influence contained in itself the potentiality of all that is noblest and best in modern civilisation and modern life.

All these considerations, and others besides these, might be urged. But I have no intention of dealing with the evidences of Christianity this afternoon. I am speaking as a Christian to Christians. It is a practical, and not an intellectual conviction, which I wish to enforce. I would desire to dwell on the magnitude of the alternative offered. No ingenuity, and no indifference, can bridge over the gulf which separates the view of human life taken by Festus from the view of it taken by S. Paul—the view taken by the upright and respectable man of the world who lives only in the present, and the view taken by the Christian whose soul is dominated with the presence of God, with the consciousness of sin, with the conviction of eternity. God forbid that we should set ourselves up as judges of others; God forbid that, possessing (as we believe we possess) a wider vision and a fuller light, we should think meanly or speak lightly of the upright ruler, of the honest citizen, in whom nevertheless the religious motive is scarcely perceptible, if perceptible at all. Honesty, truth, uprightness, whatever in human life is lovely and of good report, is consciously or unconsciously the very reflection of the perfect attributes of God Himself. We wrong God, when we wrong such men as these.

But still the fact remains. Here are two antagonistic views of human life and human destiny. Men may strive to patch up a hollow compromise between them; but no truce is real, because no meeting-point is possible. It is the alternative of sanity and madness, of light and darkness, of life and death. You have decided that the Christian view is sanity, is light, is life. The decision must not be, cannot be, inoperative. It has altered your entire point of view. It will pervade your whole being. It will influence the thoughts and actions of every day and every hour. It may not change the outward business of your life, except in a very few cases. There is no reason why it should. But it will infuse into it a wholly different spirit. It will breathe the breath of heaven into the work of earth.

All this stands to reason. It cannot be a matter of indifference, whether you are responsible only to the judgment of human society with its caprices, its prejudices, its misunderstandings, its narrowness, its blindness; or to an all-seeing eye, which overlooks nothing, misinterprets nothing, misjudges nothing, which scans motives, desires, tendencies, not less than overt acts. It cannot be a matter of indifference, whether the wrong-doing is simply a violation of physical order which may be attended with inconvenient results, simply a breach of some social compact which your fellow-men are bound to resent in self-defence; or a rebellious defiance of the All-holy, All-righteous God, an act of base ingratitude towards a loving Father in Heaven. It cannot be a matter of indifference, whether He, Who appeared in our flesh and walked upon our earth more than eighteen centuries ago, was (I shudder to apply the term even as a bare hypothesis) a lunatic—a lunatic, I say, for there is no escape from the dilemma; all His words and all His work, His aims, His aspirations, His promises, His whole life and teaching, were, on this hypothesis, built upon a mere delusion—; or whether He was indeed the great Teacher of the truth, the Only-Begotten of God, Whom the Father in His infinite mercy sent down to live our life and die our death, that He might rescue us from our prison-house of sin. It cannot be a matter of indifference, whether this life is our entire life, whether intelligence, consciousness, conscience, personality—all that we call ourselves—shall vanish at the touch of death, evaporating in gases and crumbling into dust; whether therefore it is the true and sole aim of wise men to play out their little part here as decently, as respectably, as successfully as they can; or whether there is an eternal hereafter, before which the triumphs of the present are just nothing at all.

This is the tremendous alternative. Did I exaggerate, when I called it a contrast between light and darkness? There is no halting between two opinions here, no passing to-and-fro at convenience; for the chasm is broad, and it is fathomless. Accept therefore the alternative which you have chosen, with all its consequences. Think over it, master it, live it. Men will taunt you with inconsistency. They will do so justly. But be not dismayed. Let the taunt nerve you to greater efforts. It will stimulate your actions, but it will not shake your creed. The inconsistency must necessarily be the greater, as the ideal is the higher. Festus was no doubt much more consistent than S. Paul. The standard of Festus was the ordinary standard of honourable and upright men; and, it would seem, he did not fall far short of it. The standard of S. Paul was absolute self-negation; he is constantly bewailing his shortcomings, his feebleness, his worthlessness. The mere voluptuary is far more consistent than either. Indeed it is difficult for sense-bound men, like ourselves, to project themselves into the eternal, the infinite; it is difficult, amidst the surroundings of earth, to live as citizens of Heaven. But this is the far-off goal, towards which you will ever be striving. The seal of immortality is stamped upon you. Do not forget this. Endure to be called madmen, when you stand before the judgment-seat of a Festus. This is inevitable. Only remember, that you are the sons of God, you are the redeemed of Christ, you are the temples of the Spirit, you are the heirs of eternity.

XX.

THE MESSAGE TO LAODICEA.

Unto the angel of the church of the Laodiceans write; These things saith the Amen, the faithful and true witness.

REVELATION iii. 14.

Third Sunday after Epiphany, 1878.

THE Revelation of S. John was written, as everyone allows, after the Epistles of the other Apostles included in the Canon of the New Testament. A great change has passed over the history of the Gospel, since the period recorded in these earlier writings. Death has deprived the Church of three great leaders. S. James in Jerusalem, S. Peter and S. Paul in Rome, have been crowned with the martyr's crown. Of the chief Apostles—the pillars of the Church—S. John only survives. The doom has been pronounced on the once Holy City. The eagles are gathered about the carcase of the dying or the dead. Jerusalem has fallen, or is even now falling. 'Old things are passed away.' The temple services, the Mosaic ritual, have ceased for ever. The original home of Christianity is a mass of ruins. The surviving disciples of the Lord—and, foremost among them, John the son of Zebedee—go forth to settle among the Gentiles. 'Behold, all things are become new.'

Henceforth the Churches of Asia Minor are the centre of life and activity in the Christian community. These brotherhoods had from the first received more than their proportionate share of attention from the earliest and greatest teachers of the Gospel. They had been founded by S. Paul, and they had been watered by S. Peter. Their names, their histories, their privileges, their failings, are recorded for the instruction of later ages alike in the Epistles of the great Apostle of the Gentiles, and in those of the great Apostle of the Circumcision. We may well suppose that there was something eminently hopeful, or something eminently critical, in the state of these Asiatic Churches, that so much labour should have been bestowed upon them by their Apostolic teachers. For now, when S. John, driven into exile by the catastrophe which has overtaken the Holy City, is compelled to seek a new home, it is in this same region that he fixes his abode. These Churches of Asia Minor are henceforth his special care. To them he is commissioned to deliver his Lord's messages from his retirement, or his banishment, in Patmos, rebuking, comforting, instructing, exhorting each individually according to its special needs and its special failings.

It has been thought by some that the letters to the Seven Churches are prophetical of seven successive stages in the history of Christendom. It is much more probable that the simpler view of their bearing is the correct view. They are words of warning and encouragement addressed to the immediate wants of the several communities; and they are varied accordingly. They present to us the Churches in a later stage of growth than the Epistles of S. Paul or S. Peter. They exhibit manifold diversities of type, which only lapse of time could develope. One is steeped in poverty, and yet is rich withal. Another abounds in wealth, and yet is a miserable pauper. The imminent peril of one is the bigotry and narrowness of Judaism; the besetting temptation of another is the license of Gentile profligacy. One is commended for its zeal against false teaching; another is reproved for its indifference to heresy. In one there is a falling-off from the fervour of its earliest love; in another the last works are more than the first. The

Churches have passed through several years of experience. They have been tested by the fiery trial of persecution; or they have undergone the not less searching ordeal of prosperity. With all these diversities of character they serve as types, as illustrations, of the different features, which may distinguish Christian communities from time to time. Only in this sense should they be regarded as prophetical.

The message to Laodicea is perhaps the most striking of the series. In other Churches definite failings are rebuked, and definite good deeds are praised. In Laodicea no positive sin is named, and no positive excellence is singled out. In other Churches errors of doctrine are denounced. In Laodicea no heresy is so much as hinted at. We are told nothing here of the hateful deeds of the Nicolaitans, as at Ephesus and Pergamos; nothing of the Jews falsely so called, the synagogue of Satan, as at Smyrna and Philadelphia; nothing of the woman Jezebel, the false prophetess, who seduces the servants of the Lord, as at Thyatira; nothing of the doctrine of Balaam, who taught Balak to cast a stumblingblock in the way of the children of Israel, as again at Pergamos; nothing of those false teachers who sounded the depths of Satan, as again at Thyatira. The Church of Laodicea was, so far as we are informed, perfectly orthodox, perfectly respectable.

And yet in the uncompromising sternness of the rebuke, in the sustained severity of the denunciation, this letter far surpasses all the others. Standing last of the seven, it derives a singular emphasis from its position. It is the Lord's parting message to all His Churches.

And for this reason too it has a wider application than the rest. The special circumstances of the other Churches give a special character to the messages addressed to them. Hence they contain lessons more especially adapted to exceptional crises of a Church, as, for instance, when it is directly assailed by persecution from without, or when it is insidiously undermined by false teachers from within. The Laodicean Church, on the other hand, represents the unobtrusive and indefinite temptations of ordinary times and ordinary men—the false security, the easy indifference, the unruffled self-satisfaction, of individuals and of Churches, when they are not roused to a sense of their true condition by any unwonted circumstances.

Of Laodicea two historical notices are preserved, bearing on her condition at this time, and illustrating the message in the Apocalypse—the one in secular history, the other in an Apostolic Epistle.

Only a few years before S. John wrote, a heavy blow had fallen on Laodicea. The whole region is highly volcanic; earthquakes were and are frequent here. On this occasion however the shock was more disastrous than usual. The city was in great part thrown down. But the Roman historian, who records the incident, adds another fact also of importance. It was usual for these cities of Asia Minor, when suffering under such calamities, to receive aid from the imperial treasury. Laodicea neither asked nor obtained any such relief. So great were her own material resources, that she recovered herself from the blow without any assistance from without. It was a proud satisfaction, we may well imagine, to this easy, prosperous commercial city thus to show her independence and self-sufficiency before an admiring world.

The notice of Laodicea in an Apostolic Epistle, written within two or three years of this event, is hardly so flattering. Giving directions to the Colossians, S. Paul charges them to interchange letters with their neighbours of Laodicea. At the same time he sends this message to the Church of the Laodiceans; 'Say to Archippus, Take heed to the ministry which thou hast received in the Lord, that thou fulfil it.' The misgiving, which prompts this warning, does not stand alone. In other passages of the same Epistle the Apostle betrays uneasiness about the Church of Laodicea, as well as about the neighbouring Church of Colossæ. He speaks of the conflict, the mental solicitude, which they cause him. He says that Epaphras also is very anxious about them, always struggling, always wrestling for them in his prayers, that they may stand firm in the faith. Evidently they are in a very critical state, when S. Paul writes.

The message in the Revelation is the sequel both to the laudatory notice in the Roman historian, and to the uneasy misgiving of the Christian Apostle. We see from it into what a spiritual condition the Laodiceans had passed through their national prosperity mentioned by the one. We learn also from it that there was only too much ground for the anxious forebodings entertained by the other. 'Thou sayest, I am rich, and increased with goods, and have need of nothing; and knowest not that thou art wretched, and miserable, and poor, and blind, and naked. I counsel thee to buy of Me gold tried in the fire, that thou mayest be rich; and white raiment, that thou mayest be clothed, and that the shame of thy nakedness do not appear; and anoint thine eyes with eyesalve, that thou mayest see.'

It is the great work of God's word to contrast the real with the apparent, to strip away all conventional disguises, and to reveal the truth in things moral and spiritual. This agent is described elsewhere under the image of a keen, double-edged knife, piercing, probing, dividing with infinite skill and precision, anatomizing and laying bare the inmost thoughts and desires of the heart. This 'Word of God'—as the Apostolic writer uses the term—this Divine Voice, speaks to us in many ways. Sometimes it whispers to us in the secret communings of our own hearts; sometimes it deafens us with the thunderclap of a sudden and cruel catastrophe. Sometimes it addresses us through the utterances of inspired Prophets or Apostles, when the old familiar text which we have slurred over time out of mind with listless eyes, appears suddenly ablaze, each several letter traced out in lines of fire by the visible hand of an invisible power on the palace walls, an unwonted and an unwelcome guest breaking in upon the banquet of our pride and self-complacency. Sometimes it pierces us through the taunts of an enemy of the faith, scoffing at the contrast between the selfish, mundane life which we lead, and the sublime creed of self-renunciation which we profess. But, from whatever side the knife may strike, the hand which wields it is the same.

Has it ever happened to any here, that in the midst of your false security, when all seems going on well with you, when you have got to look upon yourself—your comfortable position, your high character, your reasonable orthodoxy, your orderly and religious life—with no small complacency and self-satisfaction, its keen, cold edge has been suddenly felt. A message has come to you, as it came to the Church of Laodicea, startling you out of your apathy. You know at once from Whom it has come. There is a directness, there is a distinctness, there is a searchingness, about the message, which cannot be misunderstood. It is the voice of the Amen—the voice of the Faithful and True Witness. You recognise—you cannot help recognising—its truth and its fidelity. It tells you that, though you fancied yourself spiritually rich, you are miserably poor; though you thought you were clothed in comfortable and seemly raiment, you have been going about in shameful tatters; though you were proud of the range and the keenness of your vision, you were wholly blind. The prosperous, easy, self-complacent, self-admiring man finds himself to be after all utterly beggared in that which alone is true wealth. Struggle as you will, you cannot dispute the verdict. Your own conscience subscribes to it, and your own judgment seals it.

1. It tells you that you are *poor*. You thought that you had all the appliances needed for any emergency which might arise, that you were prepared by Christian principles for all the possible catastrophes of human life. Were you not rich in the precious treasure, well-stored with religious maxims, well-versed in religious services? So long as you

were prosperous, these served your turn very well. But the message came—came in the sudden blow which scattered your stores of worldly wealth, or in the cruel bereavement which snapped the thread of your deepest affections and your fondest hopes. And then the truth flashed upon you; then you made a discovery of your real self. The fountain, which flowed freely in the sunshine of prosperity, was frozen hard and dry by the winter of affliction. It was a painfully bitter experience to you to find that your religion, of which you thought so highly, was so inadequate, so conventional, so unmeaning, so hollow and unsubstantial after all. You sought God, and you could not find Him. You had to begin to build up your religious life anew from its foundations.

2. It tells you also that you are *naked*. You have set great store on your irreproachable character: you have guarded your fair fame with scrupulous care. You were proof against the assaults of direct opposition; you could have battled bravely with the storms of adverse fortune. These might do their worst and succeed; and yet you could have preserved a dauntless courage; your spirit would not have been broken. But you wore a proud and sensitive self-consciousness, the mantle of a stainless and unblemished reputation. You persuaded yourself that no man could rob you of this. And as long as you were

so clothed and so protected, you could bear any vicissitudes that might overtake you. The moment came, which stripped you of your comely robe—perhaps through some trifling neglect or inadvertence of your own, perhaps through accidental circumstances over which you had no control. A misunderstanding of an ambiguous word, a misinterpretation of a doubtful act, a mistaken identity, an anonymous libel, a malicious scandal, has torn to shreds the garment which you had woven for yourself with so much care, and which you prized so highly. And you are left bare and defenceless, exposed to the chilling scorn and the scoffing taunts of an unsparing world.

3. Again; it tells you that you are *blind*. Under ordinary circumstances you see your way clearly enough. You have no doubt about the path you ought to pursue. You have no moral difficulties, no inward struggles. You have enough of conscience, enough of insight, enough of moral discrimination, to steer your course through the common shoals and quicksands of life. But a great crisis comes, a trial of unwonted perplexity. And under the intensity of the moral struggle you break down. It is a conflict between two opposing claims; or it is, more likely, a conflict between an obvious duty on the one hand, and a strong affection, or a mastering aversion, on the other. If your spiritual life had been what it ought

to have been, what it seemed to others to be, what even you yourself thought it to be, the decision would not have cost you a moment's perplexity. As it is, you hesitate, you waver, you cannot see your way. Your moral vision grows more and more indistinct. The light within you is darkness.

In this hour of adversity or bereavement, in this downfall of your shattered reputation, in this agony of intense moral conflict, you find out your real self. The Faithful and True Witness speaks directly to you: 'Thou art wretched, and miserable, and poor, and blind, and naked.' He denounces for the past, and He advises for the future. 'I counsel thee to buy of Me gold, that thou mayest be rich; and white raiment, that thou mayest be clothed; and anoint thine eyes with eye-salve, that thou mayest see. As many as I love, I rebuke and chasten.' 'This sense of destitution, of nakedness, of blindness, this humiliating self-revelation, this very bitter scourge— what is it, but an instrument of mercy in My hands, bringing thee to a knowledge of thyself and of God?' 'Be zealous therefore, and repent.'

But what is the cause of this hapless condition? How shall we explain this poverty in wealth, this nakedness in sumptuous clothing, this blindness in keen vision? The image in the sequel is the answer to this question.

'I know thy works, that thou art neither cold nor hot; I would thou wert cold or hot.' The words are at first sight startling. It is not uncommonly, I imagine, assumed that these words 'hot' and 'cold' stand for 'good' and 'bad;' that they denote the godly and the godless respectively. Thus the text seems to countenance the idea that there is more hope for the reckless profligate, than for the respectable citizen who is without any deep sense of religion; or in other words, that the bad man is better than the partially good. Such an interpretation is burdened with difficulties. It even involves a contradiction in terms. Scriptural teaching and moral instinct alike repudiate it. The words 'hot,' 'lukewarm,' 'cold,' therefore cannot mark different degrees on the moral thermometer. The metaphor must be otherwise explained. It is doubtless taken from the practice of mixing hot or cold water with the ordinary wines drunk by the ancients, according to the season of the year or the hour of the day. Each had its proper time, its proper use, its proper quality. Each was good in its way; each answered its purpose. But the tepid, lukewarm water is useless, insipid, nauseous. The palate and the stomach alike reject it. Thus the hot and the cold represent those who set themselves in different ways to realise some ideal, who make it their business to act up to some standard.

The standard may fall short of the Gospel ideal. The aim may not be the Christian aim. But the vigorous, energetic, single-minded pursuit of it is elevating and ennobling in itself. The man of science, or the scholar, who prosecutes his researches with a devotion which seeks no reward beyond, will serve as an example of what is meant. The unconverted heathen, who availed himself of his opportunities and fulfilled his work, who was a patriotic citizen, who was an honourable and assiduous merchant, who was a brave and devoted soldier, stood on a far higher level than the apathetic, indolent, heartless disciple of Christ, in spite of his superior enlightenment and his larger advantages. He was at least not lukewarm. His life had a meaning and a use. It had a force and a savour in it.

The danger of Laodicea will be the danger of all Christian men and all Christian communities in a season of unruffled calm, of external prosperity, of settled routine. It is a danger which threatens a Church like our own, with its considerable endowments, with its well-appointed ordinances, with its legal position and its acknowledged respectability. It is a danger which threatens a country like our own, where material appliances abound, where the stream of social and political life flows smoothly and uninterruptedly, where religious ordinances are regularly performed and respected. It is a danger also which lies very near to any ordinary congregation of church-going people, exempt for the most part from the severest exigencies and the hardest experiences of life, who have their conventional duties and amusements, their conventional social and domestic engagements, their conventional religious observances; and whose spiritual life therefore runs a risk of degenerating into a conventional routine. For it is just here that convention must have no place. In the common avocations of life, even in the external ordinances of religion, it is inevitable, and it is right, that rule and habit should to a great extent prevail. But if any man's inward life has become conventional, has become crystallized, has been hardened into a dry, mechanical system, then that man is dead, though he liveth. The spiritual life must be always healthy, always fresh, always growing and expanding, always gathering fresh experiences and throwing out new developments.

If this is your danger or mine, then to us the message of the Faithful and True Witness is especially addressed; speaking ever and again in these momentary shocks which ruffle the tenour of our lives, or in these sudden flashes which startle the slumber of our consciences, rebuking our apathy, denouncing our lukewarmness, warning us to be zealous and repent.

Rebuking and denouncing and warning; but yet at the same time guiding, comforting, encouraging, speaking in tones of infinite love and assurance and hope. Close upon this stern and startling message, these words of uncompromising reproof, follows the gracious invitation, freely extended to all, closing the letter to the Laodiceans and with it the appeal to the seven Churches, speaking clearer and lingering later even than the words of condemnation and rebuke: 'Behold, I stand at the door and knock: if any man hear My voice, and open the door, I will come in to him, and will sup with him, and he with Me. To him that overcometh will I grant to sit with Me on My throne, even as I also overcame, and am set down with My Father in His throne.'

As we hear the words, we are reminded how this striking image has been transferred to the canvas by the genius of a living artist. We recall the calm, patient figure waiting at the door, the sad, earnest, reproachful look of tender compassion, the hand uplifted in the act of knocking, the ear attentive for the faintest sound of a response from within. We remember well the scene of neglect and desolation around; the door bolted and barred, the hinges and the fastenings rusted, the thorns and briars straggling across the entrance, the pathway overgrown with tangled weeds and poisonous fruits. As we gaze, we seem almost to hear the repeated knock, low but clear, sounding hollow through the empty chambers and passages. Has it occurred to us to ask ourselves whether this striking picture may not be too true a parable of our own lives—if not of the whole, at least of large portions of them—to enquire, whether this scene may not even now be enacting, and we ourselves the unconscious actors?

To keep our ears open to each sound of His voice (however soft and low), to answer the first summons of His knock (however faint and distant)—this is our most pressing need. It is very rarely that His voice will be heard clear and ringing, very rarely that His knock will startle with its loudness. But the less obtrusive appeals He makes to us day by day. At each repeated call, we are bidden to open our hearts, and lay before Him our inmost thoughts, our keenest desires, our hopes, our fears, our temptations to evil, our aspirations after good. This if we do, He will come in to us; will establish Himself an inmate in our hearts; will become our most welcome guest, and our most generous host; will cheerfully receive from us such meagre entertainment as alone we can give; will set before us in turn the lavish banquet, which His wealth alone can dispense.

This if we persevere in doing, He will not only admit us as guests to His table, He will even seat us as kings on His throne. For we shall follow in His steps, shall conform to Him, shall grow into Him, shall be one with Him, as He also is One with the Father. His kingdom shall be our kingdom, as His rule of life has become our rule of life: for He also overcame, and is set down on His Father's throne.

XXI.

THE HOLY TRINITY.

Go ye, and teach all nations, baptizing them in the name of the Father, and of the Son, and of the Holy Ghost.
S. MATTHEW xxviii. 19.

Trinity Sunday, 1871[1].

IT is a common remark, that Trinity Sunday differs from other festivals which retain a place in the Calendar of our Church in this respect, that, while they commemorate facts, it commemorates a doctrine. The contrast might perhaps be better stated, by saying, that, while they commemorate facts occurring in time, facts cognisable by the senses, facts of external history, it alone commemorates a fact which transcends all experience, which is of no special time or place, which is eternal in the heavens.

[1] Preached before the Lord Mayor and the Judges.

For, if this doctrine be a mere speculative opinion, a metaphysical definition in scholastic dogma, and not a living truth, then this day's anniversary is an idle, unmeaning solemnity, which it would be well to abandon at once and for ever.

But here, in the parting words of our Saviour, in the deed of bequest to the disciples, in the charter of inauguration of His Church, stands the command, that all henceforth who are incorporated into the family of God, all who claim the privilege of sonship in Christ, shall, as they sink beneath the water in which they bury their past lives, their corrupt affections, their worldliness, their impurity, their dishonour, from which they emerge to fresh hopes and privileges, to a new and regenerate life—that they shall, at this momentous crisis, be incorporated, not as our Version inadequately gives it, '*in* the name,' but as the stronger expression of the original requires, '*into* the name of the Father and of the Son and of the Holy Ghost.' Is this an idle form of words—this, which was first enjoined as the parting legacy of Christ to His Church, this which in obedience to His command is pronounced over each one of us at the great crisis of our lives? If not, what does it involve? What does it mean—this co-ordination, this union, this commemoration of Three in One?

But, besides being different in kind, Trinity Sunday was also a much later institution than our other great Christian festivals. The doctrine indeed was fully recognised. It was enunciated in Christ's own baptismal formula; it was taught by the fathers; it was systematized in the creeds. But still it was not specially commemorated. It was seen to be involved in all the main historical facts of the Gospel, the Incarnation, the Resurrection, the outpouring of the Spirit, and therefore it was regarded as underlying all the great Christian anniversaries. Christmas, Easter, Whitsuntide, were all alike witnesses to the Holy Trinity. So long ages elapse. To the mediæval Church we owe the institution of this festival. It is even said that this was especially an English usage, that an English archbishop first established it as a regular anniversary, and that from England it spread throughout the Western Church. It had a precarious, fluctuating recognition before; it was a local, but not a general festival: it was celebrated sometimes before, sometimes after, the great cycle of Christian seasons, before Advent or after Whitsuntide. At length it was generally adopted, and definitely fixed in its present position, as the crowning anniversary of the Christian year.

And rightly so fixed. For, if we have followed the course of the Christian seasons, we have been led to the very threshold of such a commemoration. Without this termination to the series, we should experience a sense of incompleteness, of inadequacy. On Septuagesima we were invited to contemplate the marvels of creation: we were bidden to cast our eyes backward to the first beginnings of all things, and forward to the final consummation of all: this vast universe in its origin, in its plan, in its destination, is one mighty chorus hymning with myriad voices the glories of its Creator, Architect, Father. To the thoughtful mind the marvellous discoveries of science would add a richness and a fulness to the voice of the Church. The minute organisms revealed by the microscope, and the intricate relations analysed in the laboratory, the distant worlds traversed by the astronomer, and the countless ages recorded by the geologist, all swell the triumphant strain, which rises from far and near, from present and from past, to the throne of Heaven—the song of praise and thanksgiving to Him the Eternal, Him the Omnipotent, Him the Invisible, Him the Beginning and the End.

Thus our thoughts were directed, first of all, to God the Father, the Creator. Then came the season which is dedicated especially to the Son. The two great historical facts in the life of the Incarnate Word were brought before us in succession. Good Friday and Easter Day directed our thoughts to the Passion and the Resurrection—the crowning act of transcendent love, and the crowning revelation of infinite hope. We were taught, how God sent down His Eternal Word, Who was with Him from the beginning, to become man, to die as man, that He might rescue mankind from sin, to rise as man, that He might be the first-fruits of a glorified humanity. This was the anniversary of the revelation of God the Son, God the Redeemer.

And, finally, on Sunday last we were invited to commemorate that great manifestation, when the infant Church was baptized with the Holy Ghost and with fire, as the historical revelation of the third Person in the Blessed Trinity, Whose mysterious, impalpable influence is diffused through the hearts and consciences and intellects of men, prompting in them whatsoever is true, whatsoever is pure, whatsoever is honest, whatsoever is lovely, in theology and in science, in contemplation and in feeling and in active life. This is the celebration of God the Spirit, God the Sanctifier, on Whitsunday.

And now we are asked to sum up all these lessons in one, and to realise the Unity of the Eternal Godhead, under this threefold Personality, Septuagesima, Easter, Pentecost, all unite in this day's commemoration.

What then, we ask, is the purpose of Trinity

Sunday? What is the proper use to make of it? What lesson, or lessons, ought it to leave behind?

1. First of all, it is a witness to the importance of beliefs. And is not such a witness needed at the present time? To hear men talk, one would suppose it an acknowledged axiom, that the ideas, the sentiments, the opinions, of individuals or of society exercised no influence at all on their well-being. It is not uncommonly, though loosely and thoughtlessly said, that, while it is important what a man does, it does not matter what a man thinks. If this means nothing more than that the mere adherence to certain dogmatic forms, which do not touch the man's heart and do not influence the man's life, is nothing worth, then it may be accepted. If it means only that God alone—the All-Seeing—can read the workings of a man's heart, and measure the degree of guilt attaching to false opinion, that it is idle and presumptuous in us to anticipate His verdict, then too we need not find fault with it. If it is merely another way of expressing the fact, that men's actions are often very much better and often very much worse than their professed or even than their genuine opinions, then also we may concede the point; for daily experience confirms it. But if it is intended to assert—and in a loose way this does seem to be its intention—that, while a man is responsible

for his actions, he is wholly irresponsible for his thoughts; that he need not give himself any concern whether he has right or wrong opinions, or no opinions at all, on moral and religious questions; that such opinions are powerless, or almost powerless, so far as regards any effect on the man's life and conduct; that society at large has no interest in securing right views or in correcting wrong views, because neither the one nor the other has any practical bearing on its welfare, because men would act very much as they act now, whatever views they might hold—if this be its intention, then it is a doctrine which we must repudiate with all the energy and all the indignation and all the strength which we can command, as the most dangerous of all heresies, destructive to individuals and to commonwealths, a flat denial of the truth-seeking instincts of our nature, a direct contradiction of common experience and of universal history.

For does not history teach us, that nations and societies have been profoundly and lastingly influenced by the ideas, the beliefs, which they have adopted? Dynasties have come and gone; institutions have flourished and have decayed. But a religious belief, a moral idea, surviving all changes, living and fructifying, has influenced for good or for evil successive generations, aye and successive races, of men. This silent, invisible thing, which we call an idea, has been found more potent far than all the elaborate machinery of states, and all the complex appliances of society. Nay, have we not seen how, at its mere touch, elaborate systems have melted away and time-honoured constitutions crumbled into dust? Imponderable though it be, on whatsoever things it has fallen, it has ground them to powder.

And, when we pass from the effects on society to the effects on individuals, we cannot say that these are small. It is true that you may often see a man, who seems destitute of any definite religious beliefs, whose speculative opinions, if logically carried out, would tend to moral indifference, exemplary and upright in his private life, a conscientious man of business, a patriotic citizen. But trace his career back, and what do you generally find? Why, that his habits have been formed under religious influences which he has since renounced; that a standard has been set to him by early principles, from which he has since broken loose; that his character, in short, is the result, not of the opinions which he now holds, but of the opinions under which he was brought up. It is only in the second generation that the effects of unbelief make themselves felt. The first rises superior to its worst influences by virtue of antecedent training. The next is brought up in its atmosphere, and the poison diffuses itself through the moral system. It is a patent fact, though a grave moral enigma, of which revelation indeed promises a future and final adjustment, but which present experience nevertheless teaches to be painfully true, that 'the fathers eat sour grapes, and the children's teeth are set on edge.' It was not the heated imagination of a Christian preacher, but the calm and deliberate opinion of a rationalist philosopher, which pronounced it to be the universal teaching of history, that ages of scepticism and unbelief have always been ages of moral decay.

Therefore it is not indifferent, you citizens and patriots, for the welfare of the state and of the society in which you live, what religious opinions you hold yourselves, and what you disseminate among others. It cannot be unimportant, you fathers and mothers, for the well-being of your children, whether or not you educate them to believe in a God, Who is a righteous Father and a loving Redeemer and a sanctifying Spirit.

It is not unimportant—nay, it is vastly important —even if you look only to their welfare here. And, as for the hereafter, God be your witness, as God shall be your judge.

There are two false views of creeds. One of these I have already described. It attaches no importance to beliefs, and therefore to creeds, as the expressions of belief. It regards them with cold indifference, perhaps even with supercilious contempt. They are not practical, and therefore they are not worth considering. This is the spirit of the Sadducee.

The other view is directly opposed to this, and yet it is hardly less dangerous. It affects to set the highest value on creeds, and it ends in degrading them. We may look upon creeds as rigid forms of words, to be carefully learned, to be tenaciously maintained; and nothing more. The spirit may be wanting, while the form is jealously guarded. We may hold them vastly important, not because they contain the expression of eternal truths—truths, which sinking into the heart and pervading the spirit will permeate and leaven and purify the whole life of the man—but only because they have been handed down, because we find them there. We may treat them as though they had some magical value, independently of their reception into the heart; they are not appropriated; they are simply *worn*; worn as phylacteries, worn as badges of doctrinal superiority, and flaunted in the face of others, as a reproach to their heterodoxy. This spirit it is, which reproduces the Pharisees of old; this it is, which by a natural reaction, evokes and encourages the indifference and the coldness of the Sadducee.

But the Spirit of the Gospel, the Spirit of Christ, is alien alike from the one and the other. Creeds are important to us; they are important, not for the condemnation of others, but for the edification of ourselves; they are important, not because the repetition of any form of words—however sacred and however true—can act as a theological charm and avert the consequences of a selfish heart or an immoral life, but because, duly apprehended, they teach us the true nature of God, and His work for us and our relations to Him; and so teaching us, act as a regenerating influence, detaching us from our corrupt passions and our paltry ambitions, and drawing us from earth to heaven.

There are two main influences, by which society is moulded. The one of these is its laws and institutions; the other is its ideas and sentiments and beliefs. We are under no temptation, as citizens and as Englishmen, to disparage the former of these. Individually, and collectively, we are reminded every day and every hour how much we owe to them— our lives, our property, our freedom of action, our opportunities of progress, our material well-being in its manifold aspects. Without them, we should be utterly helpless; we should be left at the mercy of blind chance. But they do more than this. Not only our material, but also our moral welfare is very largely and beneficially influenced by them. Laws are wholesome restraints upon us; they supply a valuable moral training. They also serve as moral landmarks—rough landmarks, it may be, but highly valuable as far as they go.

And to-day, when the chief administrators of our laws, and the leading representatives of public order, are present in this congregation, we shall not be likely to ignore or to underrate our obligations to this influence. But if the ceremonial of to-day is intended, as I cannot doubt it is intended, to teach us any lesson at all, it must surely be this; that law renders homage to a higher power; that it acknowledges its own imperfections; that it looks up to those eternal principles of duty and order and self-restraint, which are the expression of the mind of God, as the Great Original, of which it is only a partial, shadowy image, the Fountain-Head, from which it derives its truest inspiration. In short it bears testimony to the importance of belief.

And indeed history is our witness, that not even the most perfect administration of law, and the most complete elaboration of political machinery, can save society from utter degradation and ruin, if this higher principle be wanting. This truth has been vindicated at infinite cost to a sceptical world, but it has been vindicated signally and beyond dispute. The

Roman Empire—the most elaborate organisation and the vastest power, which the world has ever seen— fell at length—fell, and how great was its fall, we know. At the very moment, when her great lawyers had elaborated that marvellous system of jurisprudence which has been the special bequest of Rome to an admiring world; at the very moment, when the cornice had been placed on the edifice of her political institutions, and the franchise, gradually extended, was at length granted to all the subjects of that vast empire; then, just then, unmistakable signs of decay appeared. She was seen to be tottering to her fall. And this, because despite her admirable laws, despite her political institutions, her moral principles were eaten away. She had ceased to believe in any higher power, who vindicates those principles. She was rotten at heart. This is a lesson surely, on which we Englishmen may do well in this age to ponder.

2. But Trinity Sunday is not only a protest against indifference to belief: it is also a witness to the importance of a particular belief. You are asked to-day to pledge your assent to the teaching of the Bible and the Church, first, that there is One God, Eternal, Omnipotent, All Wise and All Good; and secondly, that this One God, taking into account the inadequacies of human language and the poverty

of human thought, is most correctly conceived of and spoken of as Father, Son, Spirit; Creator, Redeemer, Sanctifier; as Three in One.

This is a difficult saying, you reply. Yes, it *is* difficult. Could you expect it otherwise? Have you ever reflected on the nature of God at all? Are you so sanguine, or are you so inexperienced, as to suppose that, with your finite faculties, you can form any adequate conception of Him, which shall be free from difficulties; that, with your limited powers of expression, you can put that conception into language which shall not be liable to misunderstanding? A very intelligible conception indeed you may form: a very simple statement you may make. But what is the result? Your deity is either a mere man like yourself on a larger scale; or it is a pure abstraction which has no moral power at all. Then do not think lightly of the Nicene faith, even as a philosophical exposition.

But it is not as such that I ask your attention to the doctrine to-day. It is as to a living truth, which shall appeal to the hearts and mould the lives. I am not speaking as to philosophers, but as to Christian men and women.

And to Christian hearts the doctrine of the Holy Trinity says this.

It tells them first, that there is One, Absolute,

Eternal Being, from Whom all things have proceeded, and unto Whom all shall return; that He dwells in the light unapproachable; that He is Infinite Power, Infinite Justice, Infinite Wisdom—above all He is Infinite Love. He is the Creator of the universe, and He is the Father of mankind. His design is stamped on the world without; His will must be the law of our life within. And He is a Person. The dream of the pantheist, even if it could be accepted by the intellect, would leave the conscience uninstructed, and the heart unsatisfied.

It tells us again that God has manifested Himself; manifested Himself in creation and in history; manifested Himself by special revelations from time to time. God the Word, God the Son, is the agent of this manifestation. As the crowning revelation of all, He became incarnate, took our nature upon Him, lived and died and rose as man. If Christ's Godhead is denied, then the union of man with God has not been effected; then our redemption is not real, and our faith is vain. The reality of our redemption carries with it the deity of our Redeemer. And we cannot conceive of an incarnation, without conceiving of a Person; we must believe in God the Son.

And lastly; it tells us, that God is present in us and about us always; that He acts upon us by this invisible Presence; that, like the pulsations of air, this mighty, unseen Influence sweeps over us, coming we know not whence, and going we know not whither; that this Presence is our teacher, our witness, our advocate, our comforter, above all our sanctifier; that so He is a Person, speaking directly to our personality, Spirit to spirit, Mind to mind.

Into this confession you were baptized, when the Threefold Name was pronounced over you. Is it, think you, a mere hard dogma, a dry scholastic form; to some a stumbling-block, to others foolishness; or is it to them that apprehend and believe, both the wisdom of God and the power of God? Is there in the ideas which it involves, nothing to instruct, nothing to exalt, nothing to regenerate, nothing to purify? God our Father, God our Redeemer, God our Sanctifier—here we have the response to all our yearnings, the cure for all our maladies, our fullest strength and our loftiest hope.

God grant, that in this life we may realise Isaiah's vision of old; that beholding the glory of the enthroned Lord, filling the temple of the world with His train, and hearing the cadence of the angelic voices, singing 'Thrice Holy to the Lord of Hosts,' we may be touched by a seraph's hand with the live coal from the eternal altar, that so our iniquity may be purged and our sin taken away. Thus, when the warfare is accomplished and the toil is done, we shall pass by an easy transition from the earthly temple to the heavenly, from the prophetic type to its apocalyptic antitype; we shall share the unclouded vision and the glorious functions of those who are full of eyes within, and rest not day and night, saying, 'Holy, holy, holy, Lord God Almighty, which was, and is, and is to come.'

XXII.

THE GREAT RENEWAL.

*And He that sat upon the throne said, Behold,
I make all things new.*
REVELATION xxi. 5.

Second Sunday after Christmas, 1875.

ANOTHER year has passed away, another year with its joys, its sorrows, its successes, its failures, with its delightful associations and its dark memories, with its toils, its trivialities, its regrets, with its partial achievements, its phantom hopes, its unrealised possibilities.

Another year has passed away. What does this mean? There has been no jar, no dislocation, in the course of nature. All things continue as they were from the beginning. The sun and the moon and the stars appear and disappear as hitherto. The earth revolves in her orbit undisturbed. The thirty-first of December passes into the first of January as noiselessly, as imperceptibly, as any one day succeeds any other. We ourselves emphasize the transition; we ring out the old and ring in the new; we celebrate the epoch with friendly welcomes and merry gatherings; we compensate for the silence of nature by stir and noise of our own. But, after all, the distinction of old and new year is only an arbitrary distinction; after all the transition is one of our own making. And yet it appeals to us, as few other occasions appeal. It touches our whole being, kindling the affections, quickening the memory, stimulating the conscience, strengthening the resolves. It does this, because, though conventional itself, it is the echo of an eternal voice, the shadow of a divine reality. It tells us that all things are moving forward with ceaseless flow; it reminds us that we ourselves are drawing near and ever nearer to the inevitable goal; it warns us that the day is far spent and the night is at hand, the night when no man can work. It takes up the Apostle's warning, and bids us remember that old things are passed and passing away; it bids us remember that the great change cometh, and even now is; it is the very herald of Him, Who sitteth on the throne, announcing to us the proclamation of our King; 'Behold, I make all things new.'

'Behold, I make all things new.' The last chapters of the last book in our Bible are not, as we might have expected, a summary of the past, but an anticipation of the future. They are a magnificent prophecy of things to come; they tell of a great renewal, when everything which mars the happiness or sullies the life of man here shall be removed; there shall be no more pain, no more sorrow, no more sin, no more death. Yes, God shall make His tabernacle with men, shall be seen of men, shall be known of men. And where God is, there no evil can coexist. Hope, not regret, is the watchword of the Christian. Forward, not backward, is the keynote of the Bible.

It was not so with the old pagan religions. The world with them was not going forward, but backward. Their ideal was not in the future, but in the past. Their prevailing religious sentiment was 'a wistful, regretful wail of despair over a happy state of mankind, which had passed away, never to return. All things were going from bad to worse. Justice had once dwelt upon the earth; she had taken wings and was never more seen. An age of gold had been succeeded by an age of silver; an age of silver had given place to an age of iron. The burden of paganism was not 'I make all things new,' but 'I make all things old.' The world was wearing out, it was hastening to decrepitude, to decay, to ruin, to hopeless, irretrievable ruin.

Sons and daughters of God, brothers and sisters of Christ, you whom the Father has adopted into His family, you whom the Redeemer has purchased with His blood, not such is the lesson which the Bible teaches to you, not such is the thought which the season will suggest to you. You have been educated in a nobler school. You have been taught to look forward. The past year has had its sorrows, its disappointments, its sufferings. It has brought its bereavements. Old faces have passed out of sight. The cheerful voice will be no more heard; the pleasant smile will be no more seen. The wise counsels and the tender sympathies are missing. The associations of half a lifetime have been suddenly snapped asunder. Aye, you cannot hide it from yourself. This last year has made a terrible blank in your life. What then? Will you say that a light has been for ever quenched; or will you not rather believe that a torch has been removed hence, to burn more brightly elsewhere, to gladden you— yes, you—with a clearer flame hereafter? Or you have had trials and annoyances of another kind during the past twelvemonth. Your business has gone wrong; your character has been attacked; your confidence has been betrayed; your affections have been spurned and blighted. An unhealed sore is festering in your heart. It has been a dark year for you. Again I say; turn your back upon the past; set your face courageously and stedfastly towards the future. What encouragements, what consolations, what hopes, what bright visions of usefulness, what glorious anticipations of bliss, may you not find there—you whom Christ has ransomed, you to whom all things are possible, you to whom nothing is denied, if you will only look forward in hope to God Who cannot fail, instead of looking backward in fond regret to a world of which you have already had little experience, which has mocked and deceived and robbed you, leaving you a prey to vain disappointment and cruel self-tortures. Or is it worse still with you? Is it some new sin which has fastened upon you? Is it some old evil habit, against which you have struggled, but not struggled manfully enough; which still retains its hold upon you; which seems still to poison the springs of your higher life; which fills you still with a sense of feebleness, of dissatisfaction, of self-loathing. Again I say; turn your back upon the past. The past will give you no strength; the past will only tempt you to indifference or to despair. But look in front of you; for there is the secret of strength, there is the promise of victory, there is the assurance of recovery, there is the clean heart and the right spirit, there is the vision of glory, there is the very presence of God Himself, 'Behold, I make all things new.'

'Behold, I make all things new.' This is the voice, which speaks to us at the opening of another year. It teaches us through the parable of the seasons. The earth is hard and barren now; it was frost-bound yesterday and it may be so to-morrow; the days are short and the nights long. But every hour which passes brings us nearer to renewal and life. Already the light is gaining on the darkness. A few weeks hence the iron hand of winter will be relaxed. The earth will once more be set free. With the spring showers and the genial sunshine, the trees will burst into leaf, and the blade will spring up from the ground. All will be freshness, will be joy, will be life, the earnest of summer flowers and the promise of autumn fruits.

'Behold, I make all things new.' This same lesson is written indelibly with a pen of iron on the very strata of the earth. The hieroglyphs, which cover these tablets of rock and which modern geology has deciphered, bear witness to this one great principle extending through countless ages. They are a long, continuous record of successive renewals, progressive quickenings, new creations, fresh types of vegetable and animal life, each higher than the preceding.

20—3

From the earliest dawn of its history, when the inert mass of the earth began to heave and seethe with the first, rude, formless forms of awakening life, till last in time man himself was planted on the earth—man endowed with speech and reason and conscience, man created in God's own image, man charged with the sovereignty over earth and all earth's creatures—these rock inscriptions still yield the same lesson. It is the republication in diverse forms of the Eternal King's one great edict. It is the announcement of re-creation, of renewal, of requickened and heightened life.

'Behold, I make all things new.' This lesson is not only engraved on the successive strata of the earth; it is written also in the successive pages of human history. Epoch has followed on epoch, race has outstripped race in the struggle for power. Populous nations have come and gone; great empires have risen and fallen. But the one law, which we trace throughout, the one principle which God has stamped on the history of mankind as the expression of His Holy will, is renewal, is progress. There may have been seasons of apparent retrogression, but they were only apparent; they have ever proved the starting points of a newer, a more vigorous, a higher life. The wild nomad peoples retired before the barbaric empires of the East; these empires yielded to the superior culture of Greece and Rome; Greece and Rome in turn disappeared to make way for the more healthy, more enduring, because more moral, influences of Christian civilisation. And Christian civilisation itself has advanced from one conquest to another.

Yes, there has been renewal, there has been re-creation throughout all the ages before man and after man: but these progressive changes, however striking in themselves, are after all only faint shadows, blurred types, imperfect, very imperfect, analogies of the great and ultimate renewal of which the text speaks. They may serve to lead our thoughts onwards; but they can never satisfy; nay, they can only increase our dissatisfaction, because, while they heighten our ideal, while they stimulate our cravings, they leave us as far as ever from the realisation. What is all this progress to me or to you, if our brief mundane life is all, if this tangible, material world has nothing beyond and above it? We have been encouraged, we have been compelled, to look out more and more into the future; and then in cruel mockery we are told that the future is nothing, absolutely nothing to us. This we cannot believe; we cannot help forecasting a time, when our great ideal shall be realised, when perfect justice shall be vindicated, when sorrow and pain and death shall cease, when the righteous shall live in the presence of God. Our own hearts, our own consciences, confirm the inviolability of the promise, 'Behold, I make all things new.'

Brethren, we cannot disguise it from ourselves. A great conflict is raging in the world now, in which we, all of us, great or humble, ignorant or learned alike, are called to take a side—an internecine conflict, a conflict between two directly antagonistic, irreconcilable views of human life and human destiny. It is vain that we try to take an intermediate position. It is vain that we would halt between two opinions. There is no standing ground between the two—only a yawning, fathomless gulf which cannot be bridged. Let me place them side by side; and then judge for yourselves which is the truer, the nobler, the more ennobling.

The materialist's view of life is this. I am the plaything of an inevitable necessity, which mocks me with an appearance of liberty; I am a mere straw, floating helplessly down the stream of time; an atom amidst a world of atoms, driven hither and thither like the rest by incontrollable forces. My thoughts, my words, my actions, are all decided for me. My conscience, my affections, my moral sense, are only the resultants of physical laws. My freewill is a mere delusion. I have no more power of choosing between good and evil, than a stone has power to choose whether it will rise or fall. I am therefore no more blameable for committing a robbery or telling a falsehood, than I am for being stricken with a fever. Justice, honesty, purity, are only social fictions—conventional arrangements, necessary for the well-being of society, but having no other force or value. I myself am here to play my little part as an actor on this narrow stage—nay, not as an actor (this would imply some power of self-determination), but as a puppet moved hither and thither by wires—with all the show of initiative power, but none of the reality. The wires will be snapped, the puppet will be broken up; and there is an end of all. Will, conscience, consciousness, all shall vanish and be no more.

In direct and irreconcilable opposition to this stands the Christian's view. I am placed here under certain conditions of life, God's natural laws. I am bound by many restrictions, am surrounded by many temptations. But I have a power given to me, which it rests with myself to use or misuse. I have a heaven-sent capacity, which I am bound to educate, and which, if duly educated, is an instrument of incalculable moral force. My conscience is a witness of God's eternal will. My consciousness is a witness of my own immortality. There is a great battle raging within and about me—a deadly conflict between good and evil. The good shall prevail in the end. It cannot do otherwise, because it is good. I am called to take my side in this struggle. The alternative is not a mock alternative. The power of choice is a real power. Can I hesitate? Shall I not frankly accept the challenge, and range myself as a fellow-worker with God? Shall I not fight manfully under the Captain of my Salvation, Who will lead me to certain victory. The course is long, but the prize is great. The struggle is hard, but the triumph is assured. There are manifold trials now, temptations, misgivings, doubts, persecutions, failures, incapacities, sinful cravings, sinful deeds. But it shall not be so hereafter. Have I not assurance of this in the magnificent vision of the future which floats ever before my eyes—a vision of infinite joy and strength and hope? 'Behold, I make all things new:'—'new heavens and a new earth, wherein dwelleth righteousness.'

MESSRS MACMILLAN & CO.'S PUBLICATIONS.

BY THE SAME AUTHOR.

ST PAUL'S EPISTLE TO THE GALATIANS.
A Revised Text, with Introduction, Notes, and Dissertations. 8vo. 12s.

ST PAUL'S EPISTLE TO THE PHILIPPIANS.
A Revised Text, with Introduction, Notes, and Dissertations. 8vo. 12s.

ST PAUL'S EPISTLES TO THE COLOSSIANS AND TO PHILEMON. A Revised Text, with Introduction, Notes, and Dissertations. 8vo. 12s.

DISSERTATIONS ON THE APOSTOLIC AGE.
Reprinted from editions of St Paul's Epistles. 8vo., cloth. 14s.

BIBLICAL MISCELLANIES. 8vo. [*Nearly ready.*]

PRIMARY CHARGE. Two Addresses, delivered to the Clergy of the Diocese of Durham, 1882. 8vo. 2s.

THE APOSTOLIC FATHERS. PART I. *ST CLEMENT OF ROME.* A Revised Text, with Introductions, Notes, Dissertations, and Translations. 2 vols., 8vo. 32s.

THE APOSTOLIC FATHERS. PART II. *ST IGNATIUS TO POLYCARP.* Revised Texts, with Introductions, Notes, Dissertations, and Translations. 2nd Edition. 3 vols. Demy 8vo. 48s.

THE APOSTOLIC FATHERS. Comprising the Epistles (genuine and spurious) of Clement of Rome, the Epistle of St Ignatius, the Epistle of St Polycarp, the Martyrdom of St Polycarp, the Teaching of the Apostles, the Epistle of Barnabas, the Shepherd of Hermas, the Epistle to Diognetus, the Fragments of Papias, the Reliques of the Elders preserved in Irenæus. Revised Texts, with short introductions and English translations. Edited and completed by J. R. HARMER, M.A., Fellow of Corpus Christi College, Cambridge, sometime Chaplain to the Bishop. 8vo. 16s.

A CHARGE DELIVERED TO THE CLERGY OF THE DIOCESE OF DURHAM, Nov. 25th, 1886. Demy 8vo. 2s.

ESSAYS ON THE WORK ENTITLED "SUPERNATURAL RELIGION." 8vo. 10s. 6d.

Uniform Edition of
BISHOP LIGHTFOOT'S SERMONS.
Crown 8vo., Cloth. 6s. each.

LEADERS IN THE NORTHERN CHURCH. New Edition.

ORDINATION ADDRESSES AND COUNSELS TO CLERGY. New Edition.

CAMBRIDGE SERMONS.

SERMONS PREACHED IN ST PAUL'S CATHEDRAL.

SERMONS ON SPECIAL OCCASIONS.

MACMILLAN AND CO., LONDON.

MESSRS MACMILLAN & CO.'S PUBLICATIONS.

WORKS BY BISHOP WESTCOTT.

Globe 8vo. 6s.

THE GOSPEL OF LIFE. Thoughts introductory to the Study of Christian Doctrine. By BROOKE FOSS WESTCOTT, D.D., D.C.L., Lord Bishop of Durham, Honorary Fellow of Trinity and King's Colleges, Cambridge.

8vo. Cloth.

THE EPISTLES OF ST JOHN. The Greek Text, with Notes. Third Edition. 12s. 6d.

THE EPISTLE TO THE HEBREWS. The Greek Text, with Notes and Essays. Second Edition. 14s.

CLASSICAL REVIEW:—"It would be difficult to find in the whole range of exegetical literature a volume at the same time so comprehensive and so compact. It possesses characteristics which will command for it the permanent attention of scholars."

Crown 8vo. Cloth.

ESSAYS ON THE HISTORY OF RELIGIOUS THOUGHT IN THE WEST. 6s.

TIMES:—"These masterly essays."
SCOTSMAN:—"A work of high excellence."

GENERAL SURVEY OF THE HISTORY OF THE CANON OF THE NEW TESTAMENT DURING THE FIRST FOUR CENTURIES. Sixth Edition. 10s. 6d.

INTRODUCTION TO THE STUDY OF THE FOUR GOSPELS. Seventh Edition. 10s. 6d.

THE GOSPEL OF THE RESURRECTION. Sixth Edition. 6s.

THE BIBLE IN THE CHURCH. Tenth Edition. 18mo. 4s. 6d.

THE CHRISTIAN LIFE, MANIFOLD AND ONE. 2s. 6d.

ON THE RELIGIOUS OFFICE OF THE UNIVERSITIES. Sermons. 4s. 6d.

THE HISTORIC FAITH. Third Edition. 6s.

THE REVELATION OF THE RISEN LORD. Fourth Edition. 6s.

THE REVELATION OF THE FATHER. 6s.

CHRISTUS CONSUMMATOR. Second Edition. 6s.

SOME THOUGHTS FROM THE ORDINAL. 1s. 6d.

SOCIAL ASPECTS OF CHRISTIANITY. 6s.

GIFTS FOR MINISTRY. Addresses to Candidates for Ordination. 1s. 6d.

THE VICTORY OF THE CROSS. Sermons preached during Holy Week, 1888, in Hereford Cathedral. 3s. 6d.

FROM STRENGTH TO STRENGTH. Three Sermons (in Memoriam J. B. D.). 2s.

MACMILLAN AND CO., LONDON.

A Catalogue

of

Theological Works

published by

Macmillan & Co.

Bedford Street, Strand, London

CONTENTS

THE BIBLE—

    History of the Bible

    Biblical History

    The Old Testament

    The New Testament

HISTORY OF THE CHRISTIAN CHURCH

THE CHURCH OF ENGLAND

DEVOTIONAL BOOKS

THE FATHERS

HYMNOLOGY

SERMONS, LECTURES, ADDRESSES, AND THEOLOGICAL ESSAYS

January 1895.

MACMILLAN AND CO.'S THEOLOGICAL CATALOGUE

The Bible

HISTORY OF THE BIBLE

THE ENGLISH BIBLE: An External and Critical History of the various English Translations of Scripture. By Prof. JOHN EADIE. 2 vols. 8vo. 28s.

THE BIBLE IN THE CHURCH. By Right Rev. Bishop WESTCOTT. 10th Edition. Pott 8vo. 4s. 6d.

BIBLICAL HISTORY

BIBLE LESSONS. By Rev. E. A. ABBOTT. Crown 8vo. 4s. 6d.

SIDE-LIGHTS UPON BIBLE HISTORY. By Mrs. SYDNEY BUXTON. Illustrated. Crown 8vo. 5s.

STORIES FROM THE BIBLE. By Rev. A. J. CHURCH. Illustrated. Two Series. Crown 8vo. 3s. 6d. each.

BIBLE READINGS SELECTED FROM THE PENTATEUCH AND THE BOOK OF JOSHUA. By Rev. J. A. CROSS. 2nd Edition. Globe 8vo. 2s. 6d.

CHILDREN'S TREASURY OF BIBLE STORIES. By Mrs. H. GASKOIN. Pott 8vo. 1s. each. Part I. Old Testament; II. New Testament; III. Three Apostles.

THE NATIONS AROUND ISRAEL. By A. KEARY. Cr. 8vo. 3s. 6d.

A CLASS-BOOK OF OLD TESTAMENT HISTORY. By Rev. Canon MACLEAR. With Four Maps. Pott 8vo. 4s. 6d.

A CLASS-BOOK OF NEW TESTAMENT HISTORY. Including the connection of the Old and New Testament. By the same. Pott 8vo. 5s. 6d.

A SHILLING BOOK OF OLD TESTAMENT HISTORY. By the same. Pott 8vo. 1s.

A SHILLING BOOK OF NEW TESTAMENT HISTORY. By the same. Pott 8vo. 1s.

THE OLD TESTAMENT

SCRIPTURE READINGS FOR SCHOOLS AND FAMILIES. By C. M. YONGE. Globe 8vo. 1s. 6d. each; also with comments. 3s. 6d. each.—First Series: GENESIS TO DEUTERONOMY.—Second Series: JOSHUA TO SOLOMON.—Third Series: KINGS AND THE PROPHETS.—Fourth Series: THE GOSPEL TIMES.—Fifth Series: APOSTOLIC TIMES.

The Old Testament—*continued.*

THE DIVINE LIBRARY OF THE OLD TESTAMENT. Its Origin, Preservation, Inspiration, and Permanent Value. By Rev. A. F. KIRKPATRICK, B.D. Crown 8vo. 3s. net.

THE DOCTRINE OF THE PROPHETS. Warburtonian Lectures 1886-1890. By Rev. A. F. KIRKPATRICK, B.D. Crown 8vo. 6s.

THE PATRIARCHS AND LAWGIVERS OF THE OLD TESTAMENT. By FREDERICK DENISON MAURICE. New Edition. Crown 8vo. 3s. 6d.

THE PROPHETS AND KINGS OF THE OLD TESTAMENT. By the same. New Edition. Crown 8vo. 3s. 6d.

THE CANON OF THE OLD TESTAMENT. An Essay on the Growth and Formation of the Hebrew Canon of Scripture. By Rev. Prof. H. E. RYLE. Crown 8vo. 6s.

THE EARLY NARRATIVES OF GENESIS. By Rev. Prof. H. E. RYLE. Cr. 8vo. 3s. net.

The Pentateuch—

AN HISTORICO-CRITICAL INQUIRY INTO THE ORIGIN AND COMPOSITION OF THE HEXATEUCH (PENTATEUCH AND BOOK OF JOSHUA). By Prof. A. KUENEN. Translated by PHILIP H. WICKSTEED, M.A. 8vo. 14s.

The Psalms—

THE PSALMS CHRONOLOGICALLY ARRANGED. An Amended Version, with Historical Introductions and Explanatory Notes. By Four Friends. New Edition. Crown 8vo. 5s. net.

GOLDEN TREASURY PSALTER. The Student's Edition. Being an Edition with briefer Notes of "The Psalms Chronologically Arranged by Four Friends." Pott 8vo. 2s. 6d. net.

THE PSALMS. With Introductions and Critical Notes. By A. C. JENNINGS, M.A., and W. H. LOWE, M.A. In 2 vols. 2nd Edition. Crown 8vo. 10s. 6d. each.

INTRODUCTION TO THE STUDY AND USE OF THE PSALMS. By Rev. J. F. THRUPP. 2nd Edition. 2 vols. 8vo. 21s.

Isaiah—

ISAIAH XL.—LXVI. With the Shorter Prophecies allied to it. By MATTHEW ARNOLD. With Notes. Crown 8vo. 5s.

ISAIAH OF JERUSALEM. In the Authorised English Version, with Introduction, Corrections, and Notes. By the same. Cr. 8vo. 4s. 6d.

A BIBLE-READING FOR SCHOOLS. The Great Prophecy of Israel's Restoration (Isaiah xl.-lxvi.) Arranged and Edited for Young Learners. By the same. 4th Edition. Pott 8vo. 1s.

COMMENTARY ON THE BOOK OF ISAIAH, Critical, Historical, and Prophetical; including a Revised English Translation. By T. R. BIRKS. 2nd Edition. 8vo. 12s. 6d.

THE BOOK OF ISAIAH CHRONOLOGICALLY ARRANGED. By T. K. CHEYNE. Crown 8vo. 7s. 6d.

Zechariah—
THE HEBREW STUDENT'S COMMENTARY ON ZECH-
ARIAH, Hebrew and LXX. By W. H. Lowe, M.A. 8vo. 10s. 6d.

THE NEW TESTAMENT

APOCRYPHAL GOSPEL OF PETER. The Greek Text of the Newly-Discovered Fragment. 8vo. Sewed. 1s.

THE AKHMIM FRAGMENT OF THE APOCRYPHAL GOSPEL OF ST. PETER. By H. B. Swete, D.D. 8vo. 5s. net.

THE NEW TESTAMENT. Essay on the Right Estimation of MS. Evidence in the Text of the New Testament. By T. R. Birks. Crown 8vo. 3s. 6d.

THE SOTERIOLOGY OF THE NEW TESTAMENT. By W. P. Du Bose, M.A. Crown 8vo. 7s. 6d.

THE MESSAGES OF THE BOOKS. Being Discourses and Notes on the Books of the New Testament. By Ven. Archdeacon Farrar. 8vo. 14s.

THE CLASSICAL ELEMENT IN THE NEW TESTAMENT. Considered as a Proof of its Genuineness, with an Appendix on the Oldest Authorities used in the Formation of the Canon. By C. H. Hoole. 8vo. 10s. 6d.

THE SYNOPTIC PROBLEM FOR ENGLISH READERS. By A. J. Jolley. Crown 8vo. 3s. net.

ON A FRESH REVISION OF THE ENGLISH NEW TESTA-MENT. With an Appendix on the last Petition of the Lord's Prayer. By Bishop Lightfoot. Crown 8vo. 7s. 6d.

DISSERTATIONS ON THE APOSTOLIC AGE. By Bishop Lightfoot. 8vo. 14s.

THE UNITY OF THE NEW TESTAMENT. By F. D. Maurice. 2nd Edition. 2 vols. Crown 8vo. 12s.

A GENERAL SURVEY OF THE HISTORY OF THE CANON OF THE NEW TESTAMENT DURING THE FIRST FOUR CENTURIES. By Right Rev. Bishop Westcott. 6th Edition. Crown 8vo. 10s. 6d.

THE NEW TESTAMENT IN THE ORIGINAL GREEK. The Text revised by Bishop Westcott, D.D., and Prof. F. J. A. Hort, D.D. 2 vols. Crown 8vo. 10s. 6d. each.—Vol. I. Text; II. Introduction and Appendix.

THE NEW TESTAMENT IN THE ORIGINAL GREEK, for Schools. The Text revised by Bishop Westcott, D.D., and F. J. A. Hort, D.D. 12mo, cloth, 4s. 6d.; Pott 8vo., roan, red edges, 5s. 6d.; morocco, gilt edges, 6s. 6d.

GREEK-ENGLISH LEXICON TO THE NEW TESTAMENT. By W. J. Hickie, M.A. Pott 8vo. 3s.

THE GOSPELS—
THE COMMON TRADITION OF THE SYNOPTIC GOSPELS, in the Text of the Revised Version. By Rev. E. A. Abbott and W. G. Rushbrooke. Crown 8vo. 3s. 6d.

SYNOPTICON: An Exposition of the Common Matter of the Synoptic Gospels. By W. G. Rushbrooke. Printed in Colours. In Six Parts, and Appendix. 4to.—Part I. 3s. 6d. Parts II. and III. 7s. Parts IV. V. and VI. with Indices, 10s. 6d. Appendices, 10s. 6d. Complete in 1 vol., 35s. Indispensable to a Theological Student.

THE GOSPELS—*continued.*
  INTRODUCTION TO THE STUDY OF THE FOUR GOSPELS.
    By Right Rev. Bishop WESTCOTT. 7th Ed. Cr. 8vo. 10s. 6d.
  THE COMPOSITION OF THE FOUR GOSPELS. By Rev.
    ARTHUR WRIGHT. Crown 8vo. 5s.
  A TRANSLATION OF THE FOUR GOSPELS. From the
    Syriac of the Sinaitic Palimpsest. By AGNES S. LEWIS. Crown
    8vo. 6s. net.
  Gospel of St. Matthew—
    THE GOSPEL ACCORDING TO ST. MATTHEW. Greek Text
      as Revised by Bishop WESTCOTT and Dr. HORT. With Intro-
      duction and Notes by Rev. A. SLOMAN, M.A. Fcap. 8vo. 2s. 6d.
    CHOICE NOTES ON ST. MATTHEW, drawn from Old and New
      Sources. Cr. 8vo. 4s. 6d. (St. Matthew and St. Mark in 1 vol. 9s.)
  Gospel of St. Mark—
    SCHOOL READINGS IN THE GREEK TESTAMENT.
      Being the Outlines of the Life of our Lord as given by St. Mark, with
      additions from the Text of the other Evangelists. Edited, with Notes
      and Vocabulary, by Rev. A. CALVERT, M.A. Fcap. 8vo. 2s. 6d.
    CHOICE NOTES ON ST. MARK, drawn from Old and New
      Sources. Cr. 8vo. 4s. 6d. (St. Matthew and St. Mark in 1 vol. 9s.)
  Gospel of St. Luke—
    THE GOSPEL ACCORDING TO ST. LUKE. The Greek Text
      as Revised by Bishop WESTCOTT and Dr. HORT. With Introduction
      and Notes by Rev. J. BOND, M.A. Fcap. 8vo. 2s. 6d.
    CHOICE NOTES ON ST. LUKE, drawn from Old and New
      Sources. Crown 8vo. 4s. 6d.
    THE GOSPEL OF THE KINGDOM OF HEAVEN. A Course
      of Lectures on the Gospel of St. Luke. By F. D. MAURICE.
      Crown 8vo. 3s. 6d.
  Gospel of St. John—
    THE CENTRAL TEACHING OF CHRIST. Being a Study and
      Exposition of St. John, Chapters XIII. to XVII. By Rev. CANON
      BERNARD, M.A. Crown 8vo. 7s. 6d.
    THE GOSPEL OF ST. JOHN. By F. D. MAURICE. Cr. 8vo. 3s. 6d.
    CHOICE NOTES ON ST. JOHN, drawn from Old and New
      Sources. Crown 8vo. 4s. 6d.

THE ACTS OF THE APOSTLES—
  THE OLD SYRIAC ELEMENT IN THE TEXT OF THE
    CODEX BEZAE. By F. H. CHASE, B.D. 8vo. 7s. 6d. net.
  THE ACTS OF THE APOSTLES. By F. D. MAURICE. Cr.
    8vo. 3s. 6d.
  THE ACTS OF THE APOSTLES. Being the Greek Text as
    Revised by Bishop WESTCOTT and Dr. HORT. With Explanatory
    Notes by T. E. PAGE, M.A. Fcap. 8vo. 3s. 6d.
  THE CHURCH OF THE FIRST DAYS. THE CHURCH OF
    JERUSALEM. THE CHURCH OF THE GENTILES. THE CHURCH
    OF THE WORLD. Lectures on the Acts of the Apostles. By
    Very Rev. C. J. VAUGHAN. Crown 8vo. 10s. 6d.

THE EPISTLES of St. Paul—

ST. PAUL'S EPISTLE TO THE ROMANS. The Greek Text, with English Notes. By Very Rev. C. J. VAUGHAN. 7th Edition. Crown 8vo. 7s. 6d.

INTRODUCTORY LECTURES ON ST. PAUL'S EPISTLES TO THE ROMANS AND TO THE EPHESIANS. By Rev. F. J. A. HORT. Crown 8vo. [*In the Press.*

A COMMENTARY ON ST. PAUL'S TWO EPISTLES TO THE CORINTHIANS. Greek Text, with Commentary. By Rev. W. KAY. 8vo. 9s.

ST. PAUL'S EPISTLE TO THE GALATIANS. A Revised Text, with Introduction, Notes, and Dissertations. By Bishop LIGHTFOOT. 10th Edition. 8vo. 12s.

ST. PAUL'S EPISTLE TO THE PHILIPPIANS. A Revised Text, with Introduction, Notes, and Dissertations. By the same. 9th Edition. 8vo. 12s.

ST. PAUL'S EPISTLE TO THE PHILIPPIANS. With translation, Paraphrase, and Notes for English Readers. By Very Rev. C. J. VAUGHAN. Crown 8vo. 5s.

ST. PAUL'S EPISTLES TO THE COLOSSIANS AND TO PHILEMON. A Revised Text, with Introductions, etc. By Bishop LIGHTFOOT. 9th Edition. 8vo. 12s.

THE EPISTLES OF ST. PAUL TO THE EPHESIANS, THE COLOSSIANS, AND PHILEMON. With Introductions and Notes. By Rev. J. LL. DAVIES. 2nd Edition. 8vo. 7s. 6d.

THE EPISTLES OF ST. PAUL. For English Readers. Part I. containing the First Epistle to the Thessalonians. By Very Rev. C. J. VAUGHAN. 2nd Edition. 8vo. Sewed. 1s. 6d.

ST. PAUL'S EPISTLES TO THE ·THESSALONIANS, COMMENTARY ON THE GREEK TEXT. By Prof. JOHN EADIE. 8vo. 12s.

The Epistle of St. James—

THE EPISTLE OF ST. JAMES. The Greek Text, with Introduction and Notes. By Rev. JOSEPH B. MAYOR, M.A. 8vo. 14s.

The Epistles of St. John—

THE EPISTLES OF ST. JOHN. By F. D. MAURICE. Crown 8vo. 3s. 6d.

THE EPISTLES OF ST. JOHN. The Greek Text, with Notes. By Right Rev. Bishop WESTCOTT. 3rd Edition. 8vo. 12s. 6d.

The Epistle to the Hebrews—

THE EPISTLE TO THE HEBREWS IN GREEK AND ENGLISH. With Notes. By Rev. F. RENDALL. Cr. 8vo. 6s.

THE EPISTLE TO THE HEBREWS. English Text, with Commentary. By the same. Crown 8vo. 7s. 6d.

THE EPISTLE TO THE HEBREWS. With Notes. By Very Rev. C. J. VAUGHAN. Crown 8vo. 7s. 6d.

THE EPISTLE TO THE HEBREWS. The Greek Text, with Notes and Essays. By Right Rev. Bishop WESTCOTT. 8vo. 14s.

REVELATION—
  LECTURES ON THE APOCALYPSE. By F. D. MAURICE. Crown 8vo. 3s. 6d.
  LECTURES ON THE APOCALYPSE. By Rev. Prof. W. MILLIGAN. Crown 8vo. 5s.
  DISCUSSIONS ON THE APOCALYPSE. By the same. Cr. 8vo. 5s.
  THE REVELATION OF ST. JOHN. By the same. 2nd Edition. Crown 8vo. 7s. 6d.
  LECTURES ON THE REVELATION OF ST. JOHN. By Very Rev. C. J. VAUGHAN. 5th Edition. Crown 8vo. 10s. 6d.

THE BIBLE WORD-BOOK. By W. ALDIS WRIGHT. 2nd Edition. Crown 8vo. 7s. 6d.

Christian Church, History of the

Cheetham (Archdeacon).—A HISTORY OF THE CHRISTIAN CHURCH DURING THE FIRST SIX CENTURIES. Cr. 8vo. 10s. 6d.

Church (Dean).—THE OXFORD MOVEMENT. Twelve Years, 1833-45. Globe 8vo. 5s.

Cunningham (Rev. John).—THE GROWTH OF THE CHURCH IN ITS ORGANISATION AND INSTITUTIONS. 8vo. 9s.

Dale (A. W. W.)—THE SYNOD OF ELVIRA, AND CHRISTIAN LIFE IN THE FOURTH CENTURY. Cr. 8vo. 10s. 6d.

Gwatkin (H. M.) EARLY HISTORY OF THE CHRISTIAN CHURCH. [*In preparation.*

Hardwick (Archdeacon).—A HISTORY OF THE CHRISTIAN CHURCH. Middle Age. Ed. by Bishop STUBBS. Cr. 8vo. 10s. 6d.
  A HISTORY OF THE CHRISTIAN CHURCH DURING THE REFORMATION. Revised by Bishop STUBBS. Cr. 8vo. 10s. 6d.

Hardy (W. J.)—**Gee** (H.)—DOCUMENTS ILLUSTRATIVE OF THE HISTORY OF THE ENGLISH CHURCH. Cr. 8vo. [*In the Press.*

Hort (Dr. F. J. A.)—TWO DISSERTATIONS. I. On ΜΟΝΟΓΕΝΗΣ ΘΕΟΣ in Scripture and Tradition. II. On the "Constantinopolitan" Creed and other Eastern Creeds of the Fourth Century. 8vo. 7s. 6d.

Simpson (W.)—AN EPITOME OF THE HISTORY OF THE CHRISTIAN CHURCH. Fcap. 8vo. 3s. 6d.

Vaughan (Very Rev. C. J., Dean of Llandaff).—THE CHURCH OF THE FIRST DAYS. THE CHURCH OF JERUSALEM. THE CHURCH OF THE GENTILES. THE CHURCH OF THE WORLD. Crown 8vo. 10s. 6d.

Ward (W.)—WILLIAM GEORGE WARD AND THE OXFORD MOVEMENT. Portrait. 8vo. 14s.
  WILLIAM GEORGE WARD AND THE CATHOLIC REVIVAL. 8vo. 14s.

The Church of England

Catechism of—
CATECHISM AND CONFIRMATION. By Rev. J. C. P. ALDOUS. Pott. 8vo. 1s. net.
THOSE HOLY MYSTERIES. By Rev. J. C. P. ALDOUS. Pott 8vo. 1s. net.
A CLASS-BOOK OF THE CATECHISM OF THE CHURCH OF ENGLAND. By Rev. Canon MACLEAR. Pott 8vo. 1s. 6d.
A FIRST CLASS-BOOK OF THE CATECHISM OF THE CHURCH OF ENGLAND, with Scripture Proofs for Junior Classes and Schools. By the same. Pott 8vo. 6d.
THE ORDER OF CONFIRMATION, with Prayers and Devotions. By the Rev. Canon MACLEAR. 32mo. 6d.
NOTES FOR LECTURES ON CONFIRMATION. By the Rev. C. J. VAUGHAN, D.D. Pott 8vo. 1s. 6d.

Collects—
COLLECTS OF THE CHURCH OF ENGLAND. With a Coloured Floral Design to each Collect. Crown 8vo. 12s.

Disestablishment—
DISESTABLISHMENT AND DISENDOWMENT. What are they? By Prof. E. A. FREEMAN. 4th Edition. Crown 8vo. 1s.
A DEFENCE OF THE CHURCH OF ENGLAND AGAINST DISESTABLISHMENT. By ROUNDELL, EARL OF SELBORNE. Crown 8vo. 2s. 6d.
ANCIENT FACTS & FICTIONS CONCERNING CHURCHES AND TITHES. By the same. 2nd Edition. Crown 8vo. 7s. 6d.

Dissent in its Relation to—
DISSENT IN ITS RELATION TO THE CHURCH OF ENGLAND. By Rev. G. H. CURTEIS. Bampton Lectures for 1871. Crown 8vo. 7s. 6d.

Holy Communion—
THE COMMUNION SERVICE FROM THE BOOK OF COMMON PRAYER, with Select Readings from the Writings of the Rev. F. D. MAURICE. Edited by Bishop COLENSO. 6th Edition. 16mo. 2s. 6d.
BEFORE THE TABLE: An Inquiry, Historical and Theological, into the Meaning of the Consecration Rubric in the Communion Service of the Church of England. By Very Rev. J. S. HOWSON. 8vo. 7s. 6d.
FIRST COMMUNION, with Prayers and Devotions for the newly Confirmed. By Rev. Canon MACLEAR. 32mo. 6d.
A MANUAL OF INSTRUCTION FOR CONFIRMATION AND FIRST COMMUNION, with Prayers and Devotions. By the same. 32mo. 2s.

Liturgy—

A COMPANION TO THE LECTIONARY. By Rev. W. BENHAM, B.D. Crown 8vo. 4s. 6d.

AN INTRODUCTION TO THE CREEDS. By Rev. Canon MACLEAR. Pott 8vo. 3s. 6d.

AN INTRODUCTION TO THE THIRTY-NINE ARTICLES. By the same. Pott 8vo. [*In the Press.*

A HISTORY OF THE BOOK OF COMMON PRAYER. By Rev. F. PROCTER. 18th Edition. Crown 8vo. 10s. 6d.

AN ELEMENTARY INTRODUCTION TO THE BOOK OF COMMON PRAYER. By Rev. F. PROCTER and Rev. Canon MACLEAR. Pott 8vo. 2s. 6d.

TWELVE DISCOURSES ON SUBJECTS CONNECTED WITH THE LITURGY AND WORSHIP OF THE CHURCH OF ENGLAND. By Very Rev. C. J. VAUGHAN. 4th Edition. Fcap. 8vo. 6s.

IN THE COURT OF THE ARCHBISHOP OF CANTERBURY. Read and others *v.* The Lord Bishop of Lincoln. Judgment, Nov. 21, 1890. Second Edition. 8vo. 2s. net.

CANTERBURY DIOCESAN GAZETTE. Monthly. 8vo. 2d.

Devotional Books

Brooke (S. A.)—FORM OF MORNING AND EVENING PRAYER, and for the Administration of the Lord's Supper, together with the Baptismal and Marriage Services, Bedford Chapel, Bloomsbury. Fcap. 8vo. 1s. net.

Cornish (J. F.)—WEEK BY WEEK. Fcap. 8vo. 3s. 6d.

Eastlake (Lady).—FELLOWSHIP: LETTERS ADDRESSED TO MY SISTER-MOURNERS. Crown 8vo. 2s. 6d.

IMITATIO CHRISTI, LIBRI IV. Printed in Borders after Holbein, Dürer, and other old Masters, containing Dances of Death, Acts of Mercy, Emblems, etc. Crown 8vo. 7s. 6d.

Keble (J.)—THE CHRISTIAN YEAR. Edited by C. M. YONGE. Pott 8vo. 2s. 6d. net.

Kingsley (Charles).—OUT OF THE DEEP: WORDS FOR THE SORROWFUL. From the writings of CHARLES KINGSLEY. Extra fcap. 8vo. 3s. 6d.

DAILY THOUGHTS. Selected from the Writings of CHARLES KINGSLEY. By his Wife. Crown 8vo. 6s.

FROM DEATH TO LIFE. Fragments of Teaching to a Village Congregation. With Letters on the "Life after Death." Edited by his Wife. Fcap. 8vo. 2s. 6d.

Maclear (Rev. Canon).—A MANUAL OF INSTRUCTION FOR CONFIRMATION AND FIRST COMMUNION, WITH PRAYERS AND DEVOTIONS. 32mo. 2s.

THE HOUR OF SORROW; OR, THE OFFICE FOR THE BURIAL OF THE DEAD. 32mo. 2s.

Maurice (Frederick Denison).—LESSONS OF HOPE. Readings from the Works of F. D. MAURICE. Selected by Rev. J. LL. DAVIES, M.A. Crown 8vo. 5s.
RAYS OF SUNLIGHT FOR DARK DAYS. With a Preface by Very Rev. C. J. VAUGHAN, D.D. New Edition. Pott 8vo. 3s. 6d.
Service (Rev. John).—PRAYERS FOR PUBLIC WORSHIP. Crown 8vo. 4s. 6d.
THE WORSHIP OF GOD, AND FELLOWSHIP AMONG MEN. By FREDERICK DENISON MAURICE and others. Fcap. 8vo. 3s. 6d.
Welby-Gregory (The Hon. Lady).—LINKS AND CLUES. 2nd Edition. Crown 8vo. 6s.
Westcott (Rt. Rev. B. F., Bishop of Durham).—THOUGHTS ON REVELATION AND LIFE. Selections from the Writings of Bishop WESTCOTT. Edited by Rev. S. PHILLIPS. Crown 8vo. 6s.
Wilbraham (Frances M.)—IN THE SERE AND YELLOW LEAF: THOUGHTS AND RECOLLECTIONS FOR OLD AND YOUNG. Globe 8vo. 3s. 6d.

The Fathers

INDEX OF NOTEWORTHY WORDS AND PHRASES FOUND IN THE CLEMENTINE WRITINGS, COMMONLY CALLED THE HOMILIES OF CLEMENT. 8vo. 5s.
Cunningham (Rev. W.)—THE EPISTLE OF ST. BARNABAS. A Dissertation, including a Discussion of its Date and Authorship. Together with the Greek Text, the Latin Version, and a New English Translation and Commentary. Crown 8vo. 7s. 6d.
Donaldson (Prof. James).—THE APOSTOLICAL FATHERS. A Critical Account of their Genuine Writings, and of their Doctrines. 2nd Edition. Crown 8vo. 7s. 6d.
Gwatkin (H. M.) SELECTIONS FROM EARLY WRITERS ILLUSTRATIVE OF CHURCH HISTORY TO THE TIME OF CONSTANTINE. Crown 8vo. 4s. net.
Lightfoot (Bishop).—THE APOSTOLIC FATHERS. Part I. ST. CLEMENT OF ROME. Revised Texts, with Introductions, Notes, Dissertations, and Translations. 2 vols. 8vo. 32s.
THE APOSTOLIC FATHERS. Part II. ST. IGNATIUS to ST. POLYCARP. Revised Texts, with Introductions, Notes, Dissertations, and Translations. 3 vols. 2nd Edition. Demy 8vo. 48s.
THE APOSTOLIC FATHERS. Abridged Edition. With Short Introductions, Greek Text, and English Translation. 8vo. 16s.

Hymnology

Brooke (S. A.)—CHRISTIAN HYMNS. Edited and arranged. Fcap. 8vo. 2s. 6d. net.
This may also be had bound up with the Form of Service at Bedford Chapel, Bloomsbury. Price complete, 3s. 6d. net.
Palgrave (Prof. F. T.)—ORIGINAL HYMNS. Pott 8vo. 1s. 6d.

Selborne (Roundell, Earl of)—
  THE BOOK OF PRAISE. From the best English Hymn Writers. Pott 8vo. 2s. 6d. net.
  A HYMNAL. Chiefly from *The Book of Praise*. In various sizes.—A. Royal 32mo. 6d.—B. Pott 8vo, larger type. 1s.—C. Same Edition, fine paper. 1s. 6d.—An Edition with Music, Selected, Harmonised, and Composed by JOHN HULLAH. Pott 8vo. 3s. 6d.
Woods (M. A.)—HYMNS FOR SCHOOL WORSHIP. Compiled by M. A. WOODS. Pott 8vo. 1s. 6d.

Sermons, Lectures, Addresses, and Theological Essays

(See also 'Bible,' 'Church of England,' 'Fathers.')

Abbot (Francis)—
  SCIENTIFIC THEISM. Crown 8vo. 7s. 6d.
  THE WAY OUT OF AGNOSTICISM: or, The Philosophy of Free Religion. Crown 8vo. 4s. 6d.
Abbott (Rev. E. A.)—
  CAMBRIDGE SERMONS. 8vo. 6s.
  OXFORD SERMONS. 8vo. 7s. 6d.
  PHILOMYTHUS. An Antidote against Credulity. A discussion of Cardinal Newman's Essay on Ecclesiastical Miracles. 2nd Edition. Crown 8vo. 3s. 6d.
  NEWMANIANISM. A Reply. Crown 8vo. Sewed. 1s. net.
Ainger (Rev. Alfred, Canon of Bristol).—SERMONS PREACHED IN THE TEMPLE CHURCH. Extra fcap. 8vo. 6s.
Alexander (W., Bishop of Derry and Raphoe).—THE LEADING IDEAS OF THE GOSPELS. New Edition, Revised and Enlarged. Crown 8vo. 6s.
Baines (Rev. Edward).—SERMONS. With a Preface and Memoir, by A. BARRY, D.D., late Bishop of Sydney. Crown 8vo. 6s.
Bather (Archdeacon).—ON SOME MINISTERIAL DUTIES, CATECHISING, PREACHING, ETC. Edited, with a Preface, by Very Rev. C. J. VAUGHAN, D.D. Fcap. 8vo. 4s. 6d.
Binnie (Rev. William).—SERMONS. Crown 8vo. 6s.
Birks (Thomas Rawson)—
  THE DIFFICULTIES OF BELIEF IN CONNECTION WITH THE CREATION AND THE FALL, REDEMPTION, AND JUDGMENT. 2nd Edition. Crown 8vo. 5s.
  JUSTIFICATION AND IMPUTED RIGHTEOUSNESS. Being a Review of Ten Sermons on the Nature and Effects of Faith, by JAMES THOMAS O'BRIEN, D.D., late Bishop of Ossory, Ferns, and Leighlin. Crown 8vo. 6s.
  SUPERNATURAL REVELATION: or, First Principles of Moral Theology. 8vo. 8s.

Brooke (Rev. Stopford A.)—SHORT SERMONS. Cr. 8vo. 6s.

Brooks (Phillips, late Bishop of Massachusetts)—
  THE CANDLE OF THE LORD, and other Sermons. Crown 8vo. 6s.
  SERMONS PREACHED IN ENGLISH CHURCHES. Crown 8vo. 6s.
  TWENTY SERMONS. Crown 8vo. 6s.
  TOLERANCE. Crown 8vo. 2s. 6d.
  THE LIGHT OF THE WORLD. Crown 8vo. 3s. 6d.
  THE MYSTERY OF INIQUITY. Crown 8vo. 6s.
  ESSAYS AND ADDRESSES, RELIGIOUS, LITERARY, AND SOCIAL. Edited by the Rev. JOHN COTTON BROOKS. Crown 8vo. 8s. 6d. net.

Brunton (T. Lauder).—THE BIBLE AND SCIENCE. With Illustrations. Crown 8vo. 10s. 6d.

Butler (Rev. George).—SERMONS PREACHED IN CHELTENHAM COLLEGE CHAPEL. 8vo. 7s. 6d.

Butler (W. Archer)—
  SERMONS, DOCTRINAL AND PRACTICAL. 11th Edition. 8vo. 8s.
  SECOND SERIES OF SERMONS. 8vo. 7s.

Campbell (Dr. John M'Leod)—
  THE NATURE OF THE ATONEMENT. 6th Ed. Cr. 8vo. 6s.
  REMINISCENCES AND REFLECTIONS. Edited with an Introductory Narrative, by his Son, DONALD CAMPBELL, M.A. Crown 8vo. 7s. 6d.
  THOUGHTS ON REVELATION. 2nd Edition. Crown 8vo. 5s.
  RESPONSIBILITY FOR THE GIFT OF ETERNAL LIFE. Compiled from Sermons preached at Row, in the years 1829-31. Crown 8vo. 5s.

Canterbury (Edward White, Archbishop of)—
  BOY-LIFE: its Trial, its Strength, its Fulness. Sundays in Wellington College, 1859-73. 4th Edition. Crown 8vo. 6s.
  THE SEVEN GIFTS. Addressed to the Diocese of Canterbury in his Primary Visitation. 2nd Edition. Crown 8vo. 6s.
  CHRIST AND HIS TIMES. Addressed to the Diocese of Canterbury in his Second Visitation. Crown 8vo. 6s.
  FISHERS OF MEN. Addressed to the Diocese of Canterbury in his Third Visitation. Crown 8vo. 6s.

Carpenter (W. Boyd, Bishop of Ripon)—
  TRUTH IN TALE. Addresses, chiefly to Children. Crown 8vo. 4s. 6d.
  THE PERMANENT ELEMENTS OF RELIGION: Bampton Lectures, 1887. 2nd Edition. Crown 8vo. 6s.
  TWILIGHT DREAMS. Crown 8vo. 4s. 6d.
  LECTURES ON PREACHING. Crown 8vo. [*In the Press.*

Cazenove (J. Gibson).—CONCERNING THE BEING AND ATTRIBUTES OF GOD. 8vo. 5s.

Church (Dean)—
  HUMAN LIFE AND ITS CONDITIONS. Crown 8vo. 6s.
  THE GIFTS OF CIVILISATION, and other Sermons and Lectures. 2nd Edition. Crown 8vo. 7s. 6d.
  DISCIPLINE OF THE CHRISTIAN CHARACTER, and other Sermons. Crown 8vo. 4s. 6d.
  ADVENT SERMONS. 1885. Crown 8vo. 4s. 6d.
  VILLAGE SERMONS. Crown 8vo. 6s.
  VILLAGE SERMONS. Second Series. Crown 8vo. 6s.
  CATHEDRAL AND UNIVERSITY SERMONS. Crown 8vo. 6s.
  CLERGYMAN'S SELF-EXAMINATION CONCERNING THE APOSTLES' CREED. Extra fcap. 8vo. 1s. 6d.

Congreve (Rev. John).—HIGH HOPES AND PLEADINGS FOR A REASONABLE FAITH, NOBLER THOUGHTS, LARGER CHARITY. Crown 8vo. 5s.

Cooke (Josiah P.)—RELIGION AND CHEMISTRY. Cr. 8vo. 7s. 6d.
  THE CREDENTIALS OF SCIENCE, THE WARRANT OF FAITH. 8vo. 8s. 6d. net.

Cotton (Bishop).—SERMONS PREACHED TO ENGLISH CONGREGATIONS IN INDIA. Crown 8vo. 7s. 6d.

Cunningham (Rev. W.)—CHRISTIAN CIVILISATION, WITH SPECIAL REFERENCE TO INDIA. Cr. 8vo. 5s.

Curteis (Rev. G. H.)—THE SCIENTIFIC OBSTACLES TO CHRISTIAN BELIEF. The Boyle Lectures, 1884. Cr. 8vo. 6s.

Davidson (R. T.)—A CHARGE DELIVERED TO THE CLERGY OF THE DIOCESE OF ROCHESTER, October 29, 30, 31, 1894. 8vo. Sewed. 2s. net.

Davies (Rev. J. Llewelyn)—
  THE GOSPEL AND MODERN LIFE. 2nd Edition, to which is added Morality according to the Sacrament of the Lord's Supper. Extra fcap. 8vo. 6s.
  SOCIAL QUESTIONS FROM THE POINT OF VIEW OF CHRISTIAN THEOLOGY. 2nd Edition. Crown 8vo. 6s.
  WARNINGS AGAINST SUPERSTITION. Extra fcap. 8vo. 2s. 6d.
  THE CHRISTIAN CALLING. Extra fcap. 8vo. 6s.
  ORDER AND GROWTH AS INVOLVED IN THE SPIRITUAL CONSTITUTION OF HUMAN SOCIETY. Crown 8vo. 3s. 6d.
  BAPTISM, CONFIRMATION, AND THE LORD'S SUPPER, as interpreted by their Outward Signs. Three Addresses. New Edition. Pott 8vo. 1s.

Davies (W.)—THE PILGRIM OF THE INFINITE. A Discourse addressed to Advanced Religious Thinkers on Christian Lines. By WM. DAVIES. Fcap. 8vo. 3s. 6d.

Diggle (Rev. J. W.)—GODLINESS AND MANLINESS.
A Miscellany of Brief Papers touching the Relation of Religion to Life. Crown 8vo. 6s.

Drummond (Prof. James).—INTRODUCTION TO THE STUDY OF THEOLOGY. Crown 8vo. 5s.

ECCE HOMO. A Survey of the Life and Work of Jesus Christ. 20th Edition. Globe 8vo. 6s.

Ellerton (Rev. John).—THE HOLIEST MANHOOD, AND ITS LESSONS FOR BUSY LIVES. Crown 8vo. 6s.

FAITH AND CONDUCT: An Essay on Verifiable Religion. Crown 8vo. 7s. 6d.

Farrar (Ven. F. W., Archdeacon of Westminster)—
THE HISTORY OF INTERPRETATION. Being the Bampton Lectures, 1885. 8vo. 16s.

Collected Edition of the Sermons, etc. Crown 8vo. 3s. 6d. each.
SEEKERS AFTER GOD.
ETERNAL HOPE. Sermons Preached in Westminster Abbey.
THE FALL OF MAN, and other Sermons.
THE WITNESS OF HISTORY TO CHRIST. Hulsean Lectures.
THE SILENCE AND VOICES OF GOD.
IN THE DAYS OF THY YOUTH. Sermons on Practical Subjects.
SAINTLY WORKERS. Five Lenten Lectures.
EPHPHATHA: or, The Amelioration of the World.
MERCY AND JUDGMENT. A few words on Christian Eschatology.
SERMONS AND ADDRESSES delivered in America.

Finlayson (T.C.)—ESSAYS, ADDRESSES, Etc. With Portrait. Cr. 8vo. 7s. 6d.

Fiske (John).—MAN'S DESTINY VIEWED IN THE LIGHT OF HIS ORIGIN. Crown 8vo. 3s. 6d.

Forbes (Rev. Granville).—THE VOICE OF GOD IN THE PSALMS. Crown 8vo. 6s. 6d.

Fowle (Rev. T. W.)—A NEW ANALOGY BETWEEN REVEALED RELIGION AND THE COURSE AND CONSTITUTION OF NATURE. Crown 8vo. 6s.

Fraser (Bishop).—SERMONS. Edited by Rev. JOHN W. DIGGLE. 2 vols. Crown 8vo. 6s. each.

Grane (W. L.)—THE WORD AND THE WAY: or, The Light of the Ages on the Path of To-Day. Crown 8vo. 6s.

Hamilton (John)—
ON TRUTH AND ERROR. Crown 8vo. 5s.
ARTHUR'S SEAT: or, The Church of the Banned. Crown 8vo. 6s.
ABOVE AND AROUND: Thoughts on God and Man. 12mo. 2s. 6d.

Hardwick (Archdeacon).—CHRIST AND OTHER MASTERS. 6th Edition. Crown 8vo. 10s. 6d.

Hare (Julius Charles)—
   THE MISSION OF THE COMFORTER. New Edition. Edited by Dean PLUMPTRE. Crown 8vo. 7s. 6d.
Harper (Father Thomas, S.J.)—THE METAPHYSICS OF THE SCHOOL. In 5 vols. Vol. II. 8vo. 18s. Vol. III. Part I. 12s.
Harris (Rev. G. C.) — SERMONS. With a Memoir by CHARLOTTE M. YONGE, and Portrait. Extra fcap. 8vo. 6s.
Hort (F. J. A.)—THE WAY, THE TRUTH, THE LIFE. Hulsean Lectures, 1871. Crown 8vo. 6s.
   JUDAISTIC CHRISTIANITY. Crown 8vo. 6s.
Hughes (T.)—THE MANLINESS OF CHRIST. By THOMAS HUGHES, Q.C. Fcap. 8vo. 3s. 6d.
Hutton (R. H.)—
   ESSAYS ON SOME OF THE MODERN GUIDES OF ENGLISH THOUGHT IN MATTERS OF FAITH. Globe 8vo. 5s.
   THEOLOGICAL ESSAYS. Globe 8vo. 5s.
Illingworth (Rev. J. R.)—SERMONS PREACHED IN A COLLEGE CHAPEL. Crown 8vo. 5s.
   UNIVERSITY AND CATHEDRAL SERMONS. Crown 8vo. 5s.
   PERSONALITY, DIVINE AND HUMAN. Bampton Lectures, 1894. 8vo. 8s. 6d.
Jacob (Rev. J. A.) — BUILDING IN SILENCE, and other Sermons. Extra fcap. 8vo. 6s.
James (Rev. Herbert).—THE COUNTRY CLERGYMAN AND HIS WORK. Crown 8vo. 6s.
Jeans (Rev. G. E.)—HAILEYBURY CHAPEL, and other Sermons. Fcap. 8vo. 3s. 6d.
Jellett (Rev. Dr.)—
   THE ELDER SON, and other Sermons. Crown 8vo. 6s.
   THE EFFICACY OF PRAYER. 3rd Edition. Crown 8vo. 5s.
Joceline (E.)—THE MOTHER'S LEGACIE TO HER UNBORN CHILD. Cr. 16mo. 4s. 6d.
Kellogg (Rev. S. H.)—THE LIGHT OF ASIA AND THE LIGHT OF THE WORLD. Crown 8vo. 7s. 6d.
   THE GENESIS AND GROWTH OF RELIGION. Cr. 8vo. 6s.
Kingsley (Charles)—
   VILLAGE AND TOWN AND COUNTRY SERMONS. Crown 8vo. 3s. 6d.
   THE WATER OF LIFE, and other Sermons. Crown 8vo. 3s. 6d.
   SERMONS ON NATIONAL SUBJECTS, AND THE KING OF THE EARTH. Crown 8vo. 3s. 6d.
   SERMONS FOR THE TIMES. Crown 8vo. 3s. 6d.
   GOOD NEWS OF GOD. Crown 8vo. 3s. 6d.
   THE GOSPEL OF THE PENTATEUCH, AND DAVID. Crown 8vo. 3s. 6d.
   DISCIPLINE, and other Sermons. Crown 8vo. 3s. 6d.
   WESTMINSTER SERMONS. Crown 8vo. 3s. 6d.
   ALL SAINTS' DAY, and other Sermons. Crown 8vo. 3s. 6d.

Kirkpatrick (Prof. A. F.)—THE DIVINE LIBRARY OF THE OLD TESTAMENT. Its Origin, Preservation, Inspiration, and Permanent Value. Crown 8vo. 3s. net.
THE DOCTRINE OF THE PROPHETS. Warburtonian Lectures 1886-1890. Crown 8vo. 6s.

Knight (W. A.)—ASPECTS OF THEISM. 8vo. 8s. 6d.

Kynaston (Rev. Herbert, D.D.)—SERMONS PREACHED IN THE COLLEGE CHAPEL, CHELTENHAM. Crown 8vo. 6s.

Lightfoot (Bishop)—
LEADERS IN THE NORTHERN CHURCH : Sermons Preached in the Diocese of Durham. 2nd Edition. Crown 8vo. 6s.
ORDINATION ADDRESSES AND COUNSELS TO CLERGY. Crown 8vo. 6s.
CAMBRIDGE SERMONS. Crown 8vo. 6s.
SERMONS PREACHED IN ST. PAUL'S CATHEDRAL. Crown 8vo. 6s.
SERMONS PREACHED ON SPECIAL OCCASIONS. Crown 8vo. 6s.
A CHARGE DELIVERED TO THE CLERGY OF THE DIOCESE OF DURHAM, 25th Nov. 1886. Demy 8vo. 2s.
ESSAYS ON THE WORK ENTITLED "Supernatural Religion." 8vo. 10s. 6d.
DISSERTATIONS ON THE APOSTOLIC AGE. 8vo. 14s.
BIBLICAL ESSAYS. 8vo. 12s.

Lyttelton (Hon. Rev. A. T.)—COLLEGE AND UNIVERSITY SERMONS. Crown 8vo. 6s.

Maclaren (Rev. Alexander)—
SERMONS PREACHED AT MANCHESTER. 11th Edition. Fcap. 8vo. 4s. 6d.
A SECOND SERIES OF SERMONS. 7th Ed. Fcap. 8vo. 4s. 6d.
A THIRD SERIES. 6th Edition. Fcap. 8vo. 4s. 6d.
WEEK-DAY EVENING ADDRESSES. 4th Ed. Fcap. 8vo. 2s. 6d.
THE SECRET OF POWER, AND OTHER SERMONS. Fcap. 8vo. 4s. 6d.

Macmillan (Rev. Hugh)—
BIBLE TEACHINGS IN NATURE. 15th Ed. Globe 8vo. 6s.
THE TRUE VINE; OR, THE ANALOGIES OF OUR LORD'S ALLEGORY. 5th Edition. Globe 8vo. 6s.
THE MINISTRY OF NATURE. 8th Edition. Globe 8vo. 6s.
THE SABBATH OF THE FIELDS. 6th Edition. Globe 8vo. 6s.
THE MARRIAGE IN CANA. Globe 8vo. 6s.
TWO WORLDS ARE OURS. 3rd Edition. Globe 8vo. 6s.
THE OLIVE LEAF. Globe 8vo. 6s.
THE GATE BEAUTIFUL AND OTHER BIBLE TEACHINGS FOR THE YOUNG. Crown 8vo. 3s. 6d.

Mahaffy (Rev. Prof.)—THE DECAY OF MODERN PREACHING : AN ESSAY. Crown 8vo. 3s. 6d.

Maturin (Rev. W.)—THE BLESSEDNESS OF THE DEAD IN CHRIST. Crown 8vo. 7s. 6d.

Maurice (Frederick Denison)—
 THE KINGDOM OF CHRIST. 3rd Ed. 2 Vols. Cr. 8vo. 12s.
 EXPOSITORY SERMONS ON THE PRAYER-BOOK; AND ON THE LORD'S PRAYER. New Edition. Crown 8vo. 6s.
 SERMONS PREACHED IN COUNTRY CHURCHES. 2nd Edition. Crown 8vo. 6s.
 THE CONSCIENCE. Lectures on Casuistry. 3rd Ed. Cr. 8vo. 4s. 6d.
 DIALOGUES ON FAMILY WORSHIP. Crown 8vo. 4s. 6d.
 THE DOCTRINE OF SACRIFICE DEDUCED FROM THE SCRIPTURES. 2nd Edition. Crown 8vo. 6s.
 THE RELIGIONS OF THE WORLD. 6th Edition. Cr. 8vo. 4s. 6d.
 ON THE SABBATH DAY; THE CHARACTER OF THE WARRIOR; AND ON THE INTERPRETATION OF HISTORY. Fcap. 8vo. 2s. 6d.
 LEARNING AND WORKING. Crown 8vo. 4s. 6d.
 THE LORD'S PRAYER, THE CREED, AND THE COMMANDMENTS. Pott 8vo. 1s.
 Collected Works. Crown 8vo. 3s. 6d. each.
 SERMONS PREACHED IN LINCOLN'S INN CHAPEL. In Six Volumes. 3s. 6d. each.
 CHRISTMAS DAY AND OTHER SERMONS.
 THEOLOGICAL ESSAYS.
 PROPHETS AND KINGS.
 PATRIARCHS AND LAWGIVERS.
 THE GOSPEL OF THE KINGDOM OF HEAVEN.
 GOSPEL OF ST. JOHN.
 EPISTLE OF ST. JOHN.
 LECTURES ON THE APOCALYPSE.
 FRIENDSHIP OF BOOKS.
 SOCIAL MORALITY.
 PRAYER BOOK AND LORD'S PRAYER.
 THE DOCTRINE OF SACRIFICE.
 THE ACTS OF THE APOSTLES.

M'Curdy (J. F.)—HISTORY, PROPHECY, AND THE MONUMENTS. 2 Vols. Vol. I. To the Downfall of Samaria. 8vo. 14s. net. [*Vol. II. in the Press.*

Milligan (Rev. Prof. W.)—THE RESURRECTION OF OUR LORD. Fourth Edition. Crown 8vo. 5s.
 THE ASCENSION AND HEAVENLY PRIESTHOOD OF OUR LORD. *Baird Lectures*, 1891. Crown 8vo. 7s. 6d.

Moorhouse (J., Bishop of Manchester)—
 JACOB: Three Sermons. Extra fcap. 8vo. 3s. 6d.
 THE TEACHING OF CHRIST. Its Conditions, Secret, and Results. Crown 8vo. 3s. net.
 CHURCH WORK: ITS MEANS AND METHODS. Crown 8vo. 3s. net.

Murphy (J. J.)—NATURAL SELECTION AND SPIRITUAL FREEDOM. Gl. 8vo. 5s.

Myers (F. W. H.)—SCIENCE AND A FUTURE LIFE. Gl. 8vo. 5s.

Mylne (L. G., Bishop of Bombay).—SERMONS PREACHED IN ST. THOMAS'S CATHEDRAL, BOMBAY. Crown 8vo. 6s.

NATURAL RELIGION. By the author of "Ecce Homo." 3rd Edition. Globe 8vo. 6s.

Pattison (Mark).—SERMONS. Crown 8vo. 6s.

PAUL OF TARSUS. 8vo. 10s. 6d.

PHILOCHRISTUS. Memoirs of a Disciple of the Lord. 3rd Ed. 8vo. 12s.

Plumptre (Dean). — MOVEMENTS IN RELIGIOUS THOUGHT. Fcap. 8vo. 3s. 6d.

Potter (R.)—THE RELATION OF ETHICS TO RELIGION. Crown 8vo. 2s. 6d.

REASONABLE FAITH: A Short Religious Essay for the Times. By "Three Friends." Crown 8vo. 1s.

Reichel (C. P., Bishop of Meath)—
THE LORD'S PRAYER, and other Sermons. Crown 8vo. 7s. 6d.
CATHEDRAL AND UNIVERSITY SERMONS. Crown 8vo. 6s.

Rendall (Rev. F.)—THE THEOLOGY OF THE HEBREW CHRISTIANS. Crown 8vo. 5s.

Reynolds (H. R.)—NOTES OF THE CHRISTIAN LIFE. Crown 8vo. 7s. 6d.

Robinson (Prebendary H. G.)—MAN IN THE IMAGE OF GOD, and other Sermons. Crown 8vo. 7s. 6d.

Russell (Dean).—THE LIGHT THAT LIGHTETH EVERY MAN: Sermons. With an introduction by Dean PLUMPTRE, D.D. Crown 8vo. 6s.

Salmon (Rev. Prof. George)—
NON-MIRACULOUS CHRISTIANITY, and other Sermons. 2nd Edition. Crown 8vo. 6s.
GNOSTICISM AND AGNOSTICISM, and other Sermons. Crown 8vo. 7s. 6d.

Sandford (C. W., Bishop of Gibraltar).—COUNSEL TO ENGLISH CHURCHMEN ABROAD. Crown 8vo. 6s.

SCOTCH SERMONS, 1880. By Principal CAIRD and others. 3rd Edition. 8vo. 10s. 6d.

Service (Rev. John).—SERMONS. With Portrait. Crown 8vo. 6s.

Shirley (W. N.)—ELIJAH: Four University Sermons. Fcap. 8vo. 2s. 6d.

Smith (Rev. Travers).—MAN'S KNOWLEDGE OF MAN AND OF GOD. Crown 8vo. 6s.

Smith (W. Saumarez).—THE BLOOD OF THE NEW COVENANT: A Theological Essay. Crown 8vo. 2s. 6d.

Stanley (Dean)—
 THE NATIONAL THANKSGIVING. Sermons preached in Westminster Abbey. 2nd Edition. Crown 8vo. 2s. 6d.
 ADDRESSES AND SERMONS delivered during a visit to the United States and Canada in 1878. Crown 8vo. 6s.

Stewart (Prof. Balfour) and **Tait** (Prof. P. G.)—THE UNSEEN UNIVERSE; OR, PHYSICAL SPECULATIONS ON A FUTURE STATE. 15th Edition. Crown 8vo. 6s.
 PARADOXICAL PHILOSOPHY: A Sequel to "The Unseen Universe." Crown 8vo. 7s. 6d.

Stubbs (Dean).—FOR CHRIST AND CITY. Sermons and Addresses. Crown 8vo. 6s.
 CHRISTUS IMPERATOR. A Series of Lecture-Sermons on the Universal Empire of Christianity. Edited by C. W. STUBBS, D.D. Crown 8vo. 6s.

Tait (Archbishop)—
 THE PRESENT POSITION OF THE CHURCH OF ENGLAND. Being the Charge delivered at his Primary Visitation. 8vo. 3s. 6d.
 DUTIES OF THE CHURCH OF ENGLAND. Being seven Addresses delivered at his Second Visitation. 8vo. 4s. 6d.
 THE CHURCH OF THE FUTURE. Charges delivered at his Third Quadrennial Visitation. 2nd Edition. Crown 8vo. 3s. 6d.

Taylor (Isaac).—THE RESTORATION OF BELIEF. Crown 8vo. 8s. 6d.

Temple (Frederick, Bishop of London)—
 SERMONS PREACHED IN THE CHAPEL OF RUGBY SCHOOL. SECOND SERIES. 3rd Edition. Extra fcap. 8vo. 6s.
 THIRD SERIES. 4th Edition. Extra fcap. 8vo. 6s.
 THE RELATIONS BETWEEN RELIGION AND SCIENCE. Bampton Lectures, 1884. 7th and Cheaper Ed. Cr. 8vo. 6s.

Trench (Archbishop).—HULSEAN LECTURES. 8vo. 7s. 6d.

Tulloch (Principal).—THE CHRIST OF THE GOSPELS AND THE CHRIST OF MODERN CRITICISM. Extra fcap. 8vo. 4s. 6d.

Vaughan (C. J., Dean of Llandaff)—
 MEMORIALS OF HARROW SUNDAYS. 5th Edition. Crown 8vo. 10s. 6d.
 EPIPHANY, LENT, AND EASTER. 3rd Ed. Cr. 8vo. 10s. 6d.
 HEROES OF FAITH. 2nd Edition. Crown 8vo. 6s.
 LIFE'S WORK AND GOD'S DISCIPLINE. 3rd Edition. Extra fcap. 8vo. 2s. 6d.
 THE WHOLESOME WORDS OF JESUS CHRIST. 2nd Edition. Fcap. 8vo. 3s. 6d.
 FOES OF FAITH. 2nd Edition. Fcap. 8vo. 3s. 6d.
 CHRIST SATISFYING THE INSTINCTS OF HUMANITY. 2nd Edition. Extra fcap. 8vo. 3s. 6d.

THEOLOGICAL CATALOGUE 19

Vaughan (C. J., Dean of Llandaff)—*continued.*
COUNSELS FOR YOUNG STUDENTS. Fcap. 8vo. 2s. 6d.
THE TWO GREAT TEMPTATIONS. 2nd Ed. Fcap. 8vo. 3s. 6d.
ADDRESSES FOR YOUNG CLERGYMEN. Extra fcap. 8vo. 4s. 6d.
" MY SON, GIVE ME THINE HEART." Extra fcap. 8vo. 5s.
REST AWHILE. Addresses to Toilers in the Ministry. Extra fcap. 8vo. 5s.
TEMPLE SERMONS. Crown 8vo. 10s. 6d.
AUTHORISED OR REVISED? Sermons on some of the Texts in which the Revised Version differs from the Authorised. Crown 8vo. 7s. 6d.
LESSONS OF THE CROSS AND PASSION. WORDS FROM THE CROSS. THE REIGN OF SIN. THE LORD'S PRAYER. Four Courses of Lent Lectures. Crown 8vo. 10s. 6d.
UNIVERSITY SERMONS. NEW AND OLD. Cr. 8vo. 10s. 6d.
NOTES FOR LECTURES ON CONFIRMATION. Fcap. 8vo. 1s. 6d.
THE PRAYERS OF JESUS CHRIST: a closing volume of Lent Lectures delivered in the Temple Church. Globe 8vo. 3s. 6d.
DONCASTER SERMONS. Lessons of Life and Godliness, and Words from the Gospels. Cr. 8vo. 10s. 6d.
RESTFUL THOUGHTS IN RESTLESS TIMES. Cr. 8vo. 5s.
LAST WORDS IN THE TEMPLE CHURCH. Globe 8vo. 5s.
Vaughan (Rev. D. J.)—THE PRESENT TRIAL OF FAITH. Crown 8vo. 5s.
QUESTIONS OF THE DAY, SOCIAL, NATIONAL, AND RELIGIOUS. Crown 8vo. 5s.
Vaughan (Rev. E. T.)—SOME REASONS OF OUR CHRISTIAN HOPE. Hulsean Lectures for 1875. Crown 8vo. 6s. 6d.
Vaughan (Rev. Robert).—STONES FROM THE QUARRY. Sermons. Crown 8vo. 5s.
Venn (Rev. John).—ON SOME CHARACTERISTICS OF BELIEF, SCIENTIFIC AND RELIGIOUS. 8vo. 6s. 6d.
Ward (W.)—WITNESSES TO THE UNSEEN, AND OTHER ESSAYS. 8vo. 10s. 6d.
Welldon (Rev. J. E. C.)—THE SPIRITUAL LIFE, and other Sermons. Crown 8vo. 6s.
Westcott (B. F., Bishop of Durham)—
ON THE RELIGIOUS OFFICE OF THE UNIVERSITIES. Sermons. Crown 8vo. 4s. 6d.
GIFTS FOR MINISTRY. Addresses to Candidates for Ordination. Crown 8vo. 1s. 6d.
THE VICTORY OF THE CROSS. Sermons preached during Holy Week, 1888, in Hereford Cathedral. Crown 8vo. 3s. 6d.
FROM STRENGTH TO STRENGTH. Three Sermons (In Memoriam J. B. D.) Crown 8vo. 2s.
THE REVELATION OF THE RISEN LORD. Cr. 8vo. 6s.
THE HISTORIC FAITH. 3rd Edition. Crown 8vo. 6s.
THE GOSPEL OF THE RESURRECTION. 6th Ed. Cr. 8vo. 6s.

Westcott (B. F., Bishop of Durham)—*continued.*
THE REVELATION OF THE FATHER. Crown 8vo. 6s.
CHRISTUS CONSUMMATOR. 2nd Edition. Crown 8vo. 6s.
SOME THOUGHTS FROM THE ORDINAL. Cr. 8vo. 1s. 6d.
SOCIAL ASPECTS OF CHRISTIANITY. Crown 8vo. 6s.
ESSAYS IN THE HISTORY OF RELIGIOUS THOUGHT IN THE WEST. Globe 8vo. 5s.
THE GOSPEL OF LIFE. Cr. 8vo. 6s.
THE INCARNATION AND COMMON LIFE. Crown 8vo. 9s.

Whittuck (C. A.)—THE CHURCH OF ENGLAND AND RECENT RELIGIOUS THOUGHT. Crown 8vo. 7s. 6d.

Wickham (Rev. E. C.)—WELLINGTON COLLEGE SERMONS. Crown 8vo. 6s.

Wilkins (Prof. A. S.)—THE LIGHT OF THE WORLD : an Essay. 2nd Edition. Crown 8vo. 3s. 6d.

Willink (A.) THE WORLD OF THE UNSEEN. Cr. 8vo. 3s. 6d.

Wilson (J. M., Archdeacon of Manchester)—
SERMONS PREACHED IN CLIFTON COLLEGE CHAPEL. Second Series. 1888-90. Crown 8vo. 6s.
ESSAYS AND ADDRESSES. Crown 8vo. 2s. 6d. net.
SOME CONTRIBUTIONS TO THE RELIGIOUS THOUGHT OF OUR TIME. Crown 8vo. 6s.

Wood (C. J.) SURVIVALS IN CHRISTIANITY. Cr. 8vo. 6s.

www.ingramcontent.com/pod-product-compliance
Lightning Source LLC
Chambersburg PA
CBHW032357230426
43672CB00007B/731